Memorandum: On Renewing Schooling and Education

Memorandum: On Renewing Schooling and Education

Paul F. Brandwein

Harcourt Brace Jovanovich, Publishers

New York and London

Requests for permission to make copies
of any part of the work should be mailed to:
Permissions, Harcourt Brace Jovanovich, Inc.,
757 Third Ave, New York, N.Y. 10017.

Library of Congress Cataloging in Publication Data

Brandwein, Paul Franz, 1912–
Memorandum, on renewing schooling and education.

Bibliography: p.
Includes index.
1. Education—United States.
2. Educational sociology—United States.
3. Community and school—United States. I. Title.
LA212.B68   1982   370′.973   81-47301
ISBN 0-15-158857-0   AACR2

Printed in the United States of America

First edition

B C D E

To the Editors: my indebtedness

William Jovanovich edited this book. But the term "edited" hides the great service he has done the reader and the author. The cut and thrust of his mind, the precision of his insight, the range of his knowledge in schooling and education, which come out of his experience as a teacher, as a Regent of the State of New York, and out of a lifetime of work in devising curriculums and modes of instruction, have enriched the scope of this work. As always, he has given advantage to the author.

To Roberta Leighton, I owe still another debt of gratitude. She has maintained the character and style of the manuscript even as she has given it the form and art which would make it more useful and appealing to the reader.

Contents

Acknowledgments

To Harcourt Brace Jovanovich, Publishers, for permission to adapt from *The Permanent Agenda of Man: The Humanities,* 1971, and *The Reduction of Complexity, Substance, Structure and Style in Curriculum,* 1977.

To John Wiley & Sons for permission to adapt widely from my "A General Theory of Instruction," published in *Science and Education* in 1979, copyright © 1979 by John Wiley & Sons, Inc.

To Jerrold Zaccharias, who sent me his manuscript (written with Saville Davis) titled, "We Need Good Schools—How to Go About It." I was obliged *not* to read the manuscript because I had good reason to believe—having discussed problems of schooling and education with Jerrold Zaccharias and his colleagues—that if I had, I might not have written this book. I hope that "We Need Good Schools" will be published soon—but the present work which I have had the good fortune to complete may well have another point of view. It resorts, perhaps, to a different universe of experience.

I have used the resources and wisdom of Lawrence Cremin and Daniel Bell, particularly in certain sections credited to them in Chapters 1, 2, and 3.

The quotations from the literature are sparse; deliberately so, for this is intended to be a small book. As John Gardner has indicated, "the fragments of one of the finest educational systems are lying about," and I have picked them up without claim to originality. In effect, the ideas have been lying "about"; they have been "in the air." But, as the reader will see, I have selected, from among many practices, those that I have observed at work, not only in the schools in which I have taught, but also in the many schools I have been privileged to observe.

In addition to the references quoted, I have listed in the bibliography additional books. They exist as a body of expert opinion of study and of practice, on the renewing of a variety of educational systems. Had someone else written this book, a different body of experts, as effective as those named here, might well have—no doubt would have—been listed.

Also, I have adopted one phrase which Jerrold Zaccharias and Mitchell Lazarus (we were associated in trying to develop a certain curriculum) were prone to use in admonishing those who would rush into change; the reader will recognize the phrase as harking back a few thousand centuries:

"First, do no harm."

xi

Memorandum: On Renewing Schooling and Education

A Necessary Prologue

Our society has developed the belief that schooling is a way of transmitting and conserving, expanding and rectifying the knowledge, values, and skills antecedent to a life of purpose, of work, of accomplishment, of personal growth.

Indeed, the literature of education is rife with statements purporting to show that schools were invented, organized, and developed to serve as agents of society (more accurately, to serve the communities that organized them), to inculcate in the young habits of good choice which were meant to sustain visions of excellence, of greatness, and of the power of knowledge and high conduct. The record will generally show that over the two centuries of their existence, schools have accommodated the aims of the communities that organized them, abiding their constraints and mirroring their rules, customs, and values. All things considered, specific communities get the kind of schools their economic and social conditions permit; it is simplism itself to blame schools for the plight of the community or of society. Nonetheless, a community and a school are inextricably associated in securing the needs of the young. Often it is the single school within a given community—not the larger school system—that is at the center of the community's constructive affection. This is surely understandable; a single school, with a relatively small population accommodates to the human scale. Its young are not lost in the mass.

In a curious way, the unbelievable growth of our society from a preindustrial nation to industrial and technological leadership—in a bare 200 years—has stood in the way of the progressive and orderly development of a school system. As part of this incredible, gigantic technological and industrial development, with its accompanying social change, our schools have not been given a time of peace to undertake the intelligent, progressive development a major social institution must have. The schools have been too busy serving the nation's growth to tend to their own. Reforms and policies directed at advancing schooling have been, of necessity, short term, if not ad hoc. All in all, the accomplishment of American schools is remarkable considering the crushing burdens, the conflicting demands, and the persistent, dark, depressing scolding to which they have been subjected. Nevertheless, in the pendulation of attack and counterattack, a *balance* in what is to be taught, and how it is to be taught, so necessary to the *balanced* development of the young, has been lost.

Our society is about to undergo a sea change. It is about to take a quantum leap into the postindustrial age, and it is now essential to permit the schools a development denied them by the exigencies of the past 200 years. It is necessary to understand that this development means nothing less than renewing of the many different modes of education to be found in society; among these modes of education, schooling is paramount, to be sure. Schooling is, nevertheless, only one of the educational systems affecting the young in any society.

What is required is *not,* as will be seen, a total invention. The problem is one of structure. The elements of effective educational systems exist, effective policies exist, as do sound theories and excellent practice in curriculum, instruction, and evaluation. Fine school systems do exist —naturally, not without their special problems.

Essential to the development of the various modes of education including schooling, is an *ecology of achievement*. The phrase refers to a healthy balance in the collaborating environments in which schooling and education exist. The nature of this balance, this ecology, is best treated in the context of certain major functions of schooling and education: *what is to be taught, how it is to be taught, to whom, when, and where.* For purposes of useful discussion, the argument proceeds thus: one obstacle at a time, one problem at a time, one facet at a time; not *all* obstacles, not *all* problems, not *all* facets. In addition, the argument proceeds in layers, one on top of the other, until we approach what appear to be signposts to certain departures from present practice in schooling and education.

If we, throughout the nation, can muster a necessary constructive affection, as we should, if we can dispel a certain hidden agenda of resentment, the genius and the means required for the renewing of our

4

educational systems abound in our society. Nothing revolutionary is called for—only the next step in the constant renewing of our schooling system within many educational systems that can, and do, serve our young so that they may fulfill their gifts in the pursuit of individual excellence and special destination.

In taking this step we, throughout the nation, shall be required not to use our children as tools of our own psychosocial warfare.

1. Regarding an Ecology of Achievement in *Schooling*

Because we are resolutely a self-examining society, we reject a false ease. Because we are still young as mature societies go, we are bound to remember and honor our founding as well as our founding fathers and our youth as a nation. Because we are impatient with uneven progress, we are not tolerant of our adolescent years as we advance toward the maturity an open society requires. Because we insist on social, political, and economic maturity and stability, we lament departures from codes of self-reliance and personal choice. Because we value responsible consent and dissent, we seek consistently a balance of opposing opinion without coercion. In maturity we seek balance.

Because we are ethically hard-tried, we seek through our institutions to reconcile the claims of the individual with those of society; always we seek a discipline of responsible consent and dissent. We hold to a belief that one makes one's way through mastery of knowledge, skills, and values necessary to bring us the things we want and cherish. We have a variety of shorthand phrases for this: "Life, liberty, and the pursuit of happiness"; "The American Dream"; "The greening of America"; "making it." Others will occur to the reader. So we value knowledge and work, competence and compassion. And so we value schooling and education as prologue to a life that equates the dream with the reality. So our society, our culture, is maintained and sustained. And so we seek constantly for amelioration of a poor fit of individuals to society and to life— whether that poor fit is identified as poor health, poor status, or poor self-esteem. Disadvantage in any form becomes a stigma on the individual and on the immediate community. Further, any deviation from an expected "success" of individuals we seek or elect as our "representatives" is now signaled to us immediately in our living rooms; as is "the good life," and as are deviations from it.

We cannot, it seems, escape constant self-examination. Consequently, what has been called "the rising tide of self-expectation" is a reproach, as it were, to our own advance. But this tide of expectation came to our shores with the *Mayflower* and is embodied in its covenant, the Mayflower Compact. Perhaps since then our society has made both a contract and a covenant with its citizens: to give each individual scope consonant with his or her gifts and proclaimed destination. Equality and equity were written into quotable political, social, and economic documents; note, for example, our pledge of allegiance, the preamble to the Constitution, the first lines of the Declaration of Independence, the inauguration speeches of our presidents, the Declaration of Man. The rise of self-expectation, of aspiration to the good life, has become the *normal expectation* of Americans. What is deplored, then, is not the *rise* of self-expectation (that is, after all, "normal" ambition), but its *fall*—its failure, as it were.

Inevitably, as happens from time to time, our society comes to one of its strange turning points. Social, economic, and political problems assail us, not necessarily signaling a breakdown of the social fabric, but acknowledging a concatenation of next steps, of a nation bursting against its problems, its bonds, and surging toward unexpected solutions. But we expect (because it is our culture that makes us confident) that, given our zeal and purpose for achievement, in the end "solutions" will be found —tolerable, good, effective "solutions." And this will happen all in good time—but not time overlong, for our impatience will not tolerate the tempo of slow, steady development. Moreover, because we are an open society and the solutions to our problems are sought in the balance of contested, opposing opinion, this reform is to be sought without coercion. For good or ill, it is to be sought in the public forum, to the dismay or delight of the major contenders.

Inevitably, too, as always comes to be realized with a kind of effective surprise, education is central to the solution of the problems. Indeed, now and then we realize that education is a root function of a self-examining and self-correcting society. In effect, reformers press upon the now-vulnerable living room the idea that a well-informed public in the areas of social, economic, and political thought is necessary for "survival." Constant improvement, never-ending change of "the educational system," is pressed upon us as central to the life of a democracy.

But we do not have an *educational system;* we have many schools, some school systems, and many educational modes and systems, each a component of a specific community. There is, furthermore, a vital difference between schooling and education. Be that as it may, we seem always to be calling for reform of our "educational system."

Somehow, in the common speech, we have come to consider that the institutional form of education devised for children—namely, schooling—constitutes *the* educational system. Education is commonly defined as "a change in behavior." In considering the influence on change in behavior we need to rid ourselves of the notion that schooling specifically devised for children or minors has the impact on societal change we claim for it. The renewing of our educational systems should rightly include a major focus on schooling, but it should focus as well on other institutions, places, or influences that change the behavior of individuals with subsequent impact on changes in society.

A definition of the intent in schooling vis-à-vis education may become clearer as certain of our modes of education are limned throughout this book and the extent of education as compared and contrasted with schooling is considered. On this, as a first approximation of necessary definition, it might be said that schooling attempts to transmit the concepts, values, and skills prized by a community acting under the constraints of public custom, rule, and law (local, state, and federal). Education, on the other hand, is an enterprise that affects all of life and living and comprises all influences, in school and out, that affect and effect changes in the behavior of the individual—whether of habituation, of character, or of intellect. These changes in behavior occur throughout life and are not necessarily equated with graduations or exits from any form of endeavor, public or private. Thus, education occurs in situations and institutions outside of school—at home and with family; at church, synagogue, temple, mosque, informal religious encounters under the influence of nonchurchgoers; in one's life with peer and nonpeer groups; in chance encounters; from TV, newspapers, books, and magazines; from experience; from reaction to failure and success; definitely in a job or jobs; from crises generally; in personal contemplation and retreat—to mention only a few. Who was it who insisted that our education should insure a "habitual vision of greatness"? The habitual vision of greatness may begin at home or at school, but surely it does not, should not, must not end there.

It happens that one, and only one, of the institutions society has sensibly invented to press forward the individual's claim to the good life, for the fulfillment of self-expectation, is schooling. The argument—as old as Plato, and surely older—runs like this: the good life is inconceivable without the good society; the good society is surely impossible without the kind of education that will sustain and maintain a particular society; the aims and ends of a good society are surely envisioned in its educational policies and practices; and, conversely, educational policies and practices are implicitly if not explicitly expositions of the good life. For those who are not privy to this argument, so ably explicated by Lawrence Cremin in his Horace Mann Lecture, *The Genius of American Education,* it needs to be said that Plato's view of education gave only passing attention to schools; he did not equate schooling with education. Indeed, for him, and for scholars in the centuries following, schooling was a useful part, but certainly not all, of education. It was, Plato insisted, the community that educated, that shaped mind and character, vocation and avocation. But then, Plato did not live in our time. Nevertheless, almost everyone who attends to the young sees schooling (not education in all its aspects) as central to the transmission and transmutation, if not the preservation, of the knowledge, skills, and values held most dear.

A meshing with Platonic notions is clear in Jefferson's remark that "if a nation expects to be ignorant and free in a state of civilization, it expects what never was and never will be." But, like Plato, Jefferson, who believed so profoundly in schooling, did not consider schooling to be the chief educational instrument of society. There is, nevertheless, both conjunction and disjunction between schooling and education, and what follows here and in succeeding chapters should illuminate their interdependence—and their points of departure.

When were the two, schooling and education, confused? Perhaps in the hopes of certain reformers of society: to *reform,* we should recall, means to *reshape.* Perhaps in the statements of Horace Mann and William Torrey Harris and G. Stanley Hall, and a host of others whose policies and practices need to be synthesized into a statement of schooling vis-à-vis education. Perhaps in the writings of Ellwood P. Cubberley, a historian of institutional education, who stressed the importance of schooling as central to education. Even now there are those who would lay upon the schools the major, if not the total, educational burden of achieving equality and equity, whether in scholarly or in personal development. However this may be, from the point of view of achieving the mature development they seek, schools and school systems, generally, have not themselves been treated with equality and equity. But surely certain disciples of John Dewey (whose life was given over to laying down the template—no, the conscience—of American schooling), in freely translating and reinterpreting his thought, transmuted it so that to the uncritical mind schooling became, for general purposes, *all* of education. Thus Dewey's eminently reasonable proposition—not *conclusion,* mind you—that a school should educate the "whole child" became, in the ardor of implementation, revisionary; as Cremin suggests, the statement was transmuted to mean the school should furnish the "whole of education for the child."

This is understandable. We are generous with our interpretations of what should be done for children—especially for children—as we extend the bounds of sympathy to all. Nonetheless, the confusion has been the occasion of much unintended mischief. If we confuse the issue and concept of schooling as furnishing the "whole of education for the child" with that of schooling as educating the "whole child" (an end, by the way, that is conceivable if we marry our researches in the fields of growth and development with theory and practice in learning), we enter upon a discourse that is footless. In attempting to develop a school that is the "whole of education for the child" we aspire to a universe of social action and amelioration that is the domain of the body of political, social, and economic institutions *entire.*

If we accept this notion of schooling, we come to questions that roll upon teachers and young alike and crush them, simply because the whole of education in our complex society exceeds the capacity of the school, as presently conceived and organized. For example, the "habitual vision of greatness," which is an outcome of education, is a habit begun in the home but not finished in the school; it is *sustained* in the constant search for personhood, which is the goal of education and experience in life. Perhaps it was once conceivable in the unrecorded past to equate the years before the rites of passage into maturity as schooling cum education. Yet if it ever was, it is no longer so.

This is not to say—it is never to say—that schooling and education are apart. It is to say that *schooling* per se, to be effective in our present technocratic society, with its techno-electronic technology—a society hastening into a postindustrial era—should at least accommodate an "ecology of achievement." A school is *part* but not *all* of this ecology. That is, schooling is reasonably a part of a whole, as articulated in the whole of society and the culture that mothers it, even as the separate communities of the forest and the sea are parts and not the whole of the ecosystem. In effect, a school should be considered within and not apart from its ecology—its community, if you will. It can be seen that a community furnishes an ecology of achievement in which a school may achieve "success" or "failure." The ecology of achievement that nourishes a "successful" school characterizes a "successful" community.

It is necessary to emphasize, in another context, that formal schooling is only one of the many ways, albeit an important one, of transmitting the culture to new generations so that they in turn may transmit, expand, or correct it. The historian Bernard Bailyn, emphasizing the "entire process by which culture transmits itself across generations," eloquently stated the place of a host of influences on knowledge, attitude, and skills attained through life and living in his brief but important book *Education in the Forming of American Society*. Recall that the noted historian Lawrence Cremin, in his *The Genius of American Education,* pressed a similar point. Cremin has enlarged his view to encompass two periods of American education: one, the Colonial period; two, into the industrial period. It is the second book—*American Education: The National Experience 1783–1876,* that develops the view that more than public education was at the base of the growth of this society and this country in the social, industrial, political, economic, and religious sectors. In this important study, he emphasizes that education of a person may come out of direct or indirect, intended or unintended, efforts. He defines education as "the deliberate, systematic, and sustained effort to transmit, evoke, or acquire knowledge, values, attitudes, skills, or sensibilities, as well as any learning that results from the effort, direct or indirect, intended or unintended." Perhaps the impact of the school is lost in this definition but Cremin does not intend it to be, and makes the distinction clear.

This book is not in any way an attempt to reduce the tremendous influence of schooling on the nation's growth. Throughout, this book stresses the impact of school curriculum, instruction, and evaluation on children. Indeed, an enlargement of the function of schooling is proposed, but the distinction between the practices of schooling and education is emphasized and, where the argument permits, clarified.

The Apparently Successful School: An Ecology of Achievement

Over the past thirty years, it has been my opportunity and privilege to range the country observing schools at work. Each decade, beginning in 1948, the curricular, instructional, evaluative, and administrative practices of more than 200 schools—elementary and secondary, public and independent—have been studied in an effort to determine what it was that made a school "successful" in the estimate of visiting teachers, supervisors, administrators, and other educators (such as college and university teachers). By way of an assessment, based on the experience of over thirty years, the following may be stated:

• There are schools where the young *are* achieving satisfactorily by the exacting standards set for them by the school, by the university, by the community that supports them, and by society in general. There are schools and communities that work. It is rare to find a community that does not work and a school system within it that does. There is generally a fit between school and community.

• There *are* schools that are a reservoir of innovations in education that satisfy the requirements of an exacting, self-examining, open society.

• There *are* schools that live in harmony with the community and are "successful" by the standards imposed on them by the community and society generally.

These are the schools that harbor innovations and are "genetic pools" or libraries, as it were, of innovations, ready for use in the present or in the future. Certain of the schools observed are comprehensive schools—including the full range of curriculum, from academic to industrial areas, rich in science and humanities, adaptive to the needs of the range of students. These schools offer not only equality of opportunity, but also what is equally important, "special opportunity" for those who cannot as yet take advantage of equal opportunity (for example, children with reading difficulties, children with capacities in languages other than English). The proponents of "equal opportunity" really mean "special opportunity," as indeed they should.

Certain of these schools have "schools-within-schools" (SWS), which attend to the needs of a variety of students with disparate abilities —academic populations, primarily those destined for the university, as well as those populations otherwise destined, those who prize manual dexterity.

Over the past thirty years, I have conducted formal observations in over 600 schools and have talked with and interviewed some 120 administrators and some 2,000 teachers—singly or in groups. There are in this sample of schools and teachers those which prize innovative instruction and curriculums; there are technical and vocational schools of high excellence that do not disregard intellection; there are schools that use TV to assist instruction in exemplary fashion; there are schools that use computers and calculators (microprocessors) to assist instruction; there are schools that combine work and schooling (part-time); there are schools that tend to the "disadvantaged" and the "advantaged" in har-

13

mony; there are schools that have innovated programs in "environmental education" and have attacked problems of the so-called abuse of the environment and "misuse" of energy without attacking the social-industrial effort or the technology central to our technocratic society; there are schools with splendid programs in the "basics" that have not disregarded demanding programs in the sciences, social sciences, humanities (art, music, dance, drama), and athletics. There are schools in the inner city whose children are competent in reading and numbering, whose teachers, supervisors, and administrators are nevertheless aware that competence in these areas is not adequate and who are developing a balanced curriculum stressing social science, science, and the humanities. There are schools that individualize instruction for single students and small groups with similar interests and ability. There are schools that attend to the "gifted" and "talented." What is encouraging is that these schools exist. What is baffling is that, although their practices exist and have been described, to all purposes new programs are begun as if these schools, these practices, these "solutions," do not exist.

In short, the schools noted by way of example are pools of experience and innovation, and stand as a ready reference when past "movements" or "innovations" are to be resurrected or "new" ones introduced. These are the schools where one observes an ecology of achievement in operation. It is not overly profound to suggest that principals, supervisors, teachers, and children do *not* make a school without the close support of the adults in the community—parents and nonparents alike. That is, the school and the community are one in their aims and objectives—*ideally,* of course. But where children are concerned, is anything less than the ideal to serve as an objective?

Practices that define balance in curriculum and instruction will be discussed in later chapters, but it is here that the concept of an *ecology of achievement* as it is observed in schooling should be discussed, in brief. Schools in which an ecology of achievement is functioning have the characteristics given below (not in any order of precedence of cause or effect on achievement). These characteristics function in a meld; they are not easily isolated. Where an ecology of achievement exists—that is to say, where a balance in practice exists—the following conditions operate. To the extent that each condition is not operating at optimum, some dissatisfaction in the community and the school exists.

1. They prize knowledge, values, and skills, intellectual as well as personal development. In other words, they prize competence and compassion, and therefore view with constructive affection efforts

toward the attainment of desirable objectives. The administrators and teachers, their plans of instruction and modes of instruction, have the interest and support of the community—that is, its people and the support they command (influence, power, funds).

2. They have a balanced program supported by communities that have an established tax base. They are pleasant environments which encourage teaching and instructed learning and the personal behavior that advances them. Materials of instruction (books, films, records, machines) are carefully selected but are in good supply. Libraries are reasonably well supplied, as are laboratories and areas specially designed for the teaching of music, art, athletics, and vocational subjects.

3. Teachers are selected carefully and remunerated accordingly. They are rewarded for advancing their own education and training.

4. Parents *care* for the schooling and education of their young. The young are willing (properly motivated) because their parents value education and attend carefully to their children's progress or lack of it in school. Self-discipline thus becomes a matter of growth.

5. The superintendents, principals, and supervisors (the educational leaders) are selected for intellectual, social, and administrative excellence. They are characterized as "strong leaders" by observers. The characteristic "strong" seems to refer to an amalgam: their objectives ("goals") are clearly defined and ardently pursued; they are generally respected by their staffs (meaning that they know how to act on people to get agreement on objectives and secure a common effort toward their attainment). "Strength" also describes decent scholarship and professional skill.

6. The members of the Board of Education—elected, to be sure—are selected for interest in education and competence in administering *a system*—not an inconsiderable skill, for a system is the integrative functioning of all its parts.

7. The evaluative procedures are the result of discussion and general agreement by administrators, teachers, parents, and the Board (which represents the general community). In other words, tests of a wide variety (informal teaching tests, criterion-referenced tests, as well as standardized tests) are used to monitor the progress of children, as diagnostic of their problems, as aids to the design of special modes of instruction, as aids to securing special materials of instruction. The testing program provides feedback and is not initially or necessarily used to "reward" or "punish." It is used to advance the knowledge and skills of children and is used in both

artistic and artful fashion to secure the collaboration of parents and children in adopting the objectives agreed upon.

In short, in these schools the staff and the community have developed a system that is an ecology of achievement; all parts are interdependent. Such school systems manage people, ideas (programs of instruction and modes of instruction), and money wisely. The ends of an ecology of achievement are clear. The community achieves its purpose: excellence in schooling. The community and its schools achieve their purposes: excellence in curriculum, instruction, and administration. The young achieve their purposes: excellence as they grow in fulfillment of their powers, in personality, and in intellection. The community has recognized that excellence in schooling is a clear index of the social, political, and economic maturity of the community.

In effect, the social system in these communities contains a kind of servomechanism: a device responsive to feedback and to evaluation of the factors (1 through 7 above) necessary for the success of a school system. A relatively simple (too simple) example of a servomechanism or system (one that will be dealt with more extensively in Chapter 7) is the thermostat. No one assumes that the servomechanisms of a school or community are anywhere near as simple. The thermostat maintains a standard of heating and cooling (stable temperature) set by the occupants of a room. If the temperature rises beyond that which has been set, the thermostat "monitors" or "evaluates" the system and turns off the heat; if the temperature falls, the heat is turned on. It is a *system* designed to meet its objectives. And a system is a *closed circle,* as it were.

So, too, a community quick to respond to educational excellence or deficiency acts as a servomechanism. It approves and rewards excellence

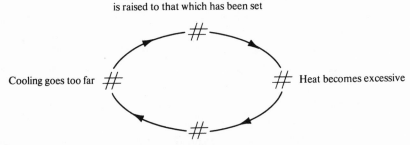

Furnace is turned on until the temperature is raised to that which has been set

Cooling goes too far

Heat becomes excessive

System is "monitored"; furnace is turned off, temperature is lowered until the desired temperature is attained

immediately and disapproves and attends immediately to deficiencies in schooling. At the same time, it takes upon itself the problems of the young that are first and properly the concern of the parents: the social behavior, the civilized behavior—the set of standards, if you will—requisite for the proper conduct of the community. In turn, the standards of the school and the community become a thermostat of the behavior fit for schooling.

A more useful analogy of an ecology of achievement is pictured in the life of a healthy forest or pond, where the ecology, the interaction of the components (organisms and physical environment), makes up a collaborative environment, a forest, a pond. If a factor essential to the life of a forest (say, water) deteriorates, the forest deteriorates. If a factor essential to the life of a school (say, support by the community) deteriorates, the school deteriorates.

Perhaps this hypothesis of an ecology of achievement can be used to account for the failure or success of a school system: *If any one of the general factors 1 through 7 listed above is not at optimum in the schooling environment, then it is to the extent of its deviation from the optimum that a given school system fails in the required set of standards that maintain excellence in schooling. As the factor found wanting is corrected and approaches the optimum, a schooling system tends to approach the standards set for it.* In effect, where the general conditions described are found and are "working," the community has invented an extraordinary social institution significant to the advance of society—in short, a *school system.*

The concept of an ecology of achievement is important from another point of view. In researches on the achievement of schools, it is now the practice to analyze and compare the range of schools over the nation. From my observations and that of other observers, it is clear that different ecologies of achievement will produce schools differing in the achievement of their students. From this point of view, valid research should compare the achievement of students existing within a given ecology of achievement (a recognizable and measurable community). Or valid research should compare the functions and achievements of students in different schools across the nation only within comparable ecologies of achievement. However, if one wishes to assess the significance of an ecology of achievement on the achievement of students, one would and should compare and contrast the variety of ecologies across the country. In other words, to measure achievement of students or teachers, it is not valid to examine the school *only;* it is essential to assess the ecology of achievement in which the school functions.

Put another way, when a community (synonym: school district) has accommodated to the practices that secure the traits of a successful school system, its eyes have been fixed simultaneously on the young and on its own obligations. With regard to the young, their fulfillment in the pursuit of their special excellence in personal growth and in learning was paramount. With regard to the community's obligations in plans of instruction and modes of instruction, there were these essential propositions: whatever was taught was to be taught well, however it was taught; whoever was taught, all were to profit; whoever was tested, the test was to be a search for improvement. There was to be proof of an individual's intellectual growth as well as growth in health and interpersonal relations.

There was a commonality of purpose and a sharing of plans to achieve an acknowledged purpose. The school, whatever its form, seemed whole, and a part of the community. The failure or success of the community was mirrored in the school and vice versa. A school system is an extraordinary organism; it learns and ever adapts to new social environments as it advances the causes of the young. But a school system, like any organism, is fed, secured, and succored by its environment.

Persistent Antecedent Questions

There are questions that have engaged minds ever since the problem of how to induct the young into a society became articulated in a body of practice called "education." Plain or not, they are antecedent questions indeed and they should be probed before we enter upon the perennial problems that fall to those who would educate the young, problems, for example, such as the following (not, of course, ordered in importance—indeed, the tranquillity of any discussion is broken by suggesting that one problem has "priority" over another):

• How do we organize an educational system that serves the *great variety* of the young—different in gifts, opportunities, and destinies?

• How do we organize instruction so that the "slow" and the "gifted" can benefit, can advance at their own pace? (Alternately: Should the young be taught in homogeneous or heterogeneous groups?)

• How do we care for the 25% of the young who, in our graded schooling system, generally get 75% of the failing marks?

- How shall we balance an incredibly rich fare of subject matters? For example, how much time shall be given over to reading and mathematics, to the humanities and arts, to the sciences, to vocational and special education?
- What are the knowledges, values, and skills necessary for a post-industrial society?
- How shall we use books, computers, TV, and the other riches of our educational technology?
- How shall we deal, if indeed we should, with problems of truth, beauty, justice, faith, and love? Is a school the place to assault the enemies of a "purposeful life," which a veritable pantheon of scholars designates as ignorance, meaninglessness, inhumanity, self-destruction, alienation, anomie, and the like?
- How do we organize the schools to offer all who attend equality and equity of opportunity in the quest for equality of achievement?
- How do we finance schooling?
- How shall we finance education?

It is not that these problems have been ignored. Indeed, useful solutions have been found to a good number of them. There are, as said earlier, exemplary schools that "balance an incredibly rich fare of subject matters" and that organize instruction "so that the 'slow' and the 'gifted' can benefit." Perhaps it is best to refer to these schools as "pilot" schools, because often they have been selected to initiate innovative practices.

The question that has occurred time and time again, and must have occurred to the reader or any observer of these exemplary or pilot schools, is: Why was it that the schools within range of the pilots did not change their own practices? A pilot school was often to be found in the midst of a number of schools that disregarded its "successful" practices. Upon reflection, the answer seems clear. Schools chosen as pilot schools in which to introduce an innovation are clearly those with the ecology of achievement described earlier: with strong administrators and supervisors, with a staff of able teachers willing to undertake the retraining necessary, and with most members of the staff—if not all—willing to make a serious study of curriculum, instruction, and evaluation necessary to institute change. Further, the pilot school is in a community in which warring factions have merged in a collaboration to attack common problems; in short, an ecology of achievement is being fashioned. Moreover, when at last the pilot school's successful achievement comes to general attention (because, for example, the problem it has solved is now critical in the community), some three to five years have already been spent by the pilot school on the solution of the problem.

Unfortunately, once the problem has risen to crisis proportion, the rush to *institute* a solution in all schools proceeds by means of what is so characteristic of our "solution" of problems in schooling: "crash programs"—and of course a crash program proceeds pell-mell. The careful planning and time applied to the overhaul of curricular, instructional, evaluative, and administrative problems that the pilot schools undertook is ignored. In effect, the program *instituted* in the pilot school is now to be *institutionalized* in the schools generally. (Perhaps the more appropriate term is "copied.") In most cases, the institutionalization fails precisely because it is copied. Even as one cannot introduce a birch tree into a desert (a full-formed ecology) or a cactus into a pine forest (an ecology patently different from that of the desert), one cannot introduce (institutionalize) a successful practice into a school where all the other factors of the ecology of achievement are not present. The failure of the introduction of individualized instruction into a school given over to the lecture-group approach is not necessarily the failure of the teaching staff, or even of the community willing to support the innovation. It is too often a "failure" due to the eagerness of the community to institutionalize the innovation. Thus the careful growth of a given staff and community is not nurtured. For example, to introduce individualized instruction is a matter of careful nurture over years (perhaps five to eight years), not a mattter of easy decision and expectation of results within a year or two.

The lesson is a hard one to learn: to introduce desirable innovation, to "change" the schools, to institutionalize new methods means first to establish an ecology of achievement in which the change, the innovation, will thrive. And to the extent that the ecology is not established, the innovation will fail, or take an exceeding amount of time and energy. However this may be, an ecology of achievement enables a community to make satisfactory response to certain antecedent questions.

The question that troubled our ancestors and still has not found a satisfactory response in most countries is: Who is to be taught? The question has been answered most recently in the United States with great force: Everyone. Schooling is to be available to all; all are meant to be able to afford it, to be served by it, to benefit by it, to have equal educational (*sic*) opportunity for equal educational (*sic*) achievement. (Note, please, "education," not "schooling." On the significant distinction that should, in the view explicated in this book, be made between "schooling" and "education," see my argument throughout. I am persuaded that schooling specifically has been confused with education generally.)

Having answered possibly the single most important question and made it part of the body of law, we are now required to consider questions, propositions, and problems that are not part of law but part of choice. The response to the question Should we afford free and equal schooling to each and all? is no longer one of *free* choice. The choice seems to be relatively free only in the *kind* of response to be made. If it is made only halfheartedly or with reservation, a healthy ecology of achievement is not attained. Certain of these perennial problems—perhaps not the most important—have already been noted. But once we begin to probe any of these so-called perennial problems we recognize that they are to be analyzed only if we resolve the "root" questions—perennial, all-important, and crucial to policy and practice in schooling. These are:

What is it that is to be taught? To what end?

How is it to be taught?

To whom is it to be taught?

Where and when is it to be taught?

And, unalterably,

What proof is there that it has been taught?

These are at once questions that encompass teaching and learning, curriculum, instruction, evaluation, and administration. These are the questions that encompass teaching and learning wherever and whenever they take place, in the school or out of school, at home, when TV is used to inform, in any mode of schooling and/or education. These are the persistent questions of which the problems stated on the preceding pages are subsets; these are the questions that are amenable to resolution in the kind of ecology we have been discussing.

When we face these questions, we discern a confusion of "instructed learning" (Jerome Bruner's phrase; see Chapter 4) with "learning." "Instructed learning" is the sure domain of schooling (not yet of TV, for example), where what is to be learned is planned for the young according to certain principles underlying curriculum and instruction by teachers in a school. Further, the response of the "learner" determines what has been learned. "Learning" per se is the domain of *all* forms of education, where what is to be learned is freely or not freely chosen but is nevertheless a part of a process within the learner, at his or her own responsibility. The early years at home—when the parent is teacher—are antecedents to appropriate schooling. The sustained, habitual visions of greatness characteristic of the "educated person," the knowledge, values, and skills that undergird habits of self-expression and habits of good choice (conduct), are antecedently to be acquired through schooling. Be that as it may, where an ecology of achievement is missing, these

21

"root questions" are often irritants leading to divisiveness, not concurrence or collaboration.

Teaching is intended to *change behavior*—self-expression and conduct both; and a change in behavior, effective behavior, to be sure, is the goal of both schooling and education. It is in the question Which behaviors are the domain of schooling and which appropriately of other educational modes, institutions, or systems and in what degree or kind? that the schools come eyeball to eyeball with a particular community, with society, and with the culture.

It is somewhat hazardous to undertake a rational discussion of almost any social problem. In the examination of social problems, we do not have the traditions of the kind of scholarship a problem-solving area should have. For example, a datum, a fact, a hypothesis, a theory put forward by a scientist is *not* accepted and acted upon; it is expected to be subjected to careful research and confirmation in critical investigation by the scientist's peers. If the hypothesis or theory is confirmed by investigation (by others than the proponent), and if, further, the hypothesis or theory explains a number of hitherto unexplained but existing facts, it is tentatively accepted by the community of scientists as useful for thought and investigation—and is then subjected to more testing. If a "fact" is true, it can be confirmed; if false, it cannot. An object is said to fall to the center of the earth not because Newton said so, but because many investigators confirmed his data and his logic, as well as his many experiments, which survived the scrutiny of good minds over time. The credential of a fact is outside the believer. But note how quickly we boost a hypothesis affecting social behavior (and this, of course, includes schooling and education) into the pantheon of fact, how we subject it to the public forum as if that were a way of making it confirmable or falsifiable. Furthermore, not all who read the results of investigations in science and society understand fully the meaning of statistical analysis. What should be our conclusion about the effect on any individual of practices that are analyzed statistically? An individual (a part of a statistic) is generally lost in the arms of the larger statistic.

If the conclusions of a physical or biological scientist are put forth tentatively (and indeed we expect them to be put forth tentatively until confirmed), why is it that the researches of the social scientist (and this includes the researches of educators) become "fact" so quickly? In terms of the tradition of scholarship, the answer is perhaps that, in the public mind, the social sciences do not yet have the standing or the traditions of the natural sciences.

In a society where astrology and other "curious disciplines" have standing, perhaps not even the traditions of the physical and natural sciences prevail. Be that as it may, schooling and education are "sciences" of practice, not of the laboratory. We do not yet know *how* the young—or, for that matter, the old—learn; we know only that they do. And this we knew before the sciences, natural or social, were established. Nevertheless, the studies of Coleman and Jencks and others did focus on the schools as part of society, but they should have emphasized attention to a single overarching element: the "success" or "failure" of a school is not to be attributed to a given school, or to communities as entities, but to the operation of discrete factors within a community that together make up an ecology of achievement. It is this ecology that characterizes not only successful schools but also successful communities.

Once we face the questions raised earlier others that have plagued us—for example, how to ensure equality of opportunity; how to educate the "disadvantaged" as well as the "gifted"; how one achieves excellence in the pursuit of one's powers; how to embrace the full spectrum of varied abilities, gifts, opportunities, destinations; how to organize curriculum and instruction effectively; how to embrace the realms of knowledge as well as the realms of inquiry that make that particular knowledge accessible—the full panoply of debate concerning schooling and education—other questions come into a credible compass.

James Bryant Conant retreated in dismay when anyone began a discussion of the "aims of education" and what constitutes "the educated man." But he, as do many respected observers of schooling and education, agreed that to speak competently about schooling per se is to focus on its nucleus: curriculum and instruction. He was constantly in search of a balance in offerings in the "comprehensive school" that would benefit all. Jerome Bruner speaks of curriculum (a plan of instruction) as a "compact delivery system of the culture." That is to say, the architecture of curriculum proceeds in at least two comprehensive steps: first, a study of the culture (the client, as it were) is necessary, then a reduction of its complexity (not its essence) so that it can be managed in the limited time and sequence and apparatus of the schools. Curriculum mirrors the culture, and instruction mirrors the curriculum in that it attempts to make the curriculum the possession of the mind and body, and, if you will, an inextricable component of the individual and his or her personality. Curriculum is, in a sense, a plan for the introduction of that comprehensive armament of knowledge, values, skills, and behaviors with which the individual attends to life and living, and, further, a plan for introducing into schooling that apparatus of behaviors (of knowledge, values, and skills) by which the community assesses its young and makes its judgment and acknowledgment of the contributions of its citizens to its commonwealth.

Curiously, when we attend to the conditions and questions antecedent to the development of an ecology of achievement, we find that in many communities school systems do not exist, only schools which are disparate parts of a town or city. We need to come down hard on new choices: Do we—in any given community—want school *systems,* or unrelated schools? And if the former, how far are we willing to go? On these questions we may have an easy conscience. The purpose of discussion (particularly in an open society)—indeed, the function of scholarship—is to go too far so that others may go far enough. Knowing how far to go is the burden of leadership and the problem of the exercise of choice by those who accept the responsibility within the precincts of an open society. And, if our answer is that, "yes," we want excellent school systems, do we then go further and say that these school systems are to be part of an excellent educational system?

As has been indicated, teaching is an art-science of practice, not yet of the laboratory. The calibrations of our instruments of inquiry are not yet refined. Too often, as Christian Gauss has reminded us, we are caught up in the "meaningless precision of numerical studies." To generalize the human being is to lose the individual, to lose what is singularly precious. This is not to say that for purposes of a study we may not generalize, but for purposes of schooling and education—that is, to change specific behaviors—we are conscience-bound to focus on the individual.

The child is an intervention in the social order. The family knows it first; the school, as an agent of society, soon thereafter. Each child is born alien, as alien to our environment, our society, our culture, as a visitor in an "encounter of the third kind." Schooling and education give the child a passport to the culture. In the school are the young who will not only receive the culture, but also create it, for a culture is constantly reborn. When the young are openly a part of the burgeoning culture, earning for themselves a discipline of responsible consent and dissent, then that culture is in constant renewal, in constant growth, and, what is more, bound in an ever-growing sympathy.

When, however, schools and children become implements of political, social, and psychological warfare, when attempts at reform *through* the schools clash head on with attempts at reform *of* the schools, the schools become a battleground, a field of stress and turbulence, of combat within one uneasy body. Then the school and the young—and in the end the society that embraces them—are in open conflict. Or, what is even more damaging than the open conflict (which is subject to resolution), there boils within individuals a grievance without easy redress. The young begin to enact what appears to be a hidden agenda; they set themselves aside in disenfranchisement. Then we say we have a "lost" generation. We mean, in effect, that we have lost them through our mismanagement of both schooling and educational enterprises; we have not diagnosed the grievance or analyzed the malady. Life has become sour, and the young and the old accuse each other: a waste. Then we resort to a phrase: the generation gap.

This need not be. For we are a gathered people. And our cry is not of evil.

2. Regarding Pertinent Lessons

At its best, schooling is a civilizing act. At best, it prepares children to conserve and transmit what is best in civilization; at best, schooling inaugurates in children the desire, and helps them invent the means, to rectify what is wrong and expand what is human and humane. At worst, a school or schooling system may become a system of rejection for those who are not able to accommodate to an unnecessarily stringent, straitened, and exacting environment.

To those who want to see an immediate change in schooling, it is necessary to say, at least for the United States, that there can be no revolution in schooling per se. Schooling is the means by which society passes on its concepts, values, and skills to its children; schooling is a means by which we conserve and transmit what society values—and what society is, whether we value it or not. A revolution in schooling, an abrupt and violent change, would therefore mean an abrupt and violent change in society. In short, for the present and the foreseeable future, schools are the agents of society. It follows then that changes in schooling in a democracy are the slow, tortuous changes coming out of the balance of opposing opinion, without coercion. In fact, American history does not record a revolution in schooling: the record is one of slow evolution. Generally speaking, the rate of change depends on the ideas available and the resources allocated. This must be a trial for the impatient, for those who seek immediate correction, an immediate amelioration of imbalance.

It must also be a trial for those who blame the schools for the imperfections of our society. The questions that are appropriate are these:

Which modern society is satisfied with the achievements of its young, in school or out? Which schooling system, anywhere on the globe, corrects the imperfections of its society? Put another way: In which country do the schools not portray the best and worst of the society?

We are caught in the grip of a depressing *déjà vu*. As in the early 1950s, we hear that high-school students are "not prepared" for work in the university. The scores on Standard Aptitude Tests (SATs), a part of the College Board examinations, are going down. (Curiously, when the scores were satisfactory, the schools were not necessarily responsible; it was merely the best of times.) We hear everywhere that the gifted are being neglected and "crash programs" are being developed. It was also thus in the 1950s. Computers and computer-assisted instruction are about to make their entry once again. It was also thus in the 1950s. And there are the "basics." So, too, in the 1950s. Perennially, the cry is that the young cannot read or number well. Careful study will show generally that 15 to 20% of our students do excellent work (comparing favorably with the best in other countries), about 15 to 20% do respectably well, about 30 to 40% do passing work, and about 20 to 25% get about 75% of the failing marks. In the latter group, about 5 to 10% attend school sporadically. The number may be higher.

The point is this: we are in a period of reform and innovation. The pendulum has swung once again. We are about to reform the schools once again. If this is said in a weary or wearying tone, it is not meant to be. It is a sad tone, reflecting the question Why aren't the excellent practices that exist—excellent curricular and instructional practices which are open to observation—embraced by all schools, public and independent?

Perhaps a light can be shed on the dilemma by examining past reforms and past innovations. And this we are obliged to do.

Schools and Society: The Avowed Hope

Must our view of schooling always be based on a vision of school and society in poor fit, of parents, children, and teachers at odds? Is this the result of our indomitable vision of human perfectability? Perhaps our vision is the result of the constant and healthy and necessary difference between the views of those who seek *revolution* (and therefore insist on instant remediation) and the views of those who are bent to the cadence of *evolution* (and see remediation as the result of point and counterpoint). Perhaps the resulting pendulation of conflict and clarification and, once again, conflict and clarification is the safety valve of struggle in an open society, reducing the chances of catastrophe. Interpreting the same data, one group sees man's inevitable descent; the other sees man's ascent.

A cranky vision would seem to insist that no matter what we do, no matter how excellent our practice, someone, some pupil, a certain group, a certain population, persists in *not* being successful. This is surely perverse. One wonders at the perversity of the population which *will not* succeed—by our measures. Might not the perversity lie in *us?* Might it not stem from our eternal assumption that somehow schooling frees ability and capacity, neutralizes error or perhaps flawed personality, corrects the heredity or the habituations of childhood, ennobles motivaion, bestows character, and frees talent?

Writing in 1846, Horace Mann, one of the great leaders in the movement to establish American public schools, was prepared to accept schooling as "universal education." However, it seems to us that *education* encompasses an ecology of achievement quite different from that of *schooling*.

Mann went further; he hoped the common schools would "create a more far-seeing intelligence and a purer morality than has ever existed among communities of men." It seems he thought of schools not only as agents of society, but also as agents of reform of society. So did others; the literature is replete with prescription for a general function or aim of schooling: to prepare the young for *complete living*. It was said that any "educational course," to use Herbert Spencer's term, is to be judged in what degree such an aim is discharged.

Nevertheless, the literature of schooling recalls to us that while one school of reform approved a steady transformation of American schooling as it attempted to serve the full range of intellectual capacity, another group of reformers considered the American school system to be a system of rejection for a significant sector of our young, particularly the poor. Thus considered, the system of schooling merited only drastic and immediate change, if not destruction. (See, for example, Ivan Illich's *The Deschooling of Society*.) Both schools of thought continued to put forth "convincing testimony" to support conflicting views, but "right" seemed generally to be on the side of the socially aggrieved, that is, the rejected.

The loud debate is aggravated by those who argue that a carefully engineered, benevolent social environment can reverse the ravages of an early disabling environment, even genetically inspired dysfunction. They argue that if intellectual ability can be to any degree overcome by schooling and education, then schooling and education, as processes, should be given their chance through the fair exercise of full and varied opportunity—even if tests (testing IQ, ability, or aptitude) indicate that a given child or group of children is handicapped. It is argued that tests, where used, should indicate how each child should be taught, because, after all, children learn in different ways, and these methods could conceivably be different for each child. This concept of modalities (ways of distinctive and idiosyncratic learning by distinct individuals) has a long history but has most recently been pressed forward with fresh evidence.

Thus, and only through individualized instruction, argue the adherents of schooling as a corrective of disadvantage (genetic or environmental), can we determine whether an environment favorable to learning can erase disadvantage. In general, the proponents of a school system whose function is to be amelioration of social ills do not question whether or not the present situation in the schools is owing to moral or social error, error in belief or love, or error in legislation, or in a confusion between the functions of schooling and of education—which includes schooling as one of its major components.

In sum, a significant number of Americans continue to believe that amelioration of initial social and intellectual inadequacies can be achieved by altering the environment through education, and most continue to assume that social and intellectual environments can be altered by changing teaching policy and practice. Here again, however, they are not speaking of *education* at all, but of *schooling*—even though schooling as presently conceived, constructed, and construed simply cannot engage the total task of education.

To alter modes of schooling to ensure greater effectiveness in teaching and learning is to alter curriculum as a plan of instruction, as well as the modes of instruction; this in turn means to alter the manner by which we conserve, transmit, rectify, and expand our knowledge and skills, our concepts and values, which are so widely accepted and generously shared. And we are urged to do this for the entire spectrum of social and intellectual capacity. Reformers of a society would press the point that the social purpose of a school system is to enlarge the bounds of sympathy, to spread self-esteem, power, and privilege over the entire range of ability, and to reduce disability in any sector.

For the sake, then, of a vision of a multitude of school and educational systems renewing themselves, joining with others to form a network of educational systems, the first on this globe, let us try to determine whether it is possible to undertake a renewing of our educational systems to meet the decades ahead—decades in which a postindustrial revolution will renew society and culture. Although our aims are those of education, of intellection, of personal growth, the problem of renewing our educational systems is a *structural* one. But structure—as all of us, as organisms, know—is at the base of appropriate, healthy, and purposive *function*. This has been forgotten, or at least lost in the heat of dispute. Without structure, an organism, an institution, a society, or an individual loses its function and inevitably loses choice as well.

Let us focus on communities that already exist, on parents who already exist, on teachers who already exist, and on children who already exist. Indeed, as said before, the elements of the finest educational system exist, lying about waiting to be picked up and organized in an ecology of achievement. When it is constructed, it is possible, perhaps, that the educational system will aim to educate, not merely to school. And so each child can become what he or she at first pretends to be—truly human, competent, and compassionate.

American schools, generally speaking, have not failed the society; in a way, a society gets the schools it wants. One might argue that American schools have been competent in managing their domain given the burdens, the constantly shifting signals and demands made by society. For example, no sooner had the schools taken on the task of curricular reform directed at attaining academic excellence (the "intellectual reform" of curriculum of 1957–1965) than they were asked to take on the task of meeting the needs of the disadvantaged (1965 through the present). Everything considered, our country could not have reached its status as a meritocracy and technocracy without the intervention of schooling and without the influence of other educational systems.

We are obligated to take the long view because social change, when it occurs, is analyzed in decades, not years. The "facts," evasive as they are, should incline us to take the long view, and we should note unfailingly the sound successes (not only the failures) in American schooling over the last 200 years. Great changes require a quantum leap—but the elements of the change come to view in discrete form; somehow they come out of the amalgam, they precipitate and accrete, and somehow they adhere to established practice. They remain in a sort of gene pool of educational practice. To press the point, it is desirable to sketch selected case studies of reform and innovation as examples of apparent failure; then perhaps it is necessary to take the long view and suggest that there exists a definable and progressive trend in schooling in which certain reforms take hold.

Case Study: A Reform of Society
Antecedent to a Reform of Schooling

The case study offered is an example of the way a social reform—a cultural reform, if you will—is effected partly by reform *through* schooling, eventually leading to a reform *of* schooling. The reform of schooling in this case study is consequent on the antecedent social reform—to wit, the Industrial Revolution.

Recall that the Industrial Revolution was not only or mainly a revolution in technology, but also one that penetrated and changed the fabric of American life. After the steam and internal-combustion engines, after the dynamo, after electricity, life and living were never to be the same. The need for labor (and therefore for immigrants), the need for raw material, the organization of the factory—indeed, of corporate industrialism—changed both the fabric and the tempo of life. Muscle gave way to machine, and to change in social structure.

The following description relies heavily on Lawrence Cremin's *The Transformation of the School: Progressivism in American Education,* an analysis of the essential effect of the reform. His is a brilliant account and integration of the thrust of American schooling in the decades bridging the last of the nineteenth and the beginning of the twentieth centuries. It furnishes considerable insight into the range of difficulties faced by American schools when they attempted to accommodate a flood of immigrant populations, and tells of the splendid service (it may unblushingly be called a success) of the schools in preparing disparate populations for citizenship. Cremin documents a substantial transformation: schools centered in subject matters, and aiming mainly at high standards of intellectual excellence, striving to define their function as *serving all the children of a society,* that, over several decades, were transformed into schools defining their function as *service to the great variety of children—varying in gifts, opportunity, and destination.* In the end, we find the public schools generally serving the needs of children and striving to accommodate a variety of subject matters not only to the great variety of abilities of the young, but also to a variety of opportunities and destinations. Yet, as Cremin suggests, the "transformation" was not completed. And the reasons may perhaps be analyzed and yield us lessons—against a coming transformation, a coming renewing of schooling.

One may well begin with the work of William T. Harris, not because an era begins with him, but because one is required to break into a cycle, or pendulate movement, somewhere. Harris, like Horace Mann, explicated and lived the educational thought of his time. In *The Pedagogical Creed of William T. Harris* he suggests that the school is the "great instrumentality to lift all classes of people into a participation in civilized life." Translated into social and educational philosophy, this meant a life of order, of self-discipline, of constancy in civil loyalty, and of respect for private property as well. Translated into educational practice, it meant mastery of the fundamentals of behavior and reading, writing, and arithmetic in elementary school and work in languages, mathematics, and classics in high school.

Among other things, to assure the command of these areas Harris organized the *graded school* with a stipulated curriculum and daily lessons. Pupils moved through quarter-years and years of work on the basis of regular examinations. Harris insisted on order, effort, work and discipline; the courses the young took were to be prescribed, not elected.

Thus Harris made the schools "work," especially in Saint Louis, where he was Superintendent of Schools, 1868–1880. Later, as United States Commissioner of Education, 1889–1906, he influenced the schools of the nation. But his attempts at precision and definition became rigid, as do most policies carried out inflexibly, and, as we shall see, his resistance to vocational education made him vulnerable. His philosophy and practice also became vulnerable as a flood of immigrants from Europe entered the schools, rural and city alike.

For decades, certainly from 1870 to 1890, however, Harris's models of efficiency ruled. What else could one do as schools swelled in enrollments (more than sixty pupils per class was not uncommon), as schools fell into serious disrepair, as untrained teachers were brought in in an attempt to meet the incredible rise in enrollments? The schools were growing and support was lacking. Soon enough the schools bent under the burden, and began to break. Newspapers took the situation in hand, and crusading reporters recounted the dismaying situation. The schools were under attack. The criticisms of the schools then—in the 1890s— were similar to those we read, or hear, or "see" (on TV) now. In short, the schools were doing a "bad job." Children could not "read or number." "Literacy" was low.

Even so, "educational" reforms were already being pressed. Frances W. Parker had instituted what was then called the "Quincy System" as early as 1875. The Quincy System attempted to make the *child*, not the *course of study*, "central" to schooling. That is, it was recognized that children varied in gifts, opportunity, and destination; they learned in different ways and at different rates. Schooling needed tailoring to individual abilities and aptitudes.

In 1876, an exposition of technical education lent itself to the spirit of reform. As Cremin recounts it, a theme of the Centennial Exposition in Philadelphia that year was the relation of education to a nation's industrial progress. One of the exhibits was that of industrial tools used at the Moscow Imperial Technical School. The literature of the exhibit concerned itself with instruction in mechanical arts (particularly the use of tools). Essentially, what was done was to analyze different trades, break them down into graded skills, and develop exercises, accompanied by models, tools, drawings, and what we now call "teacher's editions" (to assist the teacher), into a system of instruction that brought students to a standard of acceptable skill ("competency," to be sure). What was proposed by the Russians was a system where boys learned the skills of construction in workshops, after which they would become apprentices in shops where they undertook to learn *actual construction.*

It was Calvin M. Woodward, of Washington University in Saint Louis, who was active in pressing this innovation. Insisting that there was a growing demand for individuals with vocational skills, as well as for those skilled in the professions, and questioning whether the schools, colleges, and universities were equal to the demand, he concluded that the style of education then in existence did not fit students for earning a living. He was asking schools to meet the vocational needs of the young. He organized a Manual Training School in which a three-year secondary program provided more or less equal time for mental and manual labor; carpentry, patternmaking, forge work, and machine work were given equal time with history, mathematics, language, science, drawing, and the like. Soon he was a critic of the school system: it was impractical to train a minority for the learned professions while the working ("toiling") classes were ignored. Indeed, the school system of the 1870s failed to hold more than a small percentage of the population beyond the eighth grade.

Although many thought that the "new" methods of technical education belonged in technical institutions, but had no objection to including *some* technical education, they considered the primary work of public education to be "cultural"—a synonym for "nontechnical." The issue was debated in the 1880s, Woodward pressing for manual training as part of general education, others, including Albert P. Marble, of the Worcester, Massachusetts, school, decrying the movement and suggesting "its claims were exaggerated." Marble's view was that vocational education does not belong in the school; vocational training was to be done on the job.

This view was shared by many, but the view most strongly urged was that the schools were common to all and what should be provided was an education useful to all.

The crux of the matter was this: The schools were not the ground for special education, but for general education—that is, an education common to all. But Harris, while acknowledging that preparation for work was a fundamental in schooling, rejected the need to introduce apprenticeship in any form or manner into the schools. He insisted, for example, that reading was significant in the child's development, while vocational training (carpentry, bricklaying) was limited to its contribution to a specific job. In short, the "basics," as Harris interpreted them, were central to schooling.

But the rapid tide of industrialization was not to be denied, and in the 1890s to the early 1900s manual training became significant: if not in fact, at least in intention a mode of preparing the young for industry. Thus the New York Trade Schools provided instruction in plumbing, plastering, tailoring, printing, bricklaying, and the like; they did not attempt to build a curriculum with a balancing cultural thrust. The curriculum of each course was practical and led to a certificate—a result of an examination of competence in a specific trade.

Parallel to the growth of powerful industry was the growth of unionism. Spokesmen for the unions charged that the new schools turned out poor workmen who were ready to work for wages lower than those prevailing in the trade; the school graduates were often considered scabs. The hostility of organized labor increased. In the end, a committee of the American Federation of Labor, insisting that public instruction in the trades should be "privately controlled"—that is, by industry—recommended, as Cremin concludes and reports, three kinds of schools:

1. Public continuation schools for those who had already entered a trade.
2. Union-sponsored supplemental trade schools patterned after the work of the International Trades Union.
3. Public trade schools—not necessarily in separate school buildings —in which a balanced combination of general education and shop instruction would be provided.

Further, the committee recommended the creation of local advisory boards representing industry and labor.

It is necessary to remind ourselves that during these decades demands on the schools were not only for vocational education. In addition to the larger reforms in the social and educational treatment of "immigrants" and the "working classes," there were demands for reform of agricultural education.

By 1910, twenty-nine states—twenty-five of them having enacted laws concerning industrial and agricultural education since 1900—had programs advancing industrial education.

In educational reform, however, local and state efforts seem never to have been sufficient; it became clear that the federal government must somehow be involved. And so it was. An effective lobby of labor, industrial, agricultural, and teaching organizations pressed the federal government to support vocational education. In 1917, the Smith-Hughes Act provided federal aid for vocational secondary education.

The story of reform does not end here. The Smith-Hughes Act (as, indeed, the various state programs) had embraced curriculums that were craft-oriented. But technological advance, at least in the United States, was not to be denied. Once a curriculum is adopted and modes of instruction (the most difficult of habits to change) bend themselves to carry out the curriculum, teachers are apt to become isolated from the mainstream of society. So teachers of vocational subjects became isolated from the mainstream of technological innovation; their machines were soon out of mode and out of synchronization with those used in industry. From 1941 to 1948, during and after World War II, American industry (actually, American technology) recognized its responsibility for the education of its apprentices. What it had given to the schools, it took back to itself. Harold Clark and Harold Sloan, who undertook to study the phenomenon of emergent schooling in industrial sites, aptly named their report *Classrooms in the Factories*. And today, industry in collaboration with unions continues the training of its apprentices.

Society (industry) had outgrown the schools, and claimed—or reclaimed, if you will—a special function it had given to the schools. In effect, the technological society of the early 1900s had determined that specific training for special vocations was not necessarily best carried on in the schools, but society did not, in any event, take the function of general vocational training from the schools.

Cremin delineates incisively the significant aspect of the transformation, namely, the growth of progressive education—an effort to meet the social and psychological needs of the young as well as the requirements of intellection. But the progressive education movement, which will be referred to throughout this book, was, in a real sense, contiguous and continuous with the movement to "industrialize" the schools. We should note, then, the following:

• The continued influx of immigrants into the cities, with resulting poverty and squalor.

• The rise of settlement houses, such as Hull House in Chicago and the Educational Alliance in New York. These settlement houses not only cared for the physical wants of a city's needy, but also undertook educational ventures, including day nurseries and kindergartens, as well as "Americanization classes."

• The recognition that "industrialization" of the schools and the emphasis on the "basics" (reading, writing, and arithmetic) was a narrow education and a wider cultural stress was necessary. That is, the young and society were to become immersed in each other.

• The rise of schools that began to emulate the Quincy System, in which the "individual" was to take center stage.

• The rise of the progressive education movement and the progressive era in education (roughly 1910 to 1955), and the consequent development of the Progressive Education Association, with its emphasis on the needs of the learner as well as what was to be learned, with the teacher as guide and not taskmaster, with a variety of curriculums to fit the variety of abilities of the young, with extracurricular activities in all fields. In short, the sociopsychological as well as the intellection development of the child and adolescent was considered to be central.

In fact, progressive education, intended as a curricular reform, also required a drastic reform in the style of instruction and in the sociology of the classroom. For example, if a curriculum in citizenship had been introduced under the earlier system, the teacher would have been central to the process, an authority figure, the children remaining passive; the new subject matter (central to a curriculum) would have been introduced, and the method of instruction would not have been altered. Not so in the era of progressive education. Teachers were required then not only to accommodate any radically new curriculum, with new subject matter (in content and process), but also to alter their teaching style radically; classrooms were to become areas of experience where children dominated learning activity. Furthermore, this was done without the necessary change in the status of the teacher; he or she was still to be responsible for the outcome of learning. The teacher was in authority but was not to be an authority figure.

As part of the progressive education movement, in addition to accommodation to peer culture and vocational adjustment, a considerable amount of individuation of instruction involving interaction of learners with each other and with the community was central to instruction; the lecture was not a useful mode at all. The school was to become an agency for the welfare of the child, not a guarded domain given over to imparting knowledge. "Life adjustment" became a popular term in the literature of educational philosophy, policy, and practice. The school was to take on, as it were, the "entire problem of child life and master

it," as Cremin put it. "Progressivism cast the teacher in an almost impossible role, he was to be an artist of consummate skill, properly
knowledgeable in his field, meticulously trained in the science of pedagogy and thoroughly imbued with a burning zeal for social improvement." He said further: "What the progressives did prescribe made
inordinate demands on the teacher's time and ability. 'Integrated studies'
required familiarity with a fantastic range of knowledge and teaching
materials; while the commitment to build upon student needs and interests demanded extraordinary feats of pedagogical ingenuity. In the
hands of first-rate instructors, the innovations worked wonders; in the
hands of too many average teachers, however, they led to chaos."
Cremin's last statement (so simple on its surface) illuminates the complex of reasons why a certain renewing of schooling and other educational modes does not "take." For one, a rather drastic transformation
in the behavior of teachers and administrators—in style, instructional
method, and classroom management—is required. Because years are
needed to effect changes in the styles of administration and instruction
dictated by the curriculum, it is necessary for the community, the administration, and the teachers themselves to be persuaded of the effectiveness of the change. As we shall see, curricular changes (what is to be
"known" and "taught") are relatively easy to introduce, but concomitant
instructional habits (how what is to be known is to be "taught" and
"learned") are exceedingly difficult to change. Habits of instruction, of
teaching, to be sure, are rooted in the nervous system and are constantly
reinforced by social, not to say pecuniary, rewards. A swing back to the
curriculum and methods that "worked" is inevitable. If social improvement—that is, amelioration of certain ills of society—is also sought,
then the social mechanisms of "advance" and "retreat" are also brought
into play almost immediately. In effect, because time (and in my view
it takes years, perhaps a decade) is not taken to accommodate new
instructional styles to a new curriculum (which cannot achieve its aims
without alteration of instructional style), the new curriculums and the
newer knowledge, attitudes, and skills they are to accommodate fail.
This, I believe, is the single most important lesson to be learned by those
who would introduce reforms and innovations in schooling.

The majority of the members of the academic sector (at the university level, as compared and contrasted with the sector given over to
the preparation of teachers) were not inclined to favor the new curricular elements per se in the progressive education movement. They
"preferred" the college-preparatory curriculum, and, as a result, secondary school teachers were not enthusiastically part of the progressive

education movement, which remained largely a factor in elementary education. And soon, under the leadership of Bernard Iddings Bell (*Crisis in Education,* 1949) and Arthur Bestor (*Educational Waste-lands,* 1935), an attack on progressive education and what was felt to be an outcome of "life-adjustment education" was mounted. Bell and Bestor, among others, demanded stress on intellectual attainments and achievements, which were to the academic community the marks of a good society, and on decent preparation for the university.

If I have dwelt overlong on Cremin's analysis it is because I hesitate to reinvent the wheel. His work in describing the nature of a major transformation in schooling is seminal and should be examined by all who would transform schooling. And the lessons he draws are seminal as well. A cycle of reform in society, Cremin urges upon us, is pressed by society in a parallel reform through schooling. Thus the industrialization of the late nineteenth century and the early twentieth required an exceeding number of workers destined for industry, and the schools undertook to prepare them. But unless the schools are prepared (in administration, curriculum, and instruction) for the reform *through* schooling, a parallel reform *of* schooling is also required. The lesson that Cremin brings to the fore is that a society impatient for reform is often not prepared to support overlong the *reform of schooling* necessary to achieve a *reform through schooling.* Mainly, the former requires, among other things, the re-education of teachers, the building of new schools, the supply of equipment, of libraries. Yet the community at large comes to loggerheads as the course of reform falters; it regains momentum and then is blocked once again. In other words, the ecology of achievement required to sustain a reform of schooling, forged in the beginning of a movement, soon dissolves under the strains of innovation, of attack and counterattack.

A First Lesson

Having laid out the broad outline and some accommodating detail of a reform through schooling by supposedly synergistic reform of schooling, I take the privilege accorded by those who develop an argument to use it as an example—here, as an example of the uneasy but certain fit of school and society overall. Other examples will be furnished as curriculum, instruction, and evaluation are probed in the various chapters of this book. But here it is essential to draw the pertinent lesson in broad strokes:

First: the school is considered to be an agency of society.

More than that: A widely based reform of society affects the schools.

More than that: The reformers insist that the reform of society in progress be instituted, at least in part, by reform *through* schooling.

More than that: As Cremin suggests, the reform through schooling is to take place by a reform *of* schooling, that is, by a reform of curriculum, instruction, and evaluation of the effectiveness of newly introduced curriculums and modes of instruction.

More than that: Functions hitherto claimed by society are introduced into the school and made a part of the function of the school. The school then neglects its traditionally accepted functions to accommodate the special functions delegated to it. It *institutionalizes* the reform.

More than that: Other educational systems powered by different reward systems than are the schools, soon surpass the schools in the very function that was the object of the reform. Society thus institutionalizes the reform in its industrial or social educational practices; the schools fall behind in functions specially delegated to them (say, literacy, or science instruction, or attention to the disadvantaged or gifted) and are again subjected to criticism.

More than that: Society is constantly evolving new social practice and invention, hence new crises. The schools are subjected, then, almost constantly to new challenge, to new action, to new reforms. There is little time available for the reflection necessary to develop sound practice.

Thus the cycle: social reform → social reform *through* schools → educational reform *of* schools → new social reform → social reform *through* the schools.

Perhaps the pendulations that are so characteristic of school reform can be considered from another view: the persistent press upon public policy of those who hold that the school's central, even sole, function is to *impart knowledge*. Stated starkly, it is *not,* certain critics of schooling hold, the function of the school to concern itself with social reform, with the psychosocial development of the young, except, perhaps, wherein it is demonstrated that failures in development lead to disabilities in scholarship, in competence in learning the "basics" or certain subject matters. Again stated starkly, the school is to uphold standards of scholarship, and if a student fails to meet these, he or she fails. In general, successful attainment of college entrance requirements and satisfactory SAT, reading, and mathematics scores are indices of a school's success.

On the other side, again put starkly, are those who hold that children *vary* in gifts, destinations, and opportunities, and the school must accommodate the needs of all children. Psychosocial development is as important as accommodation to high standards of intellection; perhaps more so. The school is the common ground of all, of the democratic ideal; it furnishes all with the allusions that make us Americans; it is not solely the breeding ground of "elites."

So it seems that the tension existing between the two views is the reason for pendulation, thus:

A. Emphasis on knowledge (course content is significant and central) seems to give way to

B. Emphasis on children and their needs (the child, whatever his or her ability, is significant and central)

and return again to A and again to B.

Thus Harris's emphasis on course content, on discipline, on work, on the "self-active" individual came into conflict with emphasis on vocational skills to fit immigrants (who, by the way, knew little of the English tongue) into an industrial society. Again and again, we shall find the counterthrust between intellection per se and the psychosocial development of the individual as antitheses in school reform. Put simplistically, a period of emphasis on course content and intellection gives way to a period of emphasis on individual differences and needs in personal development, which in turn gives way to emphasis on course content and intellection—as if attention to personal development and to intellection were antithetical in schooling. Thus the progressive education movement, with its final thrust into "life adjustment," was counter to the demand for intellection and the course content that served it. Can these two seemingly disparate goals be harmonized? We are obligated to seek balance in the coming transformation of the schools.

A Second Lesson

We need, however, to distinguish the introduction and effect of an *innovation* from that of a *movement*. Simply, for our present purposes, an innovation is directed at one of the elements of schooling: say, improvement in reading, or mathematics, or science; improvement in course content, in self-expression, in fitness, or in certain behaviors (consideration of drug habits and the like). Perhaps it is directed at a mode of instruction: through TV or microprocessors (calculators) or, more generally, computer-assisted instruction. Perhaps it is an innovation of instruction: individuation rather than group instruction, or inquiry modes rather than lectures. A movement (such as the "industrialization of the schools"), on the other hand, affects the fabric of school and society. A movement affects a number of elements; not only the basic aims of schooling and its modes (curriculum, instruction, administration), but the elements of society supporting the school (custom, law). So the present movement for "equality of educational opportunity to assure equality of educational achievement" is a movement affecting the fabric of society and school alike. It may in the process embrace certain innovations: innovations in teaching reading to the "disadvantaged," schools-within-schools (S-W-S), open schools, alternate schools, for example. Innovations, however, are limited in their thrust. But a lesson can be learned. What is it that lies at the root of the failure of certain innovations?

Brief Histories:
TV and Programed Instruction

Recall that the essential thrust of the educational reform of the first four decades of the 1900s was to take the stress of a purely academic education (designed for college entrance) and place the developmental tasks of children at the forefront; their physical and intellectual growth, development of their personality, and the like were central to the movement. Inherent in the movement but never quite articulated was the desire to educate *all,* no matter what their status, no matter what their gifts, opportunities, or destination. Implicit and explicit in the movement erroneously called "progressive education" was the basic policy decision that the American school was a school for *all,* and, further, that each child learned in different ways peculiar and special to the abilities of the child.

In the decades after World War I, and particularly in the quarter-century 1925–1950, the thrust was toward curriculum and instruction designed to fit *all* boys and girls for "life adjustment." It fell to Arthur Bestor, Professor of History at the University of Illinois, to become the spokesman for those who thought the term and what it represented to be anathema. This group pressed for the return of the schools to education that was centered in intellection. As a matter of fact, for those students who were destined for college, the curriculum had never really changed (and today is remarkably similar, at least in form, to that of the 1940s). For these students, coursework that met college entrance requirements was central, and work intended to assure decent scores on the College Board examinations was required—and still is.

Bestor's "attack" came after 1945, following a devastating war period. Perhaps the schools, like the nation, were attempting to retrieve some balance, and that quickly. At such times it appears that we turn to methods of reform that promise quick results. We seem to turn to these methods even as we acknowledge that desirable change in a fundamental social institution is slow—evolutionary, not revolutionary. One of the responses, among many, to the pressure to return to the basics of schooling, namely, coursework or intellection, is television.

A Brief Case Study:
TV in the Classroom

Teaching through television had the promise of a quick return on investment. The idea was by this means to place excellent teachers, knowledgeable in their various subject matters, before students in the classroom, and the level of curriculum and instruction would be immediately raised. This was to be done by using a method that is clean, can be handled easily without vast expenditures of funds, and can be evaluated with effectiveness; that is, combine exceptional *people* with exceptional *ideas,* with *money* wisely spent and the whole *managed* properly and efficiently. Television teaching promised a clean, efficient *structure* in schooling.

As we shall see, almost all movements and innovations in schooling and education hinge on these four elements:

People (strong in "leadership," charismatic personality, and competent, of course)

Ideas (new, and compliant with "new" educational aims)

Money (wisely spent)

Management (competent, efficient, and accountable)

TV placed in the classroom promised these very benefits.

Within a few years, but particularly in the early 1960s, full courses "taught" by acknowledged authorities in the fields of science and mathematics were either available on film, or were beamed directly from TV studios maintained by large school systems, or were available through educational TV maintained by the community. Not to confuse the issue, we should focus on that aspect of the innovation which directly affected curriculum and instruction by replacing the curriculum then in effect. In this case, the "live" teacher was replaced by a "live" teacher on TV; in effect, what the students saw was a teacher on a TV screen.

Under the best circumstances, the TV lesson (a lecture, or lecture-demonstration in science) was given to students in a classroom with the regular teacher in attendance. At the close of the TV presentation, some ten to fifteen minutes were given over to questions by the students, or questions and an extension of the lesson by the teacher.

Under the worst conditions, the TV lesson was shown in an auditorium to a number of classes, with discussion by a "master teacher" following, or the students returned to their classrooms for brief discussion.

Evaluation by testing showed that under the best conditions of instruction the achievement of students in such courses was similar, certainly not much inferior or superior, to that achieved with a teacher in the classroom. But it is always difficult to determine how much of any achievement is due to the "halo" or Hawthorne effect—that is, the effect of higher motivation of those in the experimental group as compared with the control.

Suffice it to say, results notwithstanding, that full coursework in any subject area given by TV disappeared from the classroom within five to seven years after the enthusiastic beginning, although many school systems still possess cans of film of full courses in a number of subject areas, particularly mathematics, biology, chemistry, physics, and American history. (At this moment, I am not discussing educational TV generally. I defer a discussion of certain aspects of the educational value of this and other devices to later chapters. Surely cable TV will overcome the effects of poor TV instruction—or will it?)

Certain explanations for the almost complete demise of this particular innovation deserve attention; they illuminate our analysis of the reasons certain educational innovations such as TV instruction and computer-assisted instruction, and even movements in general, fail. The reasons embrace factors that act synergistically, affecting three populations: students, teachers, and parents (and thus the general public). The reasons also embrace the four elements that act, as it were, in an ecology of achievement: people, ideas, money, and management. (Recall that the term "ecology" refers to more than relationship and interrelationship. It refers to an interaction of factors in a system where the absence of any one factor causes a failure of the entire system.)

With regard to the student population, the unstated assumption underlying the introduction of any innovation is that it will not only improve the education of those for whom schooling is successful, but it will also engage those for whom schooling has been a failure—especially the latter. Again, for reasons that are baffling, it almost never seems sufficient for a "new" method to improve the education of those for whom schooling is successful (say, the college preparatory group); it must also increase the effectiveness of schooling for the rest, for the 25% for whom schooling is generally not a happy state. Remember that these 25% are those who in the present state of curriculum and instruction receive 75% of the failing marks. Accordingly, the school system for these students seems one of rejection.

On the other hand, an innovation that would improve the education of these 25% without affecting the acceptable level of achievement of the majority would be acceptable. But somehow the push of an innovation or a movement focuses a kind of peeved attention on one special segment of the population (almost always a population then in disregard, or "disadvantaged," or "oppressed," or a "problem") to the detriment of the population which is relatively successful (the "able," the "college-bound"). Thus a return to the basics for an "errant population" is often accompanied by a neglect of the "gifted." A return to high academic standards is accompanied by relative inattention to the nonacademic student or the "disadvantaged." We glean from this and other aspects that the elements of innovations that have promise and retain viability are those that open options for improvement to the widest range of the student population, or, better, that make provision for the entire student population. An innovation should seek a balance in options for the variety of ability at the very beginning.

It seemed that TV was just that kind of innovation—after all, it had appeal for everyone; everyone liked to watch TV. But entertainment, as we shall see, is one thing and instruction another. Instructional TV is coercive, requiring unqualified attention, sequential development, memory (particularly, immediate apprehension, storage, and recall), practice, and application. It turned out that students were "turned off" by TV instruction, which, used for instructional purposes and not entertainment per se, required a variety of elements of successful instructed learning, and was not particularly entertaining. Instructed learning should permit and, indeed, encourage interruption of the lesson, should make time for the immediate response and participation of the students—as the best classroom instruction does. In TV instruction, at least in the present state of the art, response and participation (to what is happening on the "screen") is impossible; it must be deferred; misunderstandings cannot be corrected at a given point. It is for this reason, among others, that TV instruction as given in the late 1950s and 1960s was limited in effect.

With regard to the reaction of teachers, the explanations are perhaps simpler. Teachers like to be properly prepared for the utilization of an innovation (whether TV or a new curriculum or computers); yet it turns out that the enthusiasm of the community for the introduction of an innovation almost always precludes proper preparation. Parents, Boards of Education, and school administrators all properly want the benefits of the innovation for the children *then* in school, and that immediately. These children must not miss the benefits. Hence the need for immediate introduction. Here it is that reform *through* schooling clashes with reform *of* schooling. Schools—administrators, supervisors, and teachers—are not given time to "reform" themselves before they attempt to "reform" the students.

A more subtle reason—subtle because it is the hidden agenda that is rarely discussed even as the innovation is introduced—is the uneasiness of teachers who see an innovation displacing them. In many instances the teacher's function in a TV lesson is that of caretaker, of supernumerary. The injury to professional status and to pride, not to mention economic security, is clear—but somehow not perceptible to enthusiastic reformers.

Naturally the public, mindful of its support, seeks assurance that its tax money is well spent. But the public's demand for reform through schooling—institutionalization of the reform—without allowing enough time, time for the reform of schooling necessary to make the required advance in the schooling of the young, usually results in failure.

We shall see that it is the wise and experienced school administrator—a strong educational leader, as it were—who succeeds with an innovation. It is his or her leadership that is the key. It is, given good teachers and willing students, what makes a school work.

A Brief Case Study:
Programed Instruction

In the early 1960s programed instruction was introduced. It seemed as if this innovation addressed certain aspects that had blocked the use of TV as partner in instruction in the classroom. It seemed as if the technique—a sequential, well-ordered, nonrandom presentation of subject matter—opened up options for all groups of individuals, of high or low ability. It seemed as if it could be under the control of teachers, freeing them to work with individuals. Further, programed instruction could simply be introduced by devices that were soon termed "learning machines"; again, the teacher would be freed for more important functions.

Essentially the work of Burrhus F. Skinner, Professor of Psychology at Harvard (who put together various technologies in existence and invented others), the device consisted of a machine programed for instruction, based on the principle of reinforcement. Simply put, an individual was immediately rewarded for learning, and although not punished for failure to learn, was also, in a curious way, rewarded—indeed, the student was encouraged to try again. The material to be learned was broken up into small bits, each simple to learn in itself; bit upon bit built up the whole.

In operating the machine the student pressed a button and was asked to respond to a question. If the response was correct the machine responded with "Fine" or "Correct" and made available the next question or problem. If the answer was "No, sorry," another chance was given to the student, until the correct answer was forthcoming. Certainly skill areas like arithmetic and spelling were destined to be programed; but soon almost all areas—including literature and even poetry and science—were being programed.

Certain colleges and universities embraced the "new method"; in several cases much of the instruction in areas that lent themselves to computer-assisted, or programed, instruction was given over to this "new method." Computer-assisted instruction certainly worked for college students, and it seemed clear to various agencies—federal, community, foundations, and the like—that the effort should be made to introduce it into the schools. The "new technology of learning" was hailed by the press, and several companies (Westinghouse, General Electric, and Borg-Warner, among others) embarked on a program of construction of machines (hardware) and the programs of instruction (software), particularly in the skills areas. Indeed, General Electric organized a company, General Learning, with the particular aim of advancing the new technology, particularly programed instruction. It is estimated that more than 3% of school systems—elementary and secondary—were involved in the early rush of experiment and trial. That is, pilot schools were set up in various school systems.

Note, if you please, the advantages of the method. As with TV, a teacher could present the basic principles of a subject to a class or a combination of classes. The students would then be assigned to machines for practice—and remediation, of course. The teacher would be freed to give individual attention to the "slow," the "disadvantaged," and the "gifted." Of particular appeal was the notion that the machines were "culture-fair"—that is, they did not discriminate on the basis of race. Also, they did not discriminate on the basis of ability; a student practiced till he or she "got it right." Mainly, the method had the enormous appeal that it was "individualized"—each student could work at his or her pace. Further, there was the possibility that individual programs could be prepared for those who required them—the "slow" or the "gifted." (In practice, however, most schools used programed instruction organized for instruction in grade levels, and not in individualized pacing, for which it was specially apt.)

In spite of all this—in spite of the efforts of industry, producers of hardware, and producers of software—by 1968 the thrust of the innovations in programed instruction had faltered, and by 1970 to all intents and purposes programed instruction, as a basic factor in regular instruction, had failed. Why?

The method worked: generally, the programs taught what they claimed to teach. But the first machines were relatively expensive, so access to them was limited except in the wealthiest school districts. In addition, the programs were not "schoolproof": in the hands of students too many broke down. In short, the reform was introduced before it was ready for the schools, and before teachers had been adequately trained.

However, the material programed for the machines was soon made available in workbook form. It was then accessible, cheap, and immediately available to an entire class, under the supervision of a teacher. Even so, it soon became clear that the method, which seemed to offer so many options, in fact did not. When used with an entire class the method of instruction demanded that students finish within a prescribed time. "Slow" students were penalized; "rapid" students finished long before the period was up. A sufficient number of students—and teachers

—found the material boring; it did have a certain sameness. Perhaps the most disappointing feature of a presumably "individualized" program used in the classroom by an entire class is that it is not truly individualized; students merely work at their desks. And while this is useful every now and then to practice certain skills, used every day it becomes a bore. Indeed, this is so with any method used unsparingly each day—particularly if it is not done in an interesting fashion. A lecture every day, given by an indifferent lecturer, is perhaps also boring, but even in a lecture the students have the impression that the teacher has at least prepared for them personally. (Of course, the new thrust in computer-assisted instruction now being mounted will be beneficent— or will it?)

Schools here and there have continued to use materials that were programed. But these were, in general, not prepared as software for machines, but as proper books, which were used very much as workbooks. These programed books might have been used under an "individual schedule," so that self-pacing by students would have been possible. But administering a large school is difficult unless schedules and reasonable order can be maintained. Individualization requires different administrative techniques.

There are clearly other reasons for the failure of an innovation, and these come, as Harry Broudy suggests in *The Real World of the Public Schools,* out of the psychology of teachers and parents. Broudy, who believes, as I do, that educational psychology does have a future, comments: "How market researchers, who know so much about the psychology of the housewife on the supermarket prowl, can know so little about the psychology of teachers and parents is a mystery."

Teachers do have a faith in their ability to affect the young if they are given proper opportunity for the encounter under favorable teaching conditions. Perhaps this is a "mystique," as Broudy suggests. It is nevertheless true that where machines are used teachers report themselves as feeling "devalued"; the machine has in a sense become master of the teaching process, for which the teacher has prepared himself or herself over a precious number of years. Parents, as well, feel that their children are being "devalued"; "teaching," to them, means personal attention by a *person* trained for the job, namely, a teacher. Not only are students "bored" by the machine, but also possibly, as Broudy reports, they resent machine-assisted instruction and even very good television instruction because it symbolizes a lack of concern for them as persons.

Whether this is true or not, it seems to us that the reason for "failure" does not reside in the innovation itself, but in the preparation to introduce the innovation. Many movements and innovations have embraced demonstrable improvements in curriculum and instruction. Nevertheless, in the rush to make these improvements a part of present practice, careful preparation (involving social, psychological, economic, and educational constants) of the community, the administration of the school, the teaching staff, and the students (all necessary antecedents of successful school reform) was neglected. Reform *through* schooling clashed once again with reform *of* schooling. It seems to me the latter must precede the former—in good time and with sufficient preparation, of course.

By the middle of the 1970s there was an ostensible return to the "basics," from which the elementary schools never depart. My observations of schools in the United States and over the globe over the past thirty years, as well as a careful reading of the literature, support this. But a return to the basics is not only an index of restricted budgets—as it often is—but also a holding pattern, a cry for surcease from reform and innovation; it is even a time for taking stock. It is a time when society and schools are at a turning point, even as now. So we learn, in *Looking Behind the Classroom Door,* that after John Goodlad and a team of qualified observers had visited 150 primary-grade classrooms in seventy different schools in cities in thirteen states, they found that many of the changes they had believed to be taking place in schooling "had not been getting into classrooms." They found that *most* schools, regardless of the city or kind of student enrollment, were marked by "sameness." Instruction was not individualized; machine instruction, even audio-visual equipment, was not widely used. There was little indication that the innovations of the decade of the 1950s—individualized instruction, ungraded classrooms, team teaching, inquiry learning— were being used. Generally, the teaching was overwhelmingly "group oriented" and "quietness and immobility" prevailed. Nevertheless, to say "most" is not to say "all." And, as we shall see, not to say "all" is significant. It means that advance and innovation are not only possible, but also exist.

So, too, Charles Silberman "discovered." In analyzing the great surge of reform in curriculum and instruction during 1957–1967, he reported, in his *Crisis in the Classroom:* "Things are much the same as they had been twenty years ago, and in some respects not as good as they were forty years ago."

My conclusions are somewhat different. But I must, in the coercive logic of my presentation, propose why in a different context, in succeeding chapters. Suffice it to say, for the moment, that blanket indictments of the schools leave much to be desired. To treat the schools as one system, subject to the same policy, is substantially incorrect. The schools are *not* one system; indeed, as I have stressed, we do not have *one* schooling system, and certainly not one educational system. (There are nevertheless many good schools, by common agreement.)

Why, if we do have an educational system, should the excellent practices of certain schools not prevail in all? If we did have a system, the excellent practice of a number of schools would of necessity become part of the entire system. Why in any school system in a given community should not the excellent practices of one or more schools prevail in all? For example, in my observations I noted that in certain schools in an "inner-city school system" the teaching of reading and mathematics was excellent; reading and mathematics scores were above the national average or mean. On the other hand, the scores of the inner-city schools taken as a statistical whole were below the average. The exemplary schools (pilot schools, to be sure) had student populations similar to the "problem" schools, but had adopted different administrative procedures, within an ecology of achievement. Certain of the more important procedures were:

• The teaching objectives were clear, and the administrative devices were set to achieve these goals. For example, *all* teachers were required to attend to the objectives; they were not discretionary.

• The principal and his or her supervisors were in the classrooms, not in their offices. Their personalities could be defined under the rubric "strong"; namely, they were insistent that the objectives of the school were to be met.

• Parents and community groups (Boards of Education, certainly) supported the objectives; parents "attended" to those children who were not "up to" the work and "rewarded" those who were.

Perhaps where schools are "failing," it is possibly not because they do not use the best methods available; it is because they cannot utilize the methods of the successful schools even within their own communities; or they are not obliged to undertake improvements externally devised—whether by community, university, or industrial researches, or even by the federal government. They are not, in short, part of an ecology of achievement. The schools, even if in the same community, are not, then, part of a "system."

The Transient and the Viable:
The Residual Nucleus

Are, then, movements or innovations introduced into the schools transient (short-lived) or viable (long-lived)? Are there no modest outcomes? I am required to dispel an unfortunate impression that is the residue of almost any discussion of social process or of change in an institution that is primarily social in its effects. I am obliged to question the conclusions generally derived from observation of the events that follow a perceived deficiency in schooling and an innovation that promises to fit the need. Always, the perceived deficiency in schooling that powers the innovation is observed in certain aspects of the *achievement* of the students. (I italicize *achievement* for reasons to be discussed.) It seems to me, and to other students of innovation in schooling, that the sequence runs as follows:

First Stages in Introduction of an Innovation
1. A deficiency is perceived (say, a specific deficiency in skills—reading or writing or mathematics or science—or a deficiency in health, or, broadly, a fitness for life in an industrial society; or a general failure to meet the needs of children).
2. An innovation is introduced (where skills are concerned) or a movement develops (where a broad social need is conceived).
3. Leaders appear, forces are aligned, the amelioration is pressed with vigor. It seems as if a public-relations effort is being mounted.
4. The first successes in the schools are heralded—so are failures.
5. On the basis of the first results, improvement seems possible; the innovation *through* schooling seems desirable.

Interlocking and Sequential Stages
Whatever the case for the movement or innovation, however it is introduced, the schools seem to lag behind the requirements of the reform or the speed of its introduction envisioned by the reformers. There follows:
1. An impatience with the rate of improvement and with the speed of institutionalization.
2. A perception of the relatively "poor" preparation of certain schools (synonym: staff).
3. Then reform *of* the schools, to accommodate the innovation, is pressed.

4. Generally, whatever the reform, funds and materials are not made available to the extent the schools desire.
5. Time is not available for teachers to change the habits that were, up to the time of reform, acceptable and "successful."
6. In time, society (through its institutions) takes on certain aspects of the innovation (educational TV, computerization in industry, and the like).
7. Or, if the skills and equipment are already available, the schools concentrate on the task—often to the neglect of others. For example, if there is a call to return to the basics, especially reading, the schools readily adapt. *New* instructional materials are devised, but there is already a reservoir of the skills that have been successful in the past. That is, the innovations exist and are in operation. In time, reading scores go up. But the concentration on certain aspects of schooling (say, basics) leaves other needs unmet. Concentration on reading, for example, often leaves science neglected, as well as the humanities. And soon the perceived need is to reform the schools in these areas, in the schooling of the gifted, in education in the arts and humanities, in physical fitness for all. Innovation is called for once again—as it is, indeed, today.

Always there seem to be perceived lacks, or needs, of the young which the schools are obliged to correct. Do the youth of the nation take to drugs? Somehow the schools are to correct the situation by introducing instruction on drug usage and its effects. Is venereal disease in teen-agers on the increase? The schools are to correct the situation—again by introducing instruction in the area. Is there teen-age pregnancy? The schools are to undertake "sex education." Are we in an energy crisis? The schools are to teach the essentials of the problem and its amelioration.

There is, nevertheless, little evidence that the expected ameliorative effects of instruction in these areas have the desired social effect. What seems to have the desired effect resides in an all-embracing effort of the community (including a variety of educational agencies as well as the school) engaged in devising an ecology of achievement to advance the desired solutions in the problem area. Recall that this is an "ecology" in which people, ideas, money, and management meld in a solution to the problem. It is an ecology characteristic of "schools that work."

Next Interlocking Stages: Reported Success
1. Where the schools already have the skills to attack the problem (reading, arithmetic, and the like), the deficiency is ameliorated—

in good time. But always there are the young who lag behind the others. These are the 20–30% who enter the schools already behind in their readiness for the avowed tasks of schooling (for example, the disadvantaged and the intellectually handicapped). For 70–80% of the young, the schools *are* successful in "teaching" the basics. But the failure of the schools in bringing the 20–30% to the level of the majority does attract attention. For it is that minority which does not take to schooling, or, if you will, to the plans of instruction and modes of instruction in common use. It is that minority which is "unsuccessful"; it is that minority which inordinately brings attention to itself as socially "misfit." Generally, these are the young who "drop out," who are not "fit for the job market," who have no "salable skills."

2. Or the schools meet the problem within the limits of their capacity. For example, they take on industrial training, or training in agriculture, or "job training," or "career training," or "vocational training." However, the technology of society usually passes the technology available to the schools; the schools lag behind; unions, industries, and corporations generally take on the instruction of their apprentices.

It would seem, then, that an innovation is either "successful" or "unsuccessful," disappearing in time or persevering in school practice. This is not quite the truth. It appears that an innovation cannot be said to "succeed" or "fail" in a school because of a strong or weak principal, a strong or weak staff, or a superior or inferior student body. An innovation succeeds or fails to the extent that its seed comes to rest in an environment I have called an "ecology of achievement." Foremost in that ecology is the community—characteristically informed and supportive of the school. Characteristic of an ecology of achievement are schools (within a supportive community) that have developed a servomechanism—a school system, if you will. One important answer to broad, persistent questions such as What is wrong with our educational system? is to seek the malaise not within a particular school, or schools generally, although the symptoms of distress will be evident there. It is to seek the factors of the malaise within a failing ecology of achievement and within society generally. For an ecology of achievement sometimes does not respond quickly enough; success often lulls a community to a security that does not react readily to crisis. It is these factors and an analysis of the consequences of their neglect that must be looked at. I am required, in effect, to discuss the elements that would secure an essential *balance* in at least three footholds of schooling:

1. Structure and substance of curriculum—namely, of plans *for* instruction
2. Structure and style in instructed learning—namely, of plans *of* instruction
3. Structure of evaluation—namely, devices to determine the effectiveness of curriculum and instruction

And, finally, with these in place, it is well to consider the renewing of other educational systems—as well as that educational system we call "schooling."

This may be done in the sure knowledge that throughout the country there are waiting in place the elements of the most effective educational system in the world. There are, I know, fine minds ready to undertake its construction. A newer, more effective, ecology of achievement is waiting to be forged. Perhaps the constructive affection necessary to fashion an educational system exists as well.

Our society has a certain coherence, a cement, if you will, of hard-won concepts defining the good society and hence the good life. The good society and the good life are won, our society assumes, as we win mastery of the knowledge, values, and skills necessary to bring us achievements we prize. Consequently, we give over to the school the function of assuring that our young have mastered the knowledge, values, and skills antecedent to the achievement that makes the good life possible. So we have always assumed, and so we have spoken and written. Too often (especially in the heat of social change) we have aired our disagreements and too often we have paraded our pettiness. Although this is vexing, perhaps we should not find it surprising that the search for solutions to problems of schooling and education are not even-tempered. In a way, the school is the surrogate parent of us all, and too often family disagreements are aired in frustration, openly. A certain civility, a certain comity, is lost; impulse has reign.

An open society inclined to—indeed, insistent upon—open self-examination (and therefore free expression) advances toward its humane and liberating ends alternately by conserving and transmitting its culture, then by rectifying and expanding it. But expertness implies restraint. Perhaps time will enable us to be tranquil about problems of schooling—for they will be with us as long as our society wishes the best for all. In an open society claims of individuals, of groups, of institutions, and claims of society become transmuted into political, economic, and social aims openly argued and openly analyzed; and the synthesis, if it is to survive, is equally subjected to trial.

This is all by way of saying that the reforms and innovations necessary for the transformation of the American school system—if one is really desired—will not be easily introduced; the transformation will be attended by outbursts of torment and anxiety. And it will take time— decades, not years. But it is inevitable. Our society is righting itself. In so doing, it is about to bring together three elements, *people, ideas* and *money,* and, curiously enough, *effective management* of the three. In righting itself, society will right the schools. But in the coming reform, forbearance is perhaps the first of all necessary reforms.

But we will not be effective if we assume that computers or any of a set of new technologies are *the* solution; or that a "new" mode of teaching reading, or mathematics, or the arts will suffice; or that any one reform is the answer.

What is required is an unperturbed probe into the entire business of schooling and education, that is, into the essential questions that are the business of those who teach and those who learn. What is required is perhaps a policy that will inaugurate a *balanced* view of curriculum, instruction, and evaluation, a policy that will not be subject to impulse or to the press of social and psychological warfare.

3. Regarding Present Thrusts

Social reforms usually end in renewing our educational systems, and one of the foremost subjected to public scrutiny is schooling. Society seeks to right itself, at least in part, by attempting to right the schools. This is in consequence of the fact that in a Western society, informal experience or learning achieved *at random* is not considered to be an efficient way of preparing the young in the knowledges and skills, as well as certain values, necessary to life in a complex society. There are, it is generally accepted, bodies of knowledge, of values, of skills that are to be introduced formally, and, what is more, in the kind of planned sequence a school makes possible.

The determination of which bodies of knowledge, which attitudes, which values are to be taught is given over, at least generally, if not symbolically, to a body elected by the community—a Board of Education. The authority to determine specifically what is to be taught, how it is to be taught, to whom it is to be taught, and when—and how proof of effectiveness of schooling is to be sought—is given over to specially equipped individuals, to superintendents, principals, supervisors, and teachers. At times, it has been suggested, the schools become the testing ground for the consideration of curricular and instructional materials introduced by special groups, whether political, social, ethnic, economic, or religious—each contending the correctness of its position. Each group asserts that certain content, certain values, certain skills *must* become part of, if not central to, schooling. Or specially constituted groups seek to remove certain areas of instruction from the schools. To refresh our mind so we need only consider the variety of publics that have pressed their interests on the schools. We may almost draw a generalization: when a group with special social or sociopolitical goals is organized, it seeks to have *its* knowledge, *its* values, or *its* skills become a part of the plan of instruction (the curriculum) or mode of instruction (teaching method or procedure). The assumption is that once a subject matter is taught it becomes part of the repertory of the young and affects behavior. This is not necessarily true. A further assumption is that there is a one-to-one correspondence between what is taught and what one does in life. And this is not necessarily true. What we do know is that to acquire certain knowledge, values, and skills we must utilize them persistently in practice; that is to say, their mere introduction in school programs or in random experience in life is not likely to have permanent effect. It is to say that practice and use dictate what shall be practiced and used.

For the moment, we may determine what kind of an operational model is pressed upon the schools as they plan programs of instruction and the modes of instruction that are presumed to make the program effective. The model, in turn, seems based perhaps upon a consideration of the question What constitutes the "good" or "satisfactory" life? Usually the model for the satisfactory or good life is found in the groups that have been called the "elites" of a society. (The elites are generally considered to be those in the social class favored to enjoy preferred social and economic status. But the elites are not always those with wealth, power, and prestige. In the 1960s, for example, certain groups of the young rejected—or appeared to reject—the trappings of wealth and power in the search for a different kind of prestige.) In any event, we find that groups planning programs of instruction for the schools tend to consider the education of the elites as a model for the education of the young of a society.

In short, consideration of what constitutes an appropriate program or mode of instruction often depends on answers to this question: What is the *education* of the "elite"?

The consistent error in this approach, as well as a considerable obstacle to the development of programs and modes of instruction useful in schooling, is that education is always more than schooling. The education of the elites is always more, much more, than their schooling. Against a discussion of "equal educational opportunity," I must press the point at this time that, essentially, schooling is concerned with *instructed learning,* to use Jerome Bruner's phrase, which is planned by the school to meet the vision and aims of society. Education in its complete sense is concerned not only with schooling but also with *self-*

activated learning, planned first by the family and then by the individual to meet an idiosyncratic vision of a personal life, with personal views of fulfillment. The latter, of course, need not be at odds with school or society, nor is the former always a guarantee that the individual will meet the needs of society. Further, it is never to say that certain aspects of schooling do not give opportunity for self-activated learning, or that in achieving the latter an individual does not avail himself of the rich fare of schooling. It is rare, indeed, for individuals to contemplate the *entire* curriculum and the considerable knowledges, skills, and values available to the young in a modern school system from kindergarten through the senior high-school grades. It boggles the mind.

Instructed learning is the aim, or, in general terms, is the function of schooling as presently organized. The staffs of the Board of Education and of the schools plan in considerable detail the general program, the curriculum, the modes of instruction, and the forms of evaluation that the community desires and approves. Instructed learning is planned learning, planned by administrators, supervisors, teachers with the consent of the Board of Education working within the planned program of the school: hence *instructed.* Of course, there are attempts at individualization—at self-activation—which are successful in certain communities, and will be discussed later. In the main, *instructed learning is at the heart of schooling as it exists at present.*

For the reasons that follow, instructed learning—unless greatly modified—cannot fulfill the needs of the young faced with the present and future demands of Western society. The turmoil we see about us reflects that of a society in change, a society at one of its strange turning points. But it is also a society persuaded (or perhaps only the reformers of schooling are so persuaded) that schooling, over and above its tasks of advancing instructed learning, can and should correct the habituations of childhood, neutralize if not correct flawed personality, and correct varieties of inability in learning, particularly by renewed motivations. We have somehow come to believe that success in schooling goes hand in hand with economic and other personal successes. We shall need to examine these assumptions, for, when proved, these assumptions become obstacles to effective school policy that ignores the proof, or become even greater obstacles when proof of the assumption is lacking but is assumed to exist.

On a Turning Point

The Industrial Revolution, with its consequent effects on schooling, is a matter of record. But at least three aspects of the revolution need emphasis. First, it was not a crash of events. Over eight to ten decades inventions (steam, steam engines, devices to increase horsepower, electricity, electric lighting, dynamos—in short, a variety of machines, not to mention social, economic, and political innovations) were developed and became public knowledge. Second, in the latter third of the nineteenth century, factory systems multiplied; corporate organization to combine effective people, ideas, funding, and management flourished, but this did not happen in a flash. Third, the populations which furnished the labor to serve factory and machine flooded the cities; immigration was encouraged. *The reform of schooling in the period 1870 to 1940 took just that time—seventy years.*

Thus as society was reforming itself, reform was also pressed on the schools: they were asked to turn immigrants into Americans. So it happened that the schools were overcome by a vast problem: how to school different populations with different cultural heritages in a common language and in common customs. The tools to be used were the so-called basics—reading, writing, arithmetic—the core of the elementary-school curriculum. The result was two parallel movements in schooling: a movement in "Americanization" and a movement in "industrialization" that turned the schools to programs preparing the young for places in industry. This was soon followed, in the early twentieth century, by a third movement.

Even as the schools were taking on the requirements of curriculum and instruction designed for Americanization of immigrants and for changes consequent on the Industrial Revolution, they were asked to *equalize educational opportunity for all children.* Briefly, the proponents of the progressive education movement asked schools to turn to meeting not only the *needs of an industrial society,* but also the *needs of children,* to make the fruits of democracy available to all. The progressive education movement was a turning point in American education, to say the least. To repeat, Lawrence Cremin's brilliant analysis of the progressive education movement, in *The Transformation of the School: Progressivism in American Education,* shows that significant proposals for change in curriculum and instruction were at the heart of the movement. Yet when "progressive education" and "life-adjustment" movements were assaulted by bitter critics early in the 1950s, the movements collapsed. We should be mindful of Cremin's remark that "the surprising thing about the progressive response to the assault of the fifties is not that the movement collapsed, but that it collapsed so readily."

The reasons for what appears to be a "collapse" of a given educational movement and/or innovation are found first in a failure to build a sound base (grounded in a pervasive policy governed by an ecology of achievement), and second in certain essentials of policy with regard to curriculum, instruction, and evaluation. Thus we are obliged to scrutinize the movements designed to equalize educational opportunity for all children (the progressive education movement was one; the "equal educational opportunity" movement of the present is another). It is worth mentioning, for the moment, that in the past, even as in the present, movements to offer equal educational opportunity for the young embraced two vectors:

1. Offering to all the kind of schooling previously available only to the "elites"; essentially, a college-preparation curriculum.
2. Making available vocational training (and the behaviors related to it) to those who do not care for or profit from the programs and modes of instruction available to the elites; essentially, a curriculum designed to prepare individuals for entry into an occupation immediately upon leaving secondary school, but not for entry into college and the professions. Naturally, the prospects are for a modest but "satisfactory" life.

It suffices to say that the progressive education movement followed a turning point in American society: the coalescence of a burst in industrial and technological advance and the social upheaval that accompanied it—namely, the claims of labor for equality of opportunity in achieving the quality of life that was the promise of America, and the insistence that the best possible schooling was therefore to be available to all. These were, of course, political demands, but we are here concerned with a demand made on a social institution: the school. These may be the types of movements that coalesced to energize the transformation of the school in the decades between 1870 and 1910 and are once again combining to energize a coming transformation. Again there is a coalescence of two movements: *social* and *industrial*. The public movement for equality known as the "civil-rights movement" has been in progress for at least two, perhaps three, decades. The press for equal rights for minorities has, as a matter of course, enveloped the schools.

School and society are inventing ways of equalizing *educational* opportunity (more correctly, equalizing opportunity in *schooling* and in other educational institutions) as a way of equalizing educational achievement: a turning point in social invention, to be sure. The concurrent postindustrial-movement technologies, inventing industrial methods that will surely claim the overwhelming attention of the public, have not yet come to the turning point. Nevertheless, the turning point is there for us to contemplate if we attend to the signs. And indeed we should.

A Quantum Leap

It seems that we are about to enter upon a new era of technological advance, techno-electronic in nature and postindustrial in effect. It may even be that we in the United States shall be the first to become a postindustrial society. The change will be a quantum leap, affecting more than technology. The quantum leap of society is being likened to one that occurred some 5,000 to 7,000 years ago, a period related to the birth of the city. To reflect on the caliber of the changes, it might be useful to postulate a time scale such as this:

5,000,000 years ago—postulated origins of the human as "species"
500,000 years ago—postulated origin and development of food-growing tribes
50,000 years ago—Cro-Magnon man (he/she had time to paint)
5,000 years ago—the "first" city (some would say 7,000 years ago)
500 years ago—the "first" university
50 years ago—beginning of "universal" schooling in the United States (really 70 years ago)
5 years ago—"man" steps on the moon (really 15 years or so ago)

In short, we may be the first society about to take what sociologists and anthropologists label the "5,000-year leap"—a dramatic change in the direction Western civilization is about to take. (Some students suggest that Japan may be first. Perhaps.) Early in this 5,000-year leap, this quantum jump, we may see the renewing of a variety of *educational systems,* including the renewing of the present *schooling systems,* an aggregate of some 16,000 local school "systems." Within the architecture of the renewing schooling system a structural change will be required to catalyze the tandem change in both intellectual and personal-social growth of the young. But we should not postulate a loss of initiative by local communities—the organization of a Department of Education notwithstanding. It is possible to have strong leadership without dulling local initiative. Indeed, strong leadership would catalyze the growth of school systems with time-honored local initiative.

In other words, the *balancing* of opposing opinion without coercion will be sustained (indeed, this essential of a democratic society must be sustained), but the advantages of the dynamic balance obtained within a system, especially its steady progress toward objectives that have long been the goals of education, are much to be desired. The arts of acquisition of knowledge throughout life; the lifelong search for personhood, for integrity, for identity; the sustenance of a habitual vision of greatness; the sustenance of vigorous though steady change in behavior throughout life that is the mark of the educated person—these are but a few of the vantage points of education vis-à-vis schooling.

As I have said, my analysis and direct observation of schooling in the United States does not square with the view of its major critics: that our schools have "failed" or are "failing" society. American schools which are so vulnerable to the sway of social turmoil, have managed their domain decently given the burdens, the conflicting signals, and the opposing tasks society has asked them to assume. Simply, we could not have reached—indeed, we did not reach—our enviable level (enviable from the view of societies other than ours) of social and technological advance without the intervention of schooling. Fred M. Hechinger, Education Editor of the *New York Times,* an observer whose accurate descriptions of the state of schooling and education in the United States are admirable, commented on June 10, 1980, on the three-week Salzburg Seminar in American Studies just then concluded: "An American observer pondering the nature of education in the United States is bound to find that a seminar composed of European educators and scholars leaves him with a new, more benign perspective. Viewed on home ground, the deficiencies stand out like sore thumbs. Judged by Europeans and measured against their own problems, the virtues suddenly appear like the attainment of utopian dreams."

Now a quantum leap almost always involves changes in technology and social practices in tandem. For example, the city could not have developed without technological advances that made food storage possible, which in turn made it possible for certain entrepreneurs to be freed from tillage of the land, which made it possible for artisans who had captured the new technologies to congregate in the city, which made it possible for artisans to have apprentices (that is, schools), and so on. Similarly, the sociopolitical devices that made it possible to govern cities, city-states, and nations were fully developed, making possible the "stable" life of a city.

In a similar way, the artifices of technological invention and sociopolitical invention seem to be coalescing and reinforcing each other once again. The world in which men and women are planning space colonies is as different from the world in which European nations were planning colonies across the seas as the world in which the first cities arose was different from the neolithic settlements in which the tribe was dominant. Nevertheless, the sociopolitical and technological juncture is powered, it seems, by advances addressing needs strangely similar to those of the first Industrial Revolution:

• Sociopolitical: attempts at equalizing opportunity in education to afford opportunity for securing satisfactory work to advance life and living

• Technological: attempts at improving ways of doing work to attain a more satisfactory life and living

Note that both efforts are concerned with that elusive characteristic of human effort "advancing the quality of life." It will be best to consider first the sociopolitical advance, comprising many inventions in custom and law affecting schooling. We will need to live with a sense of crisis, with a sense of paradox perhaps: the old will be in a process of transformation even though the new is not yet born. The old forces in education that provided stability will be playing out their span; the new ones will not yet have come to maturity, or may not even have begun to work.

A Note on Clarity

Phrases and meanings will need to take on clearer definition—and changing the language is never easy. The phrase "equalizing educational opportunity" has, as have all terms with sociopolitical overload, taken on a variety of meanings, two of which are central to this discussion.

First, for a number of administrators, supervisors, and teachers, as well as the public generally, it has been taken to mean "equality of opportunity for effective schooling" (note: not education, but *school-*

ing); that is, the young were to be given equally favorable environments for development in the school environment. Second, and perhaps more prominent in the public mind, it has been taken to mean "equality of opportunity in the job market." That is to say that somehow equality of opportunity for effective schooling is antecedent to and a promise of economic justice: the promise of jobs enhancing the quality of life. Again the schools were obliged to achieve goals they could not possibly reach. The schools can and should modify administration, curriculum, and instruction to give equal opportunity for *equality in achievement in schooling,* but only society can make jobs available.

Moreover, we face the ever-present danger of overzealous effort, a danger presaging chaos and failure: we turn to an overwhelming task with great energy and good will but not with patience; we want to get things done quickly, to get it over with. We need instead to examine not only what the schools have been able to do, and do well, but also what they can do, and do well. And, of course, what they cannot do. To overburden them is to court failure. Put another way, to burden the great enterprise of schooling with the greater and enormously wide-ranging, all-encompassing enterprise of education is to ensure chaos and eventual disaster.

We need to inquire into the meaning of "equality of opportunity in schooling" vis-à-vis "equality of educational opportunity." Those familiar with the literature will perhaps take issue with the phrase "equality of opportunity in schooling" rather than "equality of educational opportunity." It is the former with which we are first to be concerned; the latter requires a different focus (to be constantly evoked and discussed in this and in following chapters). The phrase made famous by the Department of Health, Education, and Welfare's Coleman Report is "equality of educational opportunity" (EEO), which is also its name; the report is often referred to as EEOR (Equality of Educational Opportunity Report). A study by Christopher Jencks and others, *Inequality: A Reassessment of the Effect of Family and Schooling in America,* is in fact Jencks's reassessment of the Coleman Report. But note Coleman's use of the term "education," and indeed he means "education," but his thesis has been applied mainly to schooling while Jencks uses "family" and "schooling," and indeed he means "family" and "schooling." Family behavior influences both schooling and education but its influence is strongly in the latter, particularly in the motivation and habituation essential to reasonably good achievement and behavior in school and out.

Coleman's study and the work of his colleagues have been of inestimable value in the necessary task of reconsidering the meaning of schooling and, most important in my view, have, in catalyzing a host of studies, led powerfully to a reconsideration of the meaning of the relationship between school and society, and thus of the true meaning of "educational system." Nevertheless, in a certain sense, it is regrettable that there is a need to focus on the confusion of terms, rather than on their clarification—but, in the view embraced here, the confusion has caused mischief. Coleman pressed his views in various publications, urging the need for attention to the social, and also racial, make-up of the schools, urging that where homogeneity of racial groups persisted, the neighborhood school should be "desegregated." His view is often stated in words he wrote in *The Public Interest* in 1966: "For those children whose family and neighborhood are educationally disadvantaged, it is important to replace this family environment as much as possible with an *educational environment*—by starting school at an earlier age, and by having a school which begins very early in the day and ends very late." (Italics added.) In effect, through his writings and speeches—of considerable influence—his purpose was to take advantage of the mix of "advantaged" and "disadvantaged" peers—boys and girls of different family background and social situation. But by 1972 Coleman was to change his mind, though only in part. In *Educational Researcher* he wrote: "There is not sufficient evidence to show that the kind of benefits to lower class children that arise from a socio-economically heterogeneous school can't also be provided by other means. I don't think a judge can say there is a prima facie evidence of inequality of *educational opportunity* on achievement grounds if there is *school segregation*." (Italics added.) In other words, an appropriate *schooling* was one that ameliorated the *educational* effects of the family, neighborhood, and social situation of the disadvantaged.

Again it seems we have run into an unintended equalization of schooling and education. I am not altogether sure that the mischief done by confusing the two in research and popular literature can be easily undone. In ancient or traditional societies where universal schooling was absent or not practiced, children (particularly sons) followed their fathers into the family occupation; *education* for the task was a family (and experiential) matter. Leonardo did not *learn* his profession in the schools. In Western societies, and those societies emulating them, elementary, secondary, collegiate, and professional *schooling* plays a considerable part in determining what trade or profession the young will follow, at least for a certain period of adult life. Schooling then is defined as what an individual learns in a place, an institution, that he or she attends. But a child cannot be said to be *schooled* at home, or by friends, or by the natural consequences of being a member of a social stratum; this is properly a part of educational experience. There are, it can be readily observed, unequal educational opportunities given to children of different social classes. This is not to disparage abilities or gifts that tend to promise equality of achievement in spite of different social strata. In my observation, schools attempt to give equal opportunity to all children in any given course of study or set of experiences, but it is also my observation that the early environment, producing a variety of habituations, may at times not be conducive to the kind of progress necessary to reach equality of educational achievement. Thus Jencks and his colleagues may be correct when they assess the *present* schooling enterprise and find it to be ineffective in providing tolerably "equal" economic success to its graduates but nonetheless stress that it is *family* and *social stratum* that are prominent in determining which of the young who have been schooled will achieve economic (job) success. Once again I must emphasize at least three aspects of the question, which apply to studies such as those of Coleman and partly to that of Jencks.

1. These studies are not of the effects of a *school system,* but of an as yet fragmented, perhaps undefined "educational system" in which certain significant aspects of education are a property of family and social stratum (or class).
2. These studies are of the *present* school and society, and not of an educational system that needs devising.
3. This book attempts to press for the distinction between schooling and education, and to emphasize the critical need for the renewing of the variety of educational systems to meet the requirements of youth and a society about to enter a new era. But it is necessary to state—with regret—that the reader will need to tolerate the disjunction and dissonance between those who speak of schooling but mean *all of education* and those who speak of education and mean *schooling in the so-called basics of reading, writing, and numbering.* Also, the reader is asked once again to bear with the cadence of this book's argument; the nature of the renewing of our schooling and educational systems which may be required will become more apparent in the chapters to come.

There are currently reports that Coleman is soon to present a study comparing public and private high schools. It is to be hoped that his statistical model or models will encompass the difference in the ecologies of achievement in which public and private schools exist and function; the ecologies are decidedly different. It is hoped that his statistical models will differentiate the environment of *schooling* (affecting most, but not all, public schools) from the environment of *education* (affecting to a considerable extent most, but not all, private schools).

It is hoped, too, that federal, state, and local initiatives will not be taken hastily in support or rejection of his latest conclusions. Sociological research, by its very nature, deals with the fragile human environment—political, social, psychological, economic, all of which are factors in creating the various ecologies of achievement considered in Chapter 1. Statistical models of vast social phenomena—designed to reflect *all* of schooling, *all* of education may not be durable, for they accommodate variables observable in the present (often the result of relatively short periods of history). Too often, different researchers do not agree on the variables; too often, sociological research places prominent sociologists, examining the same research, in opposite camps. Mainly, as has been said, statistical data hide the considerable variations among children in a given school in a given community. To lose single communities in a larger statistic is as hazardous as the loss of an individual child in the mass. One must wonder whether the conclusions of large-scale research on *education,* such as that of Coleman and Jencks, applied to a nation's *schooling* may not have adverse effects, attributable not to the research per se but to its hasty application in practice.

To re-emphasize, the interchangeable use of the terms "schooling" and "education" serves neither the purpose of research nor policy, for several reasons. "Education" almost always designates a wider area of "learning" than "schooling." Recall, by way of example, that "education" includes education by family, by church, by synagogue, temple, quasi-religious groups, and nonchurch groups, by peer groups, by newspapers, reading of all sorts, and TV; certainly it includes postsecondary education, and lifelong experience. Education is sometimes considered a property of the "social class" to which an individual is said to belong. Yet postsecondary education—whether junior college, college, university, or community center—is rarely ever called "schooling." Nor are the activities outside of school of a social class that bears the label "advantaged" or "disadvantaged" called "education," and yet they are the bone, if not the marrow, of the process. To repeat a tentative definition in another guise: Education comprises the *total* environment which continuously affects and effects changes in behavior, that is, in character, personality, habituation, intellection; it is *lifelong.* To understand the nature of the effect of educational practice vis-à-vis that of schooling, we need to consider the practices of *instructed learning,* of curriculum (plans for instructed learning) and evaluation (again of instructed learning). These constitute eminently the environment of schooling.

An interesting but common confusion between schooling and education may be discerned in a statement of Michael Harrington's, in his *Decade of Decision: The Crisis of the American System* (1980). "There is a strong relationship between *earnings and education.* But a careful study shows that education is not the *cause* of this relation since performance on tests *within any social stratum* does not affect the income of individuals within that stratum. Those who make average scores have roughly the same earnings as those who do much better or much worse. *It is membership in that particular stratum, which appears to be decisive."* (Italics added.)

Performance on certain tests, particularly tests on subject matter (whether standardized or not), *may* be the result of schooling. But membership in a social stratum is indeed *educational* and is more than schooling. Membership in a social stratum may often—*not always*—result in certain habituation in manner, motivation, speech, dress, and other aspects of personality which confer an advantage on an individual seeking certain kinds of employment. Surely the social stratum can change, if not specifically for an individual, then for his or her progeny. Membership in a social stratum is *educational* experience, not *school* experience. The Coleman Report recognizes this but also suggests that proximity in the same school environment with socially advantaged young may ameliorate the disadvantage of those denied presence in a given "advantaged" social stratum.

In any event, we may not allow ourselves the luxury of confusing schooling, a part of education, with all of education, which includes not only schooling but the educational advantages conferred by social stratum. This last need not be denied. We are obliged, however, to reduce disadvantage in schooling per se, and this is a matter of reducing disadvantage in curriculum, instruction, evaluation, and in the attitudes and skills that are part of schooling.

The requirements of justice impose on us the necessity of developing an educational system in order to reduce the hazards faced by the disadvantaged infant in order to offer opportunity for equal educational achievement as a result of schooling and education.

Education at home, and with family, and within the prerogatives of social class tends to be *private.* So does schooling and education within a private school to which parents residing in different and diverse communities send their young and thus surrender a certain scrutiny. Schooling in the public school is generally under the immediate scrutiny of a relatively small and more or less compact community.

We may digress for a moment and compare and contrast the uses of the term "research" in science and in education to note a certain dilemma. The "successes" of scientific research are not only the result of experimental method, not only the result of methods that assure effective collaboration in a given research, but are also the result of the *precision* of the terms and systematic assertions (such as theories) used to define the area of research. In addition to restricting their investigations to areas accessible to their methods, scientists define the limits of the area. Thus they cannot, and do not, investigate the "existence of God": the domain is not accessible to their modes of research. They do investigate such areas as electricity and magnetism, genetics and evolution of species. That is, they investigate areas in which models or theories have been established through observation and experiment or which can be tested by observation and experiment. Further, a discovery of new data, new phenomena, is not accepted unless confirmed. And investigation in science is directed by accepted theory, itself an explanation of confirmed observation and experiment.

Education is still an art-science of practice, not of the laboratory. For this and other reasons the scientific community often tends to look askance at educational research, although there is good reason to believe that educational research is growing in respectability; its methodology is becoming refined. The reliability of certain areas of educational research is more akin to the reliability of weather prediction than to the refined prediction of the physicist or chemist or biologist. The fields of schooling and education badly need precision in definition of terms and a careful delineation of areas accessible to their methods. In this book, it is necessary to define "equal educational opportunity" as it has been applied by the courts as a policy applicable to *schooling,* not yet to the general area of all *educational systems,* certainly not the job market; the latter is not necessarily under the control of the school. For this reason the phrase "equal opportunity in schooling for equal achievement in schooling" will be used here, rather than "equal educational opportunity for equal educational achievement." This is a reasonably important decision, and not a quibble.

From this viewpoint of clarification of the issues and of policy, it is therefore useful to separate equality of opportunity in schooling from the like in other educational systems as well as from equal opportunity in the job market.

Kenneth Keniston's foreword in Richard de Lone's *Small Futures* states another view: "For well over a century, we Americans have believed that a crucial way to make our society more just was by improving our children. We propose instead that the best way to ensure more ample futures for our children is to start with the difficult task of building a more just society."

Simplistic consideration will yield the truth that even if undertaken immediately, the task of reconstruction of society (and particularly the family) demands careful and incredibly intricate and elaborate plans over the definable short and long terms. Yet daily, each and every year, without halt, the young keep coming to our schools.

There is sufficient evidence that the young with a high-school diploma have a better initial chance of getting employment than those with elementary schooling only. There is also sufficient evidence that college graduates earn more—if not excessively more, than do high-school graduates. This is not necessarily defining competence, but reality. In their public utterances, Coleman and Jencks have clarified an essential position: their estimates of public schooling are based on what schools *do* and not on what they *can do*.

It is central to my thesis that the coming transformation of our public schools may well lie in the *combination* of the variety of opportunities available in schooling and other educational systems.

An educational system, as compared and contrasted with a schooling system, can become a servomechanism based not mainly on the model of the thermostat, but on the ecological model, which allows a greater number of variables and a wider range in their expression. An educational system embracing the ecology of achievement a nation and its society makes available in lifelong education is more likely to afford equal educational opportunity than is a schooling system. Such an educational system encompasses a *schooling system* as a major, but not sole, enterprise, with its aims clearly stated, vis-à-vis other educational systems. There are, to repeat, excellent school systems.

Such schooling systems embrace the rich experience of the best schools. The teachers', supervisors', and administrators' tasks, energies, skills, and genius, thus clarified, hence made more purposive, can be applied to meeting the needs of the great variety of children. School can then become *life* (if not *all* of life, as John Dewey's disciples proclaimed but could not practice given the restrictions of society). That is, schooling—a part of the life of the young—can prepare for variety in life, since varieties in life and living are possible in the richness of our open society.

Turning Points:
Equality of Opportunity in Public Schools

Equality of opportunity in public schooling is now a matter of law and is to be accorded to each and all. In time it will become a matter of custom; that is, it will be deeply imbedded in the culture, and future generations will wonder how it was ever otherwise.

For the point of view pertinent to this book, equality in public schooling is now considered a matter of fairness, of equity. But justice concerns itself with matters not only of equality, but of inequality as well. It is worthwhile to consider briefly the matter of justice in schooling, otherwise the present (not the last word) studies of Coleman, Jencks, de Lone, as well as others, may not be put into perspective. I lean heavily on an altogether fine but brief analysis of certain aspects of justice in relation to schooling explicated by Gordon Swanson in "As I See It . . ." in *Christopher Jencks: In Perspective.*

Discussions of excellence in achievement, accountability, or effectiveness in schooling are fruitless without a definition of the elements of justice applicable to schooling. To be sure, principles of justice embrace principles of equality and inequality. It is unarguable that each citizen of a democracy is to have equal rights to liberties guaranteed to all. Thus it is clear that any citizen is to be extended a given liberty only to the extent that it is secured for others, for each and all. Due process is a right—and within due process free public schooling. That is to say, public schooling is to be provided for all children by the state. Moreover, public schooling is to give equal opportunity for achievement to all its young. However, schooling can only guarantee certain means, not ends. Economic justice, for example, as an end may be achieved generally only when school terminates.

For a given inequality (say to become valedictorian, to take one's place in courses open to the "gifted," to become a star quarterback or Speaker of the House or President of the United States) to be considered a basic liberty, it should be, as Swanson puts it, "attached to roles open to all." Schooling is such a role. In other words, if inequality is to be deserved, it must be based on equality of opportunity, on the amelioration of disadvantage; otherwise the phrase "equal opportunity" loses its meaning: thus our attempts to ameliorate disadvantage through schooling, and, as we shall see, through preschooling.

But the fact of the matter is that schools are not faced with children equal in abilities and skills, or similar in those behaviors necessary to acquire certain skills. Schools are open to children unequal in ability seeking equal opportunity, and schooling systems now are bent to equality of opportunity on the assumption that equality of opportunity in schooling is prelude to equality in achievement, in school or out. It is this stark reality that seems to lead to misunderstanding, or at least confusion. In my observations of communities, what has emerged—as often is the case with exceedingly complex social problems—is a "terrible simplifier." The terrible simplifier—equal educational opportunity—is, too often, taken to mean sameness in treatment in curriculum and instructional modes. This simplification serves neither the children, the school, nor the community.

It is obvious, for example, that immigrant children with a language other than English must initially have *special* and *different* (not equal) treatment as compared with those competent in English—at least until they use the language with the skill required in the subject areas that form the curriculum of the school. Not until then can equal educational opportunity mean an opportunity for equal educational achievement.

It is obvious that those who have poor skills in literary and numeracy need to be brought up to the level of others. They require instruction that is *different* from others.

It is obvious that gifted or talented children require *special* treatment. The young who are talented in athletic and artistic ability are allowed to perform beyond the "norm." Should not children who can do the calculus in the sixth grade be permitted to perform beyond the "norm," too, or should they be held to a curriculum of sixth-grade arithmetic?

In other words, for the disadvantaged or the specially able, schooling may require *special* opportunity, not sameness of opportunity (synonym: similar exposure to similar curriculums and modes of instruction). So, too, for the "normal," for they are normal over a broad range of abilities, common and special.

Children are unique, each with special gifts, special opportunities, special destinations—unique destinations. The methods of statistics—normally the best instruments for the study of groups and of traits common to all—are not useful for the study of unique events, events that are not repetitive. Equal opportunity in schooling can only mean opportunity for fulfillment of special ability present in special individuals, not necessarily of a group, although groups are not excluded. Equal opportunity, then, is not to be interpreted as *sameness* in educational experience or exposure to the same subject matters, at the same

level, in equal periods of time. It should mean—should it not?—
opportunity available to *all* to reach the highest level of excellence
within their capacity. Therefore, it would mean *special* opportunities
available to each of the young to reach those levels of excellence within
the grasp of *each* individual. Otherwise, how can individuals with differences (presumably disadvantages) in background and early opportunity reach a similar level of excellence requisite for equal achievement?

Furthermore, principles of justice suggest that even in a democracy,
certain inequalities are permissible if they are *to the advantage of all.*
For example, only one person can be president of an organization at
one time; not everyone, for example, can be a doctor, lawyer, teacher,
or star athlete. Given equal opportunity to take advantage of the special
opportunities available to all, inequalities in achievement are permissible.

In such situations, different children, different students, will achieve
at different levels; a school's excellence is to be judged by the opportunities it makes available to all to reach their highest level of excellence,
that is, their highest level of achievement in pursuit of their special
powers. Some children are artistically or musically gifted. Others are
gifted in mathematics or science. Others are gifted in athletics. Still
others are writers or poets in the making. Given the thesis that a runner
develops the skills of running by running, a pianist at the piano, a gifted
mathematician by ranging far beyond the curriculum, it follows that the
treatment of some students will need to be different from that of others.

This means that we are required to face a paradox: *in schooling,
particularly where curriculum and instruction are concerned, there is
nothing so unequal as the equal treatment of unequals.** It seems to me
that to remove such inequalities as are susceptible of removal, schools
are required to assess inequalities in ability in the children at hand and
to select from curricular and instructional methods that special and
effective mix which accommodates the special mix of abilities in each
child. This is then the meaning underlying the assurance of equal opportunity in schooling, for equal achievement in schooling; to reduce
disadvantages, we are to intervene with special and beneficial oppor-

---

* Paul F. Brandwein. *The Permanent Agenda of Man: The Humanities.* New York:
Harcourt Brace Jovanovich, 1971, p. 5. It seems to me, although I cannot be sure,
that I was present, perhaps in the early part of the 1960s, at a speech when
E. Frank Brown, then Principal of Melbourne High School, Melbourne, Florida,
made use of the phrase "There is nothing so unequal as the equal treatment of
unequals." He was then, if I remember correctly, referring in particular to the
"gifted." I have used the phrase in its relation to curriculum and instruction only.

tunity to make possible equality of achievement. In the coming renewing of the schools, the policy of assuring *equal* opportunity will need to be reconciled with the practice of providing *special* opportunity for the vast majority of abilities within the school.

But the present controversy over equality in schooling resides in the assumption that equality of opportunity in schooling is prelude to equality in achievement for different ethnic and racial groups. Indeed, the major conclusions of the Coleman Report were derived from achievement tests. The inequality of the results of these achievement tests from impoverished schools (usually but not always minority schools), as compared with tests from schools in "good" or "favored" communities, led to this statement in the Report: "The first finding is that the schools are remarkably *similar* in the way they relate to the *achievement* of their pupils when the socioeconomic background of the students is taken into account." (Italics added.) And: *"Altogether, the sources of inequality and educational opportunity appear to lie first in the home itself and the cultural influences immediately surrounding the home, and in the school's cultural homogeneity which perpetuates the social influences of the home and its environs."* (Italics added.)

Note once again the comparison between educational opportunity in the home environment (where the influences are truly educational, because they are broader than permitted to the objectives and methods of the school) and the restricted environment of the school (whose function is schooling and not fitness for the total environment, a property of an "educational system").

We need to probe the meaning of equality of achievement and perhaps supplant the phrase. For in the general understanding, in the public mind, equality of educational opportunity is interpreted as meaning sameness in exposure to similar curriculums and with similar modes of instruction.

In short, I see equality of opportunity in schooling with the aim of opportunity for equality of achievement in schooling as desirable. But an examination of the nature of variety in ability and in environment leads me to suspect that at least in the initial stages, in the first decades perhaps, it will become increasingly probable that equality of opportunity will not yield equality of achievement to different ethnic and/or racial groups unless policy is directed at systematic thought toward the development of an ecology of achievement. Such a policy is essential, particularly in the coming years, where the fitness of the individual to function effectively in a techno-electronic culture may well be determined by education, in kind and degree. We are at a turning point in formulating policy in schooling and education. We are at a turning point for still another reason, for we are pressed by still another set of events.

Turning Points:
On a Coming Social Transformation

As it did in the period of the Industrial Revolution, the United States is once again about to burst its bonds. Various analysts, chief among them Daniel Bell, predict that by the beginning of the year 2000 or so we will be living in a postindustrial society. Some use the term "reindustrialization." But the characteristics of the postindustrial society (or reindustrialized society) are clearly upon us and are augury of things to come for those who wish to make the observation. The essential industrial activity of such a society will be science-based, therefore based in a sound education, not only in science, but also in language and mathematics, which are basic to communication in science-based industry; not only development of mental abilities that embrace linear sequencing, but simultaneous, holistic processing as well. To become a scientist in modern society, one needs a grasp of the history of human endeavor, of the interrelationships of people in a society, of the essential qualities of an open society, of the flow of the culture of which one is a part. To be a scientist in the twenty-first century is to forgo alchemy; it is to become fully a member of the culture.

Perhaps by the year 2000 less than 10% of the population will be engaged in manufacturing goods for the other 90% or so. The 90% of the work that will be central to the postindustrial society will be accounted for by the professional and technical service fields—education, health, publishing, research and development, distribution, data processing, transportation, and the like. Emphatically, in a postindustrial society, in an economy that is highly techno-electronic, the opportunities for advance in standards of living will be increasingly defined by education, not by schooling per se. All the young will require a minimum of a secondary schooling (or its equivalent). The kind of education that is requisite for life in the postindustrial society may well be rooted in lifelong education. Moreover, the mode and manner of schooling will undergo a slow but sure change, a carefully and systematically planned evolution to meet the needs of a postindustrial nation.

The nature of the change is worth brief analysis. In an agrarian or preindustrial society, men and women contend with nature; in an industrial society, with the machine; in a postindustrial society, informed mind will contend with informed mind. The aphorism "a sound mind in a sound body" will come to mean "a sound mind in a sound body in a sound environment." Perhaps it is simplistic to emphasize that only sound men and women can fashion sound human bodies and sound human environments; but a human environment is a sanative one.

To say that technology has changed our lives is not to say something profound; a moment's thought demonstrates the axiom. The electric light extended the day; it made active work at night possible. Between 1860 and 1945, "future shock" would have meant not only the electric light, central heating, and air conditioning, but automobiles, telephone, radio, motion pictures, television, and the airplane. Between 1945 and the present, it has come to mean television, the computer, atomic energy and atomic bombs, rockets to the moon and the planets, space stations and prolonged life in space (birth to death, that is), laser beams, "test-tube" babies, genetic engineering, or, if you wish, recombinant genetics, atomic fission and possibly fusion, solar heat, bionic hearts, augury of the bionic human. Though not a necessary accompaniment, the increases in the average life span imply problems of population and the problems that accompany increases in numbers, problems of energy, of housing, of pollution, and the like.

In number, Americans are no longer mainly engaged in the extractive industries (agriculture, forestry, fishing, mining). While it is estimated that these industries, particularly agriculture, are a large part (more than 65%) of our GNP, it is equally true that the equivalent of one farm family, with all the machines it uses, can care for the needs of some fifty or sixty city families per year. It is estimated that in the 1850s some thirty to forty farm families supplied the years' needs for food and fiber of one large city family. This is merely to emphasize that machines and their attendant technologies are now doing the work of raw muscle.

Yet individuals in most preindustrial societies are still using raw muscle power to extract life from the land. In an agrarian, preindustrial society the major part of the population—some 60 to 70%—is dependent on "natural forces"; life is answerable to soil, water, seasons. The struggle is *against,* unfortunately not *with,* nature, that is, the natural environment.* In such agrarian societies, individuals are not mainly

* I use the term "natural environment" cautiously. People in their varieties of shelter—sod house, tepee, igloo, apartment house, skyscraper—are considered by us to live as "naturally" as the bee in its hive. A liana is natural, as is a bridge. Men and women, in all their variety, are natural. In effect, to use René Dubos's term, Homo sapiens has "humanized" the environment.

or solely consumers. They are necessarily producers; the economic system of the preindustrial society requires their muscle; they add to the family's income. And because they are producers, their schooling is short. Their education is often coequivalent with "life's experience."

Bell's analysis proceeds somewhat as follows: The preindustrial society interacts with nature; the industrial society, with the machine. The peoples of preindustrial society are engaged mainly in inducing the land to grow its produce; the industrial society induces machines to till the soil and harvest the crops, and to produce its goods. In an industrial society people are not necessarily in tune with the rhythms of nature, but with the rhythms of time, of clocks; the work is technical, planned so that energy—provided by fossil fuels, hydroelectric power, atomic energy, and soon energy from space (solar energy)—is harnessed for producing goods. More goods made by fewer people is the aim; in short, to increase production is to increase efficiency.

The antecedents of a postindustrial society lie not primarily in any one industry, but in postmodern industries—that is, industries concerned with polymers, computers, electronics, genetics, solid-state physics, not to say communication, in the unbelievable blink of computerized verbal and mathematical languages. These are industries based on the availability and participation of literate and numerate people, those with capacities in language and mathematics as well as in the special symbolic languages and mathematics of physics, chemistry, geology, biology, space science, and the like. The antecedents lie in science-based industry. And science-based industry is based on knowledge, on skills, on attitudes that conform to laboratory-based theory and practice.

To make the point: Thomas Alva Edison, inventor of the electric light, the motion picture, the phonograph, and a host of other things, knew little mathematics; Alexander Graham Bell knew little of electromagnetism; Robert Fulton did not base his steamboat's mechanics on laws of thermodynamics; Luther Burbank knew little of genetics: the genius and the work of these men preceded systematic knowledge. On the other hand, modern industries, such as those given over to the manufacture of plastics, drugs, atomic energy, even farming, are based on systematic and theoretical knowledge—that is, on generalized, conceptualized knowledge—of the nature of forces, of atomic particles, of genes, of biosynthesis. To make a complex story simple in statement: A postindustrial society is based on systematic knowledge, skills, and attitudes; its central, essential resources are educated people who can conserve, transmit, rectify, and expand its knowledge and values. A postindustrial society depends on *education,* more than schooling. And so there is the need to educate all as fully as their capacities will permit.

Memorandum: On Renewing Schooling and Education

The essential person in a postindustrial society is the educated person equipped to master the machine in order to utilize the hordes of data produced by other educated individuals—the so-called professionals. Manufacturing technology in modern industry is geared to the supply of "knowledge workers" rather than to a reduced supply (in Western nations) of "blue-collar workers." Entire plants will be redesigned; traditional manufacturing will not compete. The postindustrial society is thus mainly a service economy. It is an economy based on an essential force, but with educated people supplying the work. Successful farmers now use computer-based data; they use electronically processed information on weather, soil, and crop management. The diagnoses of physicians are increasingly based on the analyses of medical technicians, who in turn use the services of machines to do micro-technical analyses employing traces of radioactive substances. Weather forecasting is done with data collected by satellite. In addition, all citizens will perhaps be required to understand enough of the technical matters and detail enhancing and coercing life so that some degree of psychological safety may be possible. Witness, for example, the anxiety produced by the failure to understand what had happened in the Three Mile Island nuclear "disaster." Witness the anxiety induced by the term "cancer."

In 1980, some seventy out of every hundred workers were engaged in services. To re-emphasize, by the year 2000 it is possible that ninety out of a hundred workers or so will be so engaged, leaving a labor force of 10% or so engaged in manufacturing.

The science-based revolution in the making—and being—is intense, affecting every facet of life. To list but a few examples:

• Computer technology is pervasive in every aspect of scholarly pursuit and research and in industrial and economic life. Indeed, the ease of record-keeping is invading privacy; records relating to private life are readily available. The computer has become part of schooling, in the availability of hand computers and for administrative purposes—scheduling, record-keeping, and the like. Soon computer-assisted instruction in schools will be in hand if . . . *if* those concerned with its introduction are wise enough to consider the capacities, abilities, and attitudes of school administrators, teachers, children, and their parents.

• Space technology is multiplying invention, including miniaturization of machines. It is out of the experimental stage; regular space shuttles will soon be instituted. Space satellites not only analyze weather, crops, and geological data, but lay open military movements. And, of course, communications satellites now bring international events into the living room, and sometimes into the school.

• The energy crisis will as a matter of course give impulse to technologies utilizing sources other than oil; inventions spawning new uses of coal, solar energy, wind, combustion engines, and other energy sources are already being patented. Researches into safer nuclear devices are flourishing.

• Efforts to protect the environment against chemical assault are also resulting in industrial innovations: improved combustion engines, new vehicles, and the like.

• Public health is, in a sense, developing into a national industry. With the practical elimination of disease caused by microorganisms (infectious disease), an attack is being mounted on organic disease. Circulatory problems (heart, blood pressure, stroke), the varieties of cancer, and the "breakdown" of function associated with aging are under study. A bionic industry is flourishing. Genetic engineering is being employed not only with the purpose of eliminating hereditary disease, but also to induce microorganisms to manufacture essential body substances—hormones and enzymes that are useful in sustaining health. A life span of 100 years or more is not out of the question.

• The "communications" industry is about to burst forth in a variety of devices to enter the home, discs as well as cassettes. In a well-planned educational system, television-inspired attitudes, which Clifton Fadiman has called "the other life," may perhaps be united with "the life of reality." Certainly audio-visual devices, attached to TV or working through TV, will increasingly furnish information and "teach" certain skills. That is to say, certain TV and audio-visual programs may well take on the characteristics of instructed learning.

The reader will surely think of other examples.

All in all, planet Earth has become a "global village." The political tremors in an underdeveloped nation and the oil policies of developing nations quickly affect the lives of Americans. The oceans no longer protect us from military attack or from social unrest half a globe away. A postindustrial society is truly based on information, and information is the property of an educated people.

It is not surprising, then, that in the United States (so too, for example, in France and Germany) the fastest growth in occupational designation has been the technical and managerial employee—if you will, the professional. These employees make up some 30% of the gainfully employed, while clerical workers approximate some 25%, skilled workers 22%, and semiskilled workers 18%. A postindustrial society is a highly technological yet interdependent group. In addition, there is an educated labor force which has changed its character. In

1900, some 3% of those twenty-five years or older had been graduated from college and about 6% had some college work. Some 13% of the population had finished high school, and 15% had only a bit of high-school work. In 1978, however, some 15% of the population had been graduated from college, and a like number had *some* college education; almost 70% had completed high school. It is perhaps predictable that by 1990 all youth will have been through high school (indeed, they may well be required to) or the equivalent. Furthermore, a secondary-school "education"—not "schooling" per se—possibly of the type limned in the following chapters, will be necessary for survival in a postindustrial society, certainly in the twenty-first century.

In the United States, then, in just a few years (say, ten to twenty) education as compared and contrasted with schooling will be the criterional attribute of the vast majority of its citizens. Have we considered the fact that children entering kindergarten this year or the next will be in their majority in the first year of the twenty-first century? Will they be prepared for a vast change in life and living?

Major Movements: "New" and "Needed"

There are ritual activities that bemuse us all. Especially during years of recession, election years, unpopular wars—and somehow in periods when a diffused and generalized dissatisfaction is not a wart on our progress—Americans are critical of their society: nothing is *just* right. Our materialism offends some of us; the homogeneity of our goals and ways, others of us; our economic and social problems, all of us. In our flaying of ourselves, we lose sight of our achievements and our rich opportunities. Our institutions are fair game for our discontent in the winters and summers of our lives, and of course the schools, so closely identified with family and person, bear more than a reasonable amount of shame and guilt. Teachers themselves are almost never satisfied with their accomplishments: there is always one child, one adolescent, one boy or girl turning adult with whom a given teacher has failed. Why not? The percentages of failure are not in batting averages, or incompleted passes, or fumbles, but in a failure to diagnose the most complex of all phenomena: the human mind, and body, and persona.

In doing all this we lose comfort. We can ponder with Thomas Hardy "the wonder and wormwood of the whole," but somehow we lose the wonder, and focus on the wormwood. Our successes are set aside, and our achievements elude us. It will remain for historians of the future—20, 40, 100, or 200 years later—to describe the wonder of our lives, the richness in cultural components, and the incredible successes, as well as the lamentable failures—but nevertheless success "beyond compare." Our country is so very young. The British are aware that they are British; the French that they are French. Late in this century Americans became aware of who they were: Americans. As Americans they began to recognize that they are what they do. And what they do, what they achieve, is, very often, the goal of people over the globe. Acts of dissatisfaction caused by failure to achieve the perceptible goals of the good life are also a part of what we do. And so we shall always seek to improve the schools and in so doing we shall always point to their imperfections—not their excellences, except in moments of ease.

As indicated, in this search for perfection of schooling, we often confuse schooling with education. We seek not only to school *all* but also to educate *all*. Imperceptibly, then growing barely perceptible, certain movements and their accompanying innovations are bursting the seed pod. To emphasize, these movements are directed not only at schooling *all,* but also to educating *all*.

Certain Strictures

An emphasis on education for all may imply slower growth in wealth and status (but longer life), probably also later marriage, a different life style, fewer children, and a slower growth in population. The increasing participation of all citizens in society is the goal—and should, in time, become a matter of course. In a postindustrial society with the professional as central, the continued, lifelong education of the older worker with technical and managerial potential cannot be ignored. Certainly we will be required to meet the needs of a greater variety of youth. It will no longer be possible to have collegiate and noncollegiate orientations only; the full range of human endeavor will require representation in our educational system.

Pause for a moment to consider, in broad outline at least, the present life-sequence, generally speaking, of course:

The first part of life is given over to *schooling.*

The second part of life is given over to *work.*

The third part of life (aging, retirement) is given over to *nothing*. That is, "nothing" as it affects utilization of most retired individuals by society.

Surely a more mature view of schooling and education needs to be fashioned: one in which the uses of formal and informal education will not be limited to the first third of life. If collegiate education means the securing of an education given over not only mainly to preparation for a vocation but also to a search for the meaning of truth, beauty, justice, love, and faith, then is not *lifelong education*—called by whatever name —to be open and to be secured by all? Under this assumption, all citizens would continue their education after high school—some in the university (meaning graduate work of all sorts), some in community centers, some in the home, and some in institutions not yet invented. This movement toward lifelong education has begun, has it not? With the techno-electronic innovations already upon us—cable TV arranged for audience participation, discs and tapes with their computer-directed technology, communications satellites that beam "educational programs" over a wide range, and a host of others in blueprint—the possibilities are enormous. Let alone the adult-education classes which are everywhere in a bewildering richness of courses and workshops. Get enough people together and a course will be arranged!

In a postindustrial society, school populations themselves will undergo a change in character. For example, a new formal division of schooling is springing up: preschool. It is estimated that some 4 million children (age 3–4) will be part of this new formal education, prior to entrance into the elementary grades.

By 1990, it is probable that all who enter secondary school will have had an elementary-school environment that will enable them to accommodate the newer requirements for graduation from high school. That is to say, the curriculums will be so varied that students with a variety of abilities will achieve the "diploma" or "certificate" attesting to different and special competencies (with certain competencies in literacy and numeracy required for graduation). The diploma will then represent many different accomplishments. And it may well be so interpreted without deprecation of its owner.

The world of the postindustrial society cannot permit the luxury of a division between the humanities and arts as compared and contrasted with the technologies, science, and mathematics. The expert will be required to have a decent capability in both (granting speciality in lifework), and members of the society that supports the expert will require a decent capability in both. For without the support of society, the expert will not flourish. In short, a balance in instruction as well as in curriculum will be required.

Given the strictures placed upon life, it will be clear that the major business of humankind will be the business of education. In other words, with expenditures in energy and resources severely cut, the investment must be in people. A "full" education of the young will no longer be a matter of choice; it will be obligatory, even mandatory. Moreover, our desire to balance schooling for all, to balance personal gifts with opportunities and destination, may well result in the fashioning of a different progression in schooling. The movement is already discernible.

A Different Progression

If everyone is to be in a school, then the needs for variety cannot be denied. Variability itself is the guarantee of our freedom, if only because an open society requires the different skills and the wide array of contributions of its people.

An educational system embodies a servomechanism that "displays" its successes and failures in constant feedback. The schools—as they exist—have not failed the majority of students; rather, the schools have been given too meager a purpose, and too meager a task, by society. To teach basic skills is relatively easy if that is demanded—as it should be. Our schools do it well enough for the 75% who do have the capacities to learn in time-honored ways.

Unfortunately, for the 25% who "fail," the schools have become systems of rejection, because those in this group cannot learn by the methods and at the rate adaptable to the majority. They require different modes of instruction and evaluation, and possibly a different structure of schooling, certainly a head start in home and preschool. These 25% are the hard-to-teach; these are children for whom repression diminishes competence. But the schools have also, in a sense, failed our most creative children, the so-called gifted and talented, those children who require the nurture of imagery, of idiosyncratic thought and achievement, of intuitive qualities that make discovery possible—those competent children for whom repression diminishes creativity.

Even casual observation will disclose that only two decades ago society did *not* demand careful attention to the needs of the disadvantaged, and only sporadically did it demand attention to the needs of the gifted.

We need now to use all we know about teaching and learning to address the problems and redress grievances.

There are other aspects of schooling that power the change that is slowly gathering momentum. My investigations and discussions with a representative group of administrators at higher levels of supervision and curriculum development press the view that a significant change is about to occur: administrators, supervisors, and curriculum directors, whose concepts and values were affected by the environment of the 1930s, are about to retire in significant numbers. The concepts and values of the Great Depression, which significantly affected schooling and educational policies, are giving way to those of later generations. Further research must be directed to this situation. Nevertheless, however this change manifests itself, we, and the new administrators, will be faced with the reality of crisis. What we will face, perhaps, is not mainly or only a crisis brought on by science and technology; it will be a crisis in values, a crisis in moral behavior. There are few who do not see the need for re-evaluation of standards affecting our conduct and our work. The nature of our conduct and our work remains central to our ethic. A central purpose of schooling and education is to focus our capacities on our modes of self-expression, on conduct, and on our lifework. One way seems to be to develop new structures to meet our newer purposes. One of these newer structures is not necessarily a restructuring of society, but a restructuring of the components of the school to meet the needs of effective schooling for all. But this effort is not to be, it seems to me, an ad-hoc effort.

It is a truism—possibly impressive because it is one of those "terrible simplifiers"—to say that we live in a world of rapid change. Not only the United States but also countries over the world pursue ad-hoc solutions in response to crises. Ad-hoc efforts applied to school reform, even empirical and pragmatic methods, conceived in our patently vigorous manner, may well be useful to meet relatively familiar problems capable of solution. But the coming transformation of the schools, involving as it does the creation of an educational system, will not be ad hoc. We will not be planting a wood lot but developing a forest, with its profound ecology. The "educational" movements in the past century were, in effect, ad-hoc movements, and a careful analysis of their "failure" will determine that in correcting one imbalance another was induced. In responding to crises they tended to correct one element—industrial preparedness, citizenship, child-centering of the schools, academic excellence, "basics," giftedness—and failed to attend to the balance, to the ecology of achievement. *Balance is all.*

As in all ecologies, balance is not static; it is dynamic, built of countervailing forces. A forest in ecological health is in constant growth, but because of its balance it can rebuild itself after crises of disease (fungal or insect-borne), or fire, or the devastations of climate. A forest is an ecosystem, its parts in balance. An educational system is in a sense a human ecosystem—its parts in balance, and capable of healing itself because the parts that make it a whole effectively balance each other. The test of an educational system is its effectiveness in achieving its social obligations. An ecology of achievement is concerned with the effectiveness of an educational system in sustaining a mature equality of educational opportunity which catalyzes the attainment of equality of educational achievement. In these terms, it is essential to use the term "schooling" in its special and important place as a *major* component of a number of educational systems forming, if you will, an educational system with divergent but open opportunities. To carry the analogy with the forest ecosystem one step further: as a tree in a forest is rooted in and nourished by its soil, so the educational system is rooted in and nourished, not by its schools only, but by society. Schooling is part of the *stem* of an educational system, but not necessarily its root.

The boundaries of an ecology of achievement—the base of the pervasive policy of an educational system—come out of a consideration of these essentials of an educational system: *equality of educational opportunity* aimed at equalizing opportunity for educational achievement; *essentiality of certain knowledge, attitudes, and skills* fitted to a society in constant growth; *excellence of performance* to ensure achievement of the aims of the educational system and society; *evaluation of theory and practice* in all sectors; *effectiveness of learning* once assurance that the means and the methods of attaining effective use of appropriate theory and practice has been secured. It is not useful to talk of a postindustrial revolution, of equality of opportunity for equality of achievement, without designing educational systems—among them schooling—to fit the change.

Too often, in considering a policy to undergird change in a school system, we focus on only one of its components, say, the structure of school buildings, the nature of the curriculum, the caliber of the staff (particularly teachers), the caliber of the administration (particularly leadership), or the system of evaluation (particularly of "minimum competence"). In a policy based on attaining an ecology of achievement, the effect of a change in *one* practice is to be calibrated in relation to a change in the whole. To talk, for example, of the caliber of the teachers is also to consider the nature of what is taught, the methods of instruction that are acceptable, the nature of the working conditions. A community gets the teachers it wants, or perhaps one should say the kinds of teachers who can adapt to its environment and its demands. Once an ecology of achievement rests on a sound structure of curriculum, instruction, and evaluation (all to be discussed in their theoretical and practical applications in the following chapters), a direction beckons.

However, a few remarks on change in structure in a new schooling system should be made here.

First, to attain equality of opportunity, it is essential to attend to the *education* of preschool young. Fitness for schooling depends on essential aspects of early training and education, as considerable research has indicated. Distinguishing between training and education is desirable: training closes options, education opens them.

Certain aspects of failure in schooling may be ascribed to failures in the home. This is not to say that education at home is not available, but that it proceeds willy-nilly. Habits are taught by imitation; that is, certain attitudes and skills are "caught," not taught. Further, the educational effect of TV has not yet been adequately assessed; most children now have TV—with indiscriminate programing, to be sure—as baby-sitter. But education or schooling at home is not to be confused with formal preschooling. The home *is* the first educational environment, more than a first school.

Failures in reaching the levels of intelligence available to a child may be a failure of the home in attending to factors of physiology—say, failure to correct an aspect of faulty physiology due to an errant gene. For example, the child may suffer from phynylketonuria (PKU), a failure to metabolize the amino acid phenylalanine. A child with unameliorated PKU disease is one who may be mentally retarded, unable to learn at the rate expected of the "average" schoolchild. Yet, PKU may be corrected by removing phenylalanine from the diet—hardly a matter of schooling.

The formal preschool has become a necessity: it is a requisite for working parents. Even more important, preschool may well be a corrective for a poor educational "start" at home. Certainly it will be more successful if the parents are involved, as certain longitudinal studies of programs such as Head Start have disclosed.

Second, schooling (generally beginning with kindergarten and ending with graduation from secondary school) is not now attuned to growth and developmental processes of the young. In a certain sense, schooling has developed in response to natural custom. It is not, for example, a fact that all children develop at the same rate. It is not a fact that the graded system accommodates the learning rate or the mode of learning appropriate for each student. It is not a fact that growth and development proceed in a steady progression of events. Development of the young is saccadic, and does not proceed in a graduated cadence. That is, growth becomes apparent in its spurts—as at three to five years of age and at puberty. Moreover, the young develop different abilities, aptitudes, attitudes, skills; the young are multifaceted, they are populations or pluralities of traits. Some children develop strongly in cognitive traits (acquisition of knowledge), others in enactive and iconic traits (athletics and the arts); some are balanced in most, some are idiosyncratic in a few. While all children can learn things in common and possibly at rates not too disparate, so that they can be placed in small groups within suites or groupings of grades, provision must be made for the young who are gifted, those who are handicapped, those who excel in the cognitive areas, those who excel in the arts, those who excel generally in all school areas, and those who do not. In the "new" schools, provision is to be made for all. (And there are a number of schools, including some I have recently visited, that are valiant in their efforts to reach all.)

Third, it follows, then, that schooling—as a basic social institution in the United States, paramount as an exemplar of the discipline of responsible consent and dissent, and of the balance of opposing opinion—might well be re-examined to consider whether its present divisions are suitable for the ensuing years. For good and sufficient reasons—particularly the consideration of lengthened life span, the availability of newer modes of instruction, and the competition of TV as another "mode of life" (often antagonistic to the aims of schooling)—the present divisions (preschool, kindergarten, primary, junior, and secondary schools) need reassessment, as does the allotment of time to each.

Fourth, since schooling is generally concerned with *instructed learning,* it needs to be developed as a center of instructed learning, with provisions not only for the learning common and essential to a citizen in an open society, but also for *individuated instruction* to accommodate difference and variety. To re-emphasize, the variety of the kinds of achievement our young are capable of is the guarantee of our freedom; there is a swath of excellence in all young in all activity we call "schooling." Achievement is not monolithic; it accommodates and rewards differences in scale in accordance with ability, and abilities vary because of past history in personal development.

Fifth, a host of devices that educate are to be utilized. That is not to say that the activities of instructed learning are to be limited to the school. An educational system requires that learning not be relegated to a place and time sequence. For example, TV used at home is an educational medium. It will be necessary for TV to make its contribution to education. In view of the availability of cassette and the disc, TV programing need no longer be haphazard and can be utilized by individuals at their convenience. But this utilization, whatever the schedule, may well be obligatory and should be evaluated. Other devices, such as computer-assisted instruction, should also be made available, at home and in school. These devices may assist either remediation or advanced preparation.

Sixth, the effectiveness of such a system requires measurement of the achievement of objectives. There are now a variety of means of testing effectiveness which may be used once the aims of an educational system are clearly established. This is not to be done by fewer measurements or tests, but by varied measurements, a variety of tests and the measurement of success in certain instructional activities as well. Similarly, the training and education of parents, teachers, supervisors, administrators, and the qualifications of members of supervising bodies, including Boards of Education and government agencies, can only be assessed and planned if we know the structure of schooling qua other educational systems and its requirements.

Nevertheless, it is essential to stress that statistical measurement requires repetitiveness of a phenomenon on which to base its generalizations. As indicated elsewhere, effectiveness of curriculum and instruction must take into account the *uniqueness* of special abilities of the young. Otherwise giftedness, talent, and varieties of excellence in performance are lost in "norms" and "means." Scores on achievement tests, IQ measures, and the like are not generally interpreted correctly by the public. The process of education as compared and contrasted with schooling should accommodate a concern for measures of effectiveness and accountability that recognize the uniqueness of an individual life. The individual is not, as said before, to be lost in the arms of the larger statistic. This error is not a property of the test per se, but of the interpretation and utilization—and *reporting*—of test results, particularly standardized tests. To be considered individually effective, the various administrators, supervisors, teachers, and other personnel in an educational system require means of competent, compassionate, and effective measurement to determine whether the educational system *entire,* as a servomechanism of society, is effective.

For a schooling system acting in concert with other educational systems to fit a postindustrial environment (socioeconomic, sociopolitical, sociopsychological) in which education must be central, we should consider an invention in schooling that has "newer" divisions—perhaps the following, or others that may prove more suitable. I intend to treat each of these divisions in greater detail in the following chapters.

• *Home school:* with the parent as teacher

The home is essentially an educational institution. Parents will need to accept responsibilities for certain aspects of the education of their young. Possibly TV and other electronic devices will be adjunct, perhaps central, to the home school. But it is here and in the preschool that the 25% who are accorded 75% of the failing marks should be accorded the beneficent environment and "education" to enable them to benefit from schooling.

• *Preschool* (perhaps ages three through five)

This might well be concerned with the basic habituations in self-expression and conduct required for the "effective and good life" in a post-industrial society.

• *Primary or common school* (perhaps ages six through ten)

This might well accommodate practices concerned with the common ("basic") aptitudes and skills required of all citizens, among them reading, writing, arithmetic, social conduct. However, this school is also to be especially concerned with the *identification of difference,* that is, special opportunities, special destinations.

• *Transitional school* (perhaps ages eleven through twelve)

This could, and perhaps should, be concerned especially with *opportunities accommodating difference.* For some, continued remediation in common skills will be required, as well as special opportunity in certain areas of talent. For others, common skills well in hand, focus may be on special opportunities undergirding differences in capacity, ability, or special bent—giftedness in the arts, in expression, in the sciences, in mathematics.

• *Secondary or preparatory school* (perhaps ages thirteen to sixteen)

This might be considered a year-round school. Each year might consist of four quarters, including a summer quarter. In this preparatory school a program of *education* might well be designed for individuals to the point when personal aptitudes have been identified by the individual, by the family, and by the school (coming out of experience in and out of school). In this sector of schooling, the school, together with the family and the student, determines the nature of the education to be pursued. For some, it may well be college-preparatory work, which should end at some "leaving age" (not necessarily the present age of "graduation"). The appropriate leaving age may well be a judgment of the school, which, with the advice of experts (or testing?) in a particular area of competence, will determine when the individual is intellectually capable of pursuing the work he or she selects and mature enough to accommodate its demands. For some, it may mean industrial or commercial programs emphasizing general skills. The same standards for judging leaving age may well be established for those who have selected themselves as fit for industrial-commercial work. In any event, secondary or preparatory schooling may be a minimum of two or three years, and this may well be the maximum for a number of the students. At the end of that period, some may wish to undertake various ways of serving the community; others may wish to enter the university. (See below and Chapter 7.)

- *Apprentice or intern school* (ages sixteen to eighteen)

Work-study programs are central to this school. If work is one of the major elements central to life, then it ought to be experienced early and under trained supervision. This period of schooling might embrace at least three divisions maintained commonly by the community, the federal government, and industry. (A system of tax credits or other incentives may need to be devised.) Students in each division might, for example, undertake a work-study program in which the actual work done is recompensed by wages; the program of studies would be related to the individual's choice of work.

In the *industrial division,* the apprentices may well follow established industrial/union/corporate practices, coupled with a prescribed program of studies.

In the *precollegiate division,* the apprentices follow a program of work available in professional areas—assisting in schools, businesses, laboratories, medical and dental establishments, publishing.

In the *arts division,* the individual undertakes training in the art particular to his or her talents; performance would also be recompensed.

In the apprentice or intern school, study and work and development toward mature behavior are central to the program.

- *Public-service year*

After leaving the apprentice or intern school, one year may well be given over to the community, city, state, or nation, as a year of service. There will be need for competent young men and women to serve in the preschool, common school, and transitional school by assisting in individual reading and mathematics programs (whether in remediation or advance); to serve in special-education programs, in hospitals, in assisting the infirm, in maintaining conservation activities, in construction—in a host of activities that enrich an open society and are enriched by collaboration. Or the young men and women may, if they wish, undertake military service. "Supervision"—if indeed it is required—is available: the increasing life span makes available a well-educated, well-trained group of mature individuals (now "retired") eager to serve society.

Naturally, this year of service, whether optional or obligatory, is to be recompensed. If done well—and why shouldn't it be?—what a magnificent contribution will be made, and what magnificent experience will be gained by the young, as well as by those competent people now retired. Again, the aim is to secure study, and work, and opportunity for growth toward maturity.

Education (defined in another context as a combination of instructed learning and self-activated learning) is, of course, not to be terminated at any age. Considering the advances in control of disease and aging, it is obviously *lifelong*. The need for a variety of teacher's aides and teachers at various levels of instruction in preschool, primary, secondary, and collegiate areas is clearly demonstrable. A postindustrial society has room for all its individuals, in productive work.

Policy and Practice

One may agree that the preparation of the young for life in a postindustrial age is essential and, of course, we are required to afford all the equal opportunity to reach their full potential in achievement assuming variety in abilities and goals. However this may be, full potential is possible when optimum conditions prevail in curriculum, instruction, and evaluation. To effect schooling and educational policy, then, is to effect an optimum environment in schooling policy, practice, and procedure. Such a policy concerns itself pervasively, with what is to be taught, how, when, where, and to whom. In turn, these aspects of an effective school system may depend on method, procedure, and technique.

Nonetheless, with a change in the structure of the school system there may well be a search for new tactics and strategies in administration, in curriculum, in instruction and evaluation. There may well be movements and/or innovations in curriculum. A few, by way of example:

• There may be attempts to secure balance in offerings; that is, to balance the cognitive with the affective areas.

• There may be attempts to reorder knowledges, values, and skills into sequential wholes related to the students' development, and not "catch as catch can." The failure of TV as an instructional mode, for example, is that it is precisely "catch as catch can."

• Surely there will be attempts to make computer-assisted curriculum and instruction a part of the whole, not just an accessory.

There may well be movements to affect the philosophy of over-all policy. For example:

• There is need for a modern axiology of schooling and education. Possibly we shall be required to re-examine the values of Horace Mann, of Herbert Spencer, even those of John Dewey. This is hardly heresy. The almost mystagogic feelings that pervade philosophies of schooling and education need rigorous critical study. Schooling and education has been politicized; their "dogmatic backbone," to use Malinowski's term, needs rethinking.

• There is a need perhaps to consider whether the school is not a place for a certain amount of education in development of a "self-concept." (See Chapters 5 and 7.) Why are schools (the temporary but daily "homes" of the young) subjected to terror and vandalism; why should a drug culture exist in the schools and undermine their efforts?

The above reflect certain categories that may lead to innovation and reform in the practice of schooling. Others will surely occur to the reader. In another context, with a change in structure of schooling, public officials, administrators, supervisors, teachers, parents will of necessity review the aims and objectives of the schools and in so doing reform them. What are they to guard against? To succumb to the ad-hoc solution, to impulse, to whim, to fancy, to haste or to climb on the bandwagon will result in the kind of pendulation of which all of us have become weary. Our guide may well be to interpose, between impulse and action, evidence, reason, and judgment:* evidence, surely, if it is available; reason, of necessity; beyond doubt, judgment based on the most competent and compassionate advice. But evidence is not always available; and so we need a guard against the politicization of our reason and judgment. Always the search is to be for balanced development: balance in curriculum, instruction, and evaluation.

The brevity of this book—an intended brevity, to be sure—permits specific discussion of certain practices I consider obstacles to a coming transformation; it does not permit a detailed description of procedure and technique. Sometimes I may be required to note two or more descriptions of policy, theory, practice, or procedure which are not in

---

* John Dewey's remark, I believe, but I am not altogether sure.

agreement. But then, we know that schooling and education are not yet sciences. Practices that seem opposed in detail are, however, often adaptable to different communities, and to different stages of the development of an ecology of achievement.

To recapitulate: the development of an ecology of achievement and of a balance in curriculum, instruction, and evaluation is essential to the renewing of schooling and education. The methods of developing an educational system embracing numerous schooling systems will be difficult and will require time, but in all probability no greater expenditure in funding will be required, given the adjustments of inflation, than is now available for the totality of services schooling and education require. What will require additional time is the establishment of adequate agreement on the essential change in behaviors—in essential knowledge, attitudes, skills—to be expected of schooling and of education. Otherwise the effectiveness of curriculum and instruction cannot and will not be measured. Otherwise we will once again undertake futile searches for tests of competency, unable to determine where the competencies of the various constituencies of a school begin and end: competencies of parents, of funding agencies, of supervisors, of administrators, of teachers, of pupils, and of other educational agencies.

There are at least two fundamental questions to be asked before beginning the dialogue essential to the invention of an educational system: What kind of a world do we want for our children? What kinds of individuals will secure such a world? This dialogue will require the contributions of competent and compassionate thought, of the constructive joust of the best minds.

Once our aims are worthy of a people who value the young as they value themselves, of a people who have advanced civilization, we may then be able to live with the contradictions that haunt great plans and great aims. We may then be able to outwit time.

4. Regarding Instruction

A Necessary Prologue

As I visit classrooms over the country, as I probe the research literature of school and educational reform, I find described two species of instruction, and, of course, hybridization along a full range. But in the "polemic" literature and in speeches at conventions and in the utterances of partisans, I find the "battle lines" drawn.

There are strong proponents of a mode of instruction in which the *teacher* (representing authority) *is the central figure,* determining *what* is to be learned in a given class period (but not determining the adopted curriculum) determining *how* it is to be learned, and (excluding standard testing) determining *whether* it has been learned. The teacher is surely a figure in authority, and central to instruction—a guardian of the archives. One sees this mode represented in its purest form in a lecture on TV—a form of instruction, to be sure. The learner is passive and is not consulted.

On the other hand, there are strong proponents of forms of instruction in which the *pupil is the central figure;* for each pupil is different in the way he or she approaches what is to be learned and how it is to be learned. How it has been learned must be determined then by methods that accommodate pupils with varying and idiosyncratic abilities or capacities in learning. In this mode, the teacher is a *guide* to the archives.

I have not found any research, embracing a sufficient number of schools, teachers, pupils, and applied and tested with validity over a sufficiently long period, that favors either extreme. It seems now that the pendulations in practice without a clear-cut experimental protocol have become counterproductive; the swings in practice advance neither teach-ing nor learning. Nevertheless, there is sufficient thought and investiga-tion to suggest that until further research (an *experimentum crucis,* to be sure) is conducted, a balance is desirable, possible, and practicable. Such a balance should not, however, jeopardize attention to varieties of abil-ity, aptitude, and interest.

This chapter, therefore, concerns itself with the *theory* and *practice* that *harmonize and balance* both species of instruction. Teachers and pupils do find domains in teaching and learning that are collaborative and reinforcing. Philosophies, researches, and practice defend such a balance.

What is suggested is a balance to be found neither in instruction—as a sole property of the teacher—nor in learning—as a sole property of the learner—but one that is to be sought in "instructed learning" in which both actively participate. The balance we seek is found in an ap-proach in which the pupil gains increasing experience in the aptitudes required to become an efficient and independent learner even as he or she gains useful knowledge, skills, and attitudes which fulfill personal gifts and opportunities in a search for excellence in personality, in char-acter, in intellection, and in destination. Such excellence is the outcome of effective instruction and wise curriculum practice. It goes without say-ing that if the "inventions" proposed in this chapter, and elsewhere, are not suitable, others will be devised. Inventive minds live and work within the fields of schooling and education. But the search for *balance* is im-posed on all—is it not?

A variety of problems will be discussed in an attempt to develop useful theory and practice, but we will also seek an answer to a major problem that has puzzled us all: why "advances" in curriculum (what is tȯ be taught) seem to "succeed," whereas "advances" in modes of in-struction (how it is to be taught) which are made part of the curriculum often "fail." I will reverse the usual order of presentation and discuss instruction first, in this chapter, and defer curriculum to the next. Cur-riculum and instruction in any given area of study need to be planned together, but the philosophy and practice undergirding each may fruit-fully be considered apart.

A teacher's task has changed radically. The explosion of knowledge accompanied by a rampant technology requires that instruction prepare the young for an unknown future, for events still in the realm of fiction.

A Certain Reality

If by some act of magic or technology one were to attend three decades of major meetings on instruction (as I have done), one would come away with perhaps three notions of instructional policy and/or theory and practice. They are:

1. A defense of the concept of schools as agents of society produces a defense of the idea that instruction should be concerned with methods, styles, disciplines, and devices that accommodate the child to the ways of society. Certain proponents of this view, though not all, suggest that one way to do this is to have teachers "teaching" and "demonstrating," as it were—that is, "telling" the young what is "out there." In effect, the teacher is to inform and thus transmit to the child what is known. Textbooks are to be used to assist the teacher in the transmission of information. As a transmitter of experience (of the history of human experience), the teacher is central to instruction. The proponents of this method express the *didactic view* of instruction.

2. The best way to accommodate children to the ways of society is not for teachers to "tell" children what is known, but to have children "discover for themselves." That is, the teacher is to invent ways by which children discover what is "out there," what is known and perhaps what is unknown. This is considered the *heuristic,* or discovery, *mode.* By way of example: with the "discovery approach," the laboratory and field trip are to become central; so are methods of creative writing; so are methods that induce the learner to paint, to practice and perform on an instrument, and the like. Learning is to be mainly "by doing." The lecture and the textbook furnish background; they are to be springboards for discovery.

3. An artistic and useful combination of both didactic and heuristic modes is most effective, in the interests of a total economy of funds and time and energy. The argument is old: *ars longa, vita brevis.* Because knowledge is exploding at a tremendous rate, doubling every twelve to fifteen years, it is impossible for the young to discover for themselves all that is necessary. If they did engage in "learning by discovery," they would "rediscover" the wheel. Judicious "telling" and artistic transmission of certain aspects of the history of experience are not only necessary, but mandatory. Textbooks are useful, indeed necessary, so that the learner may "stand on the shoulders of others."

Nevertheless, exponents of both the didactic and heuristic modes suggest that the teacher is to be a model of competence and compassion; that what he or she does speaks more loudly than what is said; that he or she is, then, to use what has been called the *affective mode*. The affective mode comprises all those methods that make the teacher sympathetic to the young; the teacher's acts are to be those of *constructive affection*.

These three arguments are not straw men set up to be devastated. In effect, these views (with slight modifications representing special philosophies) furnish the substance of argument at teachers' meetings and national conventions. They are important and useful ways of looking at schooling and education.

What is the reality?

By the fourth- to sixth-grade level of schooling, teachers "talk" (lecture, if you will) about 40 to 60% of the time, giving the rest of the time over to an activity (in which the student takes part) closely corresponding to and illustrative of the teacher's presentation. In junior high school the time given over to teachers' presentations (mainly lectures) is approximately 60 to 70%; in the senior grades, 70 to 90%, particularly in classes in physics, government, history, and economics. The textbook is found to be central in all fields where subject matter (or what is lectured) is central to the curriculum. This is not to deny the fact that children do learn from a teacher's talk, particularly if it is interesting. Learning from the talk of adults is indeed a form of learning by imitation. Nevertheless, instruction by the lecture approach is teaching mainly by the linear-verbal method. There are students who take easily to the linear-verbal activities affecting percepts and concepts; there are those who do not.

The model of teaching that is exemplified by the lecture may be diagramed thus:

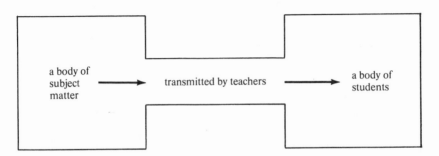

a body of subject matter → transmitted by teachers → a body of students

Although knowledge is generally transmitted by the teacher and by reading, the activity permitted students (closely corresponding to and illustrative of the teacher's presentation) is in a real sense *directed by the teacher* (or by the textbooks and workbooks he or she uses). The activity takes the form of discussions (in which the teacher is central— asking questions, directing a panel); or it is directed by the teacher (writing, laboratory work, films, filmstrips); or it takes the form of tests, to determine how effective the student's apprehension of the lecture-lessons or the teacher-directed activity (laboratory work, field trips, reading) has been. Put another way, the effectiveness of instructed learning is determined by tests prepared by the teacher which reflect the teacher's approach. The model described embodies a style of instruction that may be called "teacher-centered" or "teacher-dominated."

A model embodying another style of instruction is that usually called "child-centered" or "discovery-centered" or an "inquiry" model. In the discovery style of instruction the teacher also plays an active role. He or she is a guide to learning, not a guardian of the archives. He or she presents information that the learners cannot get themselves and orchestrates the materials of instruction, but the activity corresponding to the topic of the presentation—textbooks, films, filmstrips, laboratory work, field trips—is left more and more, as the teacher's style permits, to the initiative of the student. The style may be diagramed this way:

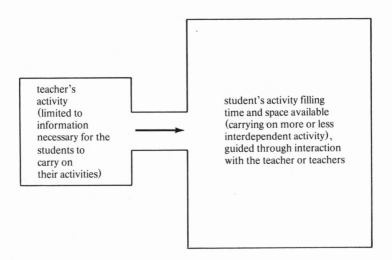

teacher's
activity
(limited to
information
necessary for the
students to
carry on
their activities)

student's activity filling
time and space available
(carrying on more or less
interdependent activity),
guided through interaction
with the teacher or teachers

In this model it is clear that because the activity occurs within a school, within a particular period of time, within a given plan, the results of the heuristic or discovery activity are generally foreordained. In other words, it is rare (that is, improbable) that the discovery would be of a new phenomenon, even where gifted children are involved. The teacher's activity (presentation) precedes the learner's activity; the learner's activity is more or less self-initiated, guided by the teacher or individuals (paraprofessionals) who assist the teacher. Some examples—simple ones, to be sure—are useful to make the point.

In a simple lesson on perspective a teacher may illustrate the principle *by example.* The children may examine an outdoor scene and be asked how they might show that one tree is in front of another. The teacher would then illustrate the technique. In succession, the teacher might ask the children to draw the same scene, then a fresh scene in another place, and finally a scene of their own choosing. The teacher would *not* draw the last two scenes but would be available for advice. The last two are successively designed to give more opportunity for heuristic activity. As the child matures, as the young student enters junior high and secondary school, more and more time may be given over to heuristic activity in all subject areas. The learner is thus given increasing time for self-activation (synonym: self-actualization).

Note that in the last two drawings the children may be said to be "discovering" for themselves. In the first their activity corresponds in mirror image, as it were, to that of the teacher. The degree of correspondence to the teacher's example makes it a matter of *imaginative imitation;* the further away from the teacher's example the child goes, the greater the chance for discovery and creativity—*imaginative invention.*

In a lesson in reading, the teacher may ask the child to read a selection the teacher has just read; then may ask the child to read another selection from the same book; then may—indeed, should—ask the child to select a book of his or her own or write his or her own story. This is common practice in a good reading program. In visual arts, music, and dance, children may design their own dances, write their own songs, paint their own vision. All students, in all their variety, are thus given opportunity to express their idiosyncratic modes. The heuristic approach is fairly common in those subject matters requiring simultaneous processing (for example, the arts) rather than linear-verbal (for example, the social sciences). But the approach is not as common in science, mathematics, and the social sciences.

It would seem then that there are at least two species of instruction: the *didactic* (or informing) approach and the *heuristic* (or discovery) approach. The didactic approach is centered presumably in telling, lecturing, demonstrating, reading—that is, in *receiving* the knowledge and wisdom of others. Of course, there is often exchange and discussion between the giver and the receiver. The heuristic approach is centered presumably in discovering for oneself, in probing and investigating one's sources and environment. To investigate may involve reading what has been discovered, or discussing questions of interest with those who "know." But essentially the didactic approach presumably places responsibility for the dissemination of what is known on the teacher (as present guardian of the archives). It is the teacher who knows, and it is most economical of the process of teaching-learning for him or her to present what is known, as it is organized in a curriculum. The heuristic approach places responsibility on the learner (as future guardian of the archives). It is the learner whose business it is to learn, and one learns best by being active in learning, by discovery.

As usual, where evidence is lacking, the polemic takes over. One of the proponents of the discovery approach, Jerome Bruner (often considered a prime mover, with Jerrold Zaccharias, in the resurgence of this approach in the 1955–1965 period), has this to say, in *The Relevance of Education,* and it is well worth noting:

You cannot consider education without taking into account how a given culture gets passed on. It seems to me highly unlikely that given the centrality of culture in man's adaptation to his environment—the fact that culture serves him in the same way as changes in morphology served earlier in the evolutionary scale—that, biologically speaking, one would expect each organism to rediscover the totality of its culture—this would seem most unlikely. Moreover, it seems equally unlikely, given the nature of man's dependency as a creature, that this long period of dependency characteristic of our species was designed entirely for the most inefficient technique possible for regaining what has been gathered over a long period of time, i.e., discovery.

Robert Gagne, writing in *The Conditions of Learning,* states:

Obviously, strategies are important for problem solving, regardless of the content of the problem. The suggestion from some writings is that they are of overriding importance as a goal of education. After all, should not formal instruction in the school have the aim of teaching the student "how to think"? If strategies were deliberately taught, would not this produce people who could then bring to bear superior problem-solving capabilities to any new situation? Although no one would disagree with the aims expressed, it is exceedingly doubtful that they can be brought about by teaching students "strategies" or "styles" of thinking. Even if they could be taught (and it is possible that they could), they would not provide the individual with the basic firmament of thought, which is subject-matter knowledge. *Knowing a set of strategies is not all that is required for thinking; it is not even a substantial part of what is needed. To be an effective problem solver, the individual must somehow have acquired masses of structurally organized knowledge. Such knowledge is made up of content principles, not heuristic ones.*

Lee Cronbach has perhaps given the definitive statement on the matter, in "The Logic of Experiments in Discovery":

In spite of the confident endorsements of teaching through discovery that we read in semi-popular discourses on improving education, there is precious little substantiated knowledge about what advantages accrue. We badly need research in which the right questions are asked and trustworthy answers obtained. When the research is in it will tell us, I suspect, that inductive teaching has value in nearly every area of the curriculum, and also that its function is specialized and limited. The task of research is to define that proper place and function. Honest research is hard to do, when learning by discovery is the battlecry of one side in the ardent combat between educational philosophies. We have, on one hand, the view of education as cultural transmission, which hints strongly that it is the teacher's job to know the answers and to put them before the pupil. On the other, we have the view of education as growth, arguing that the only real and valuable knowledge is that formulated by the pupil out of his own experience. The second position, which appeals to liberal, humanitarian, and instrumentalist biases, has a long history. In the last thirty-cdd years the bias favoring do-it-yourself learning has been very strong, as educators and psychologists have united in attacks on teacher dominance and pupil conformity. Consequently, we have had almost none of the cut-and-thrust debate needed to define issues and to expose implications of fallacies of the evidence.

The whims and fads, twists and turns of uncritical practice have pushed us always to extremes. In one elementary-school classroom I observed, children were engaged mainly in discovery by activities that offered them tiny increments of experience in search of meaning, for seeing wholes. For over a year, they had been quite active in discovery, in problem-solving, but had gained little of what Gagne suggests is significant in problem-solving. To repeat, he says: "To be an effective problem solver, the individual must somehow have acquired masses of structurally organized knowledge. Such knowledge is made up of content principles, not heuristic ones." As David Ausubel, particularly, and others have had occasion to remind us, we have enough experience and research to know that one good economical way of learning a principle, or concept, is that of being told about it—of course by means of imaginative and instructive "telling."

101

Design of a "Model" of Instruction:
Theory and Practice

One may theorize simply: a teacher teaches and a learner learns. But learners learn different things in any "lesson," and sometimes not what the teacher intends. Many workers have postulated that potent methods of instruction emphasize methods in which the student is active in learning. There is a respectable body of research that suggests that learning is most "effective" when it is carried on by the learner, but the same body of research does not dispute the importance of an "effective" teacher. In his *The Process of Education* Bruner holds the essential position, stated in a variety of ways throughout this influential book, that insofar as is possible a method of instruction should have the objective of leading the child to discover for himself.

Indeed, most innovations in instruction have as their aim methods that place the act of learning in the child's hands. Thus, programed instruction had the learner working through a body of information on his or her own, guided by a program of sequential steps. So did computer-assisted instruction, a form of individualized instruction. And so, above all, did individualized instruction.

A decent amount of research on methods of instruction supports a hypothesis that what is learned actively by the young, what the learner initiates as learning activity, what he or she responds to actively, is effective in retention by the learner of what is learned.

Those who practice measurement of "achievement" postulate a kind of "theory of instruction"—if only to systematize the practice of measurement. In sum, the objective of instruction is a change in learned behavior, and what is retained (as a result of instruction) is recalled in response to appropriate stimuli or devices. (But how does one know whether what is recalled is the result of instruction by a teacher in a given school or learned outside of school?) Moreover, if one analyzes at random the theoretical assumptions of those who have written for a variety of journals, one recognizes a kind of "theory of effectiveness of instruction": what is taught can be determined by the number of acceptable responses to certain test situations presented to the learner.

In the absence of decent knowledge of how neurons or cerebral cell assemblies undertake the art we call "learning"—that is, in the absence of a validated theory of learning—a tentative theory of instruction may be useful, if only to emphasize the limitations of our knowledge and our practice. If the theory is inept, those who are better equipped than I will no doubt hasten to state one embracing what is known.

The absence of a theory hinders not only research but also speculation leading to invention of fruitful hypotheses. A field of knowledge is theory-dependent; without a useful theory, research is often fragmented. Often a fruitful theory directs observation and experiment.

The following statement, from a study commissioned by the National Science Foundation, published in 1979, is to the point:

Another area of great concern to education is the weakness of its research base. As these studies point out in several instances, there seems to be a lack of general direction, a lack of sufficient background of educational theory that would give direction to and provide the basis for the development of dependable research findings. It is obvious, particularly from the report of the Center for Science and Mathematics Education, that a large proportion of educational research is noncumulative and is often inconclusive or even contradictory. Some of this may be attributable to faulty design, inadequate research conceptualization, or some other factors. However, it seems probable that there are other more general factors involved. *Certainly problems of definition and the absence of a substantial theory base are a major part of the problem and contribute largely to the fragmentation and ineffectiveness of much research effort.* It might also be conjectured that at least some of the problem is due to the extreme complexities involved in educational problems. For example, in studies of student learning, it might be argued that the impact of any single variable is likely to be very small considering the total universe of variables which affect each student so that significant observable change as a result of the manipulation of a single variable is unlikely. Herein may lie some of the reasons for much inconclusive educational research. It may imply the need for far more sophisticated and comprehensive research designs and far greater precision in identifying, limiting, defining, and measuring research variables. [Italics added.]

Recall that a theory is fundamentally an orderly explanation of confirmed observation. We require a theory of instruction, perhaps a conceptual scheme—a statement that is adequate enough as a target to draw the fire of cogent, informed analysis. Teachers require a synthesis, however ephemeral, if only because, daily, teachers must teach. We cannot turn away students because as yet we lack a theory that is elegant and free from noise. Because the theory offered in this chapter is based on observation of classroom teaching, and on an analysis of research in education, it is in one sense a *factual* theory. It is also normative, because if the practice of teaching on which the theory is based is an acceptable one, it indicates what *ought* to be done. I hasten to modify that dangerous "ought." A social theory, as a theory of instruction, is constructed within a social environment, and ours is that of an open society, a democratic society, to be sure. The aims of such a society are generally humane and liberating, and are codified in rule, law, and custom. The elements of justice which are the breathing space of any social theory are generally those discussed in the previous chapter. In a word, the most extensive liberties we ought to wish for ourselves ought to be compatible only with our desire to extend those liberties fully to all. A theory of instruction, then, falls within these "oughts," but should not at the same time be confused with a theory of society, or a theory of education, or schooling, within which a theory of instruction is a subset. As a subset it need not repeat all the humane and liberating purposes coded in the honorable social intent of schooling or education.

There are, of course, such rubrics as "teaching through inquiry" and "teaching through discovery"; and, in similar rubrics, such as "learning as a change in behavior" and "learning by doing," what is required of the act of instruction is summarized as theory in a kind of shorthand. On analysis, "teaching through inquiry" and "learning by doing" seem to be tactics, or even strategies, of instruction, but are not general enough to form a theory entire.

Jerome Bruner, too, with brilliant, incisive strokes, painted the difficulties of fashioning a theory of instruction. But his *The Process of Education* is an arrow pointing in that direction; so, too, is his *On Knowing: Essays for the Left Hand,* which should be read with both *The Process of Education* and his later statements in *Toward a Theory of Instruction.* Although he describes certain credentials of a theory of instruction, he does not state in these works a theory of teaching in a systematic assertion, however tentative. Yet his statements complement each other in attending to what is significant in instruction, and in the general areas of education. Remember his suggestion that perhaps the most effective methods of instruction lead the child to discover for himself. This statement points to theory precisely because it defines and explicates the kinds of practice we call "teaching." In this remark, Bruner sums up considerable learning theory and, in a sense, "states" a theory of instruction (as different and distinct from a theory of learning).

Philip Hosford, in *An Instructional Theory: A Beginning,* makes a prodigious effort to analyze the researches, the criteria for, the components of, and the limits that would constrain a theory of instruction vis-à-vis other areas of schooling—for example, curriculum. But, to our loss, he, too, does not state a theory of instruction in a *systematic assertion,* in my view, an altogether necessary effort.

In a considerable body of work, David Ausubel has laid the foundations for a cognitive theory of teaching and learning. Beginning with his *The Psychology of Meaningful Verbal Learning* and later, with his colleagues Joseph Novak and Helen Hanesian, in *Educational Psychology: A Cognitive View,* as well as in a comprehensive series of studies, he has described with precision methods that aid the learner in acquiring the foundations of intellectual skills and the cognitive structures required for the meaningful reception transmission, manipulation, and transformation of conceptual structures and verbal knowledge. In his *A Theory of Education* Joseph Novak builds on Ausubel's theory of meaningful reception-learning and offers a number of valuable theoretical models relating the teacher, the learner, and the social environment in which knowledge plays a key role. The two works summarize in incisive fashion the body of work centered in cognition. It would not be wide off the mark to stress that the works are concerned in the main with schooling and with instructed or planned learning.

On the other hand, Carl Rogers, a psychologist concerned with psychotherapy, has considered human learning from the viewpoint of the characteristics of the teacher, whether in school or not. He suggests, in *On Becoming a Person,* that human learning is advanced by the Empathy (understanding), Congruence (genuineness or authenticity), and Positive Regard (valuing) which are part of the teacher's professional and human repertory. Recall that the parent is a teacher-at-home and the professional teacher is the teacher-in-school—and, in a way, all of us "teach" our peers or those with whom we have relationships, small or large. Rogers and his colleagues emphasize the affective side of teaching, while Ausubel and his colleagues emphasize the cognitive aspects. Neither would, of course, ignore either aspect—and, in my experience, has not in public utterances or writing. The theory that needs developing should combine the affective and cognitive—that is, should concern itself with concepts, values, attitudes, and skills in all areas of knowledge.

In simplified form, a theory of instruction, applied to formal schooling and planned education, may be as follows:

In any act of teaching, a new environment is created; in responding to the altered environment (by initiating activity involving the manipulation and transformation of concepts, values, or skills) an individual learner gains demonstrably in capacities and abilities not achieved through prior experience but specified in the given act of teaching.

To emphasize, this theory applies whether the act is one of instructed learning, which is part of schooling, or one intended to change behavior in situations that are part of the educational environment. It is clear that a theory of curriculum goes hand in hand with a theory of instruction, but at present and within the circumscribed observations available, theories of instruction, curriculum, and evaluation should be considered as separate but related. So, too, aims of education. On this more needs to be said, and it is done in Chapter 5 for *curriculum,* in Chapter 6 for *evaluation,* and in Chapter 7 for *aims of education.*

An Accounting

One of the difficulties in assuring productive examination and discussion of instruction, or so it seems, is that "learning" is too capacious a term. It occurs everywhere; it seems to occur whenever a learner perceives and reacts to an altered environment, whether that alteration is intended or unintended. Hence the term "instructed learning"* is useful, for that is what we are concerned with in schools and classrooms; but note, please, instructed learning as it affects the capacities of individual learners. A theory of instruction should not lose the individual within the class. Learning does not occur only in classrooms; it occurs wherever the mind contemplates its environment. A theory of teaching needs to be concerned with *instructed learning* or *intended teaching.*

Jean Piaget's considerable contributions have led to a paradigm which is somewhat to this effect: The teacher creates situations through which children discover structure. That is, of course, a statement of a theory of teaching, but it seems to account for children's activity in the area of cognition. The theory stated refers to all aspects of instructed learning, those related to intellection per se as well as those related to psychosocial areas, areas of personal development, and the like. A general theory should attempt to embrace Piaget's thinking as expressed in this statement. Surely it should embrace John Dewey's paradigm "learning by doing."

It is well to remember that Piagetian theory is not based on instructed learning but on "learning" resulting from everyday random experience. Unlike everyday random experience, schooling is an intervention in which nonrandom, planned experience is of the essence. As a case in point, the protocol and reasoning behind certain of Piaget's exper-

---

* "Instructed learning," a term used by Jerome Bruner, infers and implies that in any act of learning in schools, instruction is planned as a change of the environment designed for the purposes of learning and is part of the act of learning. Hence *instructed* learning. Bruner's term clarifies many ambiguities, but it indicates especially that the learning has been initiated by instruction.

iments are not applicable to school situations, because in those experiments, he was not concerned with the interventions of instructed learning. I have not been able to confirm, for example, certain of his experiments on "de-centering" in school situations. Margaret Donaldson, in her remarkable little book *Children's Minds,* also finds certain of Piaget's experiments wanting.

If there is no active or overt response, one might assume that learning is not taking place, for whatever reason: the inappropriateness or inadequacy of the new environment, or of the instructional material (textbooks, laboratory manuals, workbooks), lack of ability, lack of prior preparation of the students, failure of appropriate reinforcement, for instance. If there is no response by an individual learner, one would need to assume that instruction has not been effective or attention has not been given to the task at hand. If no response was given, one could not assume that an act of instruction had taken place, if only because a response is a measure of the act of instruction. To repeat, the theory postulates an active or overt response by an individual learner.

Skinner makes the point again and again that contingencies of reinforcement (conditions that reward a learner*) act significantly, if not primarily, in the improvement of learning. The learner is indeed reinforced if he or she "gains capacities not achieved through prior experience." Nevertheless, the learner is also reinforced by approval from the teacher. In turn, the teacher is reinforced if "in responding to the altered environment the learner gains demonstrably in capacities not achieved through prior experience." The teacher thus reinforces the learner and, in turn, the teacher is reinforced by the student—and not by the time-honored "apple polishing." A systematic assertion of a theory of instruction with a Skinnerian thrust might be as follows:

Appropriate contingencies of reinforcement invented by the teacher result in gains in demonstrable capacity in a given learner; in turn, the gains in capacity demonstrated by the learner function as contingencies of reinforcement for both teacher and learner.

The climate of the classroom, or the climate of any environment given over to instructed learning, affects learning. Apparently children identify with teachers (with the parent-as-teacher as well) and often model their behavior on them. To a number of observers and experimenters the teacher's behavior is of considerable importance in developing learning activity and making it effective. The environment created by the teacher is an act of instruction; the teacher's behavior and per-

* For example: the shade of an oasis in a desert is a reward (a contingency of reinforcement) for one who is weary of the heat and drought of the desert.

sonality are part of the environment even if the teacher transfers some of his teaching to a device—a book, a machine, a laboratory, a film, an assignment. The teacher's approval, if the teacher is liked and respected by the learner, gives sanction to the device. One of the reasons, perhaps, for failure of the teaching environment created by television is the relative absence of contingencies of reinforcement, particularly the opportunity to weigh the validity of one's response—that is, to feel immediate satisfaction or reinforcement as one "learns." According to Rogers, the empathy, genuineness, and positive regard of the teacher for the pupil (and vice versa) are significant in securing a change in behavior and this, too, may not operate in a "lecture" on TV.

Put simply, research generally suggests that if the learner "likes" the teacher, he or she is generally more likely to accept the changed environment; he or she will "like" to learn. Nevertheless, in the classroom one cannot isolate cognitive elements from psychomotor elements from affective or conative elements. The act of instruction unifies the various modes and postures of learning even as it unifies process and product, concept-seeking and concept-forming.

A theory of instruction should account for practices acknowledged as "teaching" or "instruction," or catalyze their more appropriate definition. The place of the lecture (the planned act of informing the learner by a teacher) must therefore be considered. Clearly, the lecture is an integral part of instruction throughout the world. Perhaps it would be more useful to consider the lecture, where it informs but does not analyze or synthesize the experience of students developed in response to a prior teaching act, as part of the materials of instruction. The theory proposed suggests that the act of instruction *is* consummated by a response ("responding" or "initiating activity"), *and must be consummated by a response*. The general theory of instruction proposes that the evaluation of the act of instruction lies in the amount of effective, meaningful learning activity (the response) that is carried on by an individual learner, whether that activity be reading, investigating in the field or laboratory, writing a composition or poem, reacting to a film or a presentation on TV, reporting on a museum trip, reciting a poem, playing a game (chess or football), engaging in a debate, painting a picture, performing on an instrument, participating in a discussion, or one learner teaching another. It might be more appropriate to consider the lecture *plus* the time spent by the learner in study of the materials suggested in the lecture as the period of instruction, where the lecture approach is the major instructional activity.

Still, how is one to know what increments are the result of the lecturer's instruction and which the effect of the materials studied or peers consulted? We need to consider what is patent: when a teacher is engaged in "telling" (lecturing or explaining) and when there is no apparent response by the learner (then acting as "listener"), the teacher cannot know whether instruction is going on. Put another way, a gain in a learner's capacity *must be* consequent upon the specified act of instruction, consequent in an observable, demonstrable manner through acceptable response, if the learner's gain is to be credited to the specified act of instruction. It is for this reason, perhaps, that television per se cannot be credited with "teaching" or "instruction," because a specified act of learning cannot generally be directly related to the act of "watching" the special program designed for instruction. Perhaps cable TV, with its devices directed at assuring individual responses, can correct this deficiency.

We need to re-emphasize that the postulate of learning as meaning an *overt response* by the learner is nothing new: remember that the learner's response was central to Dewey's thought, so, too, to Piaget's, so, too, to Comenius's, so, too, to teachers over the centuries. That is perhaps what Comenius was saying when he remarked, in essence, "When the teacher teaches less, the learner learns more." Whenever I have had the privilege of observing a great teacher, I have noted that students are engaged in "working," "doing," "acting," "responding by word or deed," "investigating," "inquiring," "initiating activity," "inventing," "probing."

A general theory of instruction should include within its framework, or give an accounting of, or be in accord with, the "folklore" of learning and the variety of systematic assertions based on research in learning. It should not contradict what is presently "known" of the way learning occurs, all cognizance being taken of the fact that we do not know how learning occurs.

To learn must mean to do something "new"—whether this be a modification of an old act or not. Hence the emphasis on a *new* environment. But note: to be useful instruction, this new environment should be created from recognizable objects or familiar events not necessarily from "problems" created by unfamiliar objects or events. If one studies the advance of science over a long period of history, one notices particularly that discovery is directed by observation of objects and events, not necessarily by "problems" per se. It seems that mental activity in the learner is not generally or even necessarily directed by "problems" per se. Thus, if the object or event is not recognized by a learner, a problem is not recognized and so cannot be stated. Further, if a concept embracing the problem is not available, the problem may not be clarified—unless the learner is sophisticated, a scholar, a scientist. Were this not true, one would be at a loss to explain why Aristotle did not propound such problems as: What is the nature of the virus? Or: What is the relationship of the atomic number to the properties of the atom? We emphasize, with Gagne and others, the requirement that the learner have sufficient background ("structurally organized knowledge") to recognize an object or event, and so recognize a problem.

Similarly, if a child has not had some acquaintance with an object or event under discussion, he or she cannot begin to respond to a "new environment," whether in a group or in an individual situation. In a classroom I once observed a teacher who asked a child to make a three-dimensional model of a paramecium, from clay. But the child had never seen a paramecium. The "failure" of the child was indeed not a failure; it was not a failure in learning, but a failure of instructed learning. Generally speaking, unless psychological problems intervene (that is, the need for attention), a child does not state what he or she believes to be "wrong." When the child is wrong, it may be due to a lack of prior effective instructed learning.

In the more sophisticated sense, we give children problems in order to induce problem-solving activity; but the problems are usually ours. With the present preposterous workload of administrators, supervisors, and teachers, the latter rarely have the opportunity to determine whether the learner has had the experience to enable him or her to grasp the problem. Often, "slow" students are those whose failure to grasp the problem is a failure in prior experience with the objects or events undergirding the problem and with their analyses and synthesis of these objects and events. A teacher must endeavor to build a structure in which the child's prior and continuing experience in problem solving is taken into account. Children in school are generally rewarded for problem doing, not problem solving, which is in its finest sense "a relentless pursuit of a belief in proof or disproof," as John Dewey implied.

Of what use, then, is the theory I have developed and which I propose as guide, against a better formulation or demonstrable proof? A theory of instruction can and should direct administrative procedures affecting the structure or form of instruction, its sequences and provisions, and these in turn should determine practice and style in the classroom, that is, what teachers and pupils do together. The mark of a competent learner is partly a measure of a certain skill in independent learning activity, that is, independent of the overseer's activity of an adult, whether teacher or parent. The young do leave school; then they are, or should know how to learn and be, "on their own." A structure and style in modes of instruction should instruct the young in developing independence in learning—a self-discipline, to be sure. But this, I insist, needs to be accomplished in a progression, as the learner matures. A considerable gift of schooling is surely an inculcation in the learner of the habits of learning, of solving new problems, of the acquisition of skills of acquiring, interpreting, and gaining new capacities, new attitudes, new values, new skills. And these are acquired by practice, by response, not by passiveness. The learner, away from the school and teachers, having practiced and applied again and again, practiced and failed again and again, has indeed practiced and succeeded in finding his or her own idiosyncratic mode of learning, and with it a skill in independent learning. Learning does involve a kind of conflict between new and old facts and concepts and a kind of reconstruction or coalescence of new facts into new concepts. To become an independent learner is to become comfortable with the alternating conflict, reconstruction, and coalescence that the creation of fresh concepts requires.

The young do take their teachers with them as kinds of "inner parents" who are models of self-activation or self-actualization. The need is, then, to develop in the young habits of independence in learning, independence in seeking solutions to new problems—inevitably new. Of course, since the parent is a teacher, what is useful as a style in the classroom also points to a style in the one-to-one correspondence in teaching style and practice in the home.

As I have indicated, the theory I have stated is based on a considerable body of evidence. The essence of the theory as it directs teaching (and, consequently, learning) is that the learner is an essential participant in the teaching act. That is, without the learner's active participation (an overt response and a demonstrated change in behavior)—whether by overt activity in response through dialogue and discussion or through an experiment, field trip, project, or role play—the teacher cannot evaluate the effectiveness of instruction. I am indebted to Professor James J. Jelinek, of Arizona State University, for his analysis of certain characteristics of responsible interaction between teacher and student. In a personal communication, he suggests that instruction (to be a dialogue) should:

- Become not a deposit of *one* person's ideas, but a confirmation that the ideas are understood
- Be not merely an exchange of ideas as a kind of calisthenics in which the learner is manipulated
- Be a search for the validity of ideas, not the imposition of ideas
- Be not an example of domination by a teacher, or by an instructional mode

- Be an effort to educate (from *educare,* meaning "to bring forth")
- Furnish evidence that the learner perceives the material as useful, as a means to an end
- Indicate that the learner is active in the learning process, reinforces the teacher, and thus participates actively in making the substance and structure of the discipline his or her own. And, of course, through active participation in learning, the substance and structure of a discipline become one's own.

A study I made of eighty-two "successful" teachers, made through observation in classrooms, and published under the title *The Gifted Student as Future Scientist,* supports the point: the learner's activity is central to the efficiency of instructed learning. What the teachers did not do was, and is, as important as what they did do. A comparison, however brief, of certain aspects of what was done and what was not done clearly demonstrates a difference in a conception of schooling, therefore of the act of teaching, in style and practice. These teachers did not employ the lecture or the narrative mode of instruction for more than 40 to 50% of their lessons. Naturally, their students were prepared for active participation in the classroom (for example, discussion, laboratory work, painting, or music) by prior practice (homework, reading, practice of instruments, or painting at home). I stress work at home (homework, to be sure) as an important practice. Just as the teacher prepares for a lesson, so, too, must the student. For example, these teachers *did not:*
- Use a method of narration, or demonstration, or lecture, with students participating solely by note-taking
- Place their students in the position of listeners only, of trainees. They understood that training too often closes options for discovery, while education opens such options.
- Minimize the creative powers of their students; they encouraged individual adaptations. (Their behavioral objectives—developed for each lesson—permitted departure where a student's creative thought required it.)
- Place sole stress on memorization of the content (although memorization is part of learning), but encouraged memorization of detail useful in exposition of an argument, useful in the defense of the student's position
- Set aside attempts at a balance of *opposing opinion* (where a "balance" was a part of the discipline, as in the social sciences), or set aside attempts to secure rigorous evidence, again as part of the discipline (science), or set aside individual self-expression, again as part of the discipline (literature, art, music)

These teachers *did,* for example:

• Place themselves in the position of guides to learning, not of guardians of the archives

• Inculcate in their students the notion that the state of teaching/learning devolved responsibilities on the learner as well as on the teacher. Thus, they insisted on careful preparation by students for their function in the coming lessons, even as they prepared carefully for their function as teachers.

• Nurture a situation in which acts of knowing, of cognition, replaced transfer of information to be memorized

• Encourage authentic activity, reflection, questioning, and reconstruction of subject matter. In short, they encouraged critical thinking.

• Emphasize personal responsibility for self-expression and conduct

In brief, where response of the student to an act of instruction is required, and where the student *expects* to respond and is prepared to respond (by his or her own work in anticipation of instruction), the atmosphere of the classroom is entirely different from that in which the teacher is the sole actor and the students are passive, recipient not respondent. To emphasize: TV "instruction" or the pure lecture fails precisely in this consideration: the learner is passively a recipient, not actively a respondent. Neither TV nor the lecture stops long enough for the "learner" to pause, to think, to re-examine, or even to reread, as a book, or newspaper, or magazine permits. The educational policy of the teachers who were considered excellent by administrators, supervisors, parents, and students, as well as other teachers, is based on a conceptualization of a model of instruction aimed at assisting their students in achieving independence in learning, in problem solving. Of course, these teachers modulated their teaching activity in relation to the maturity of their students. It is this kind of modulation of experience, of maturity, it is this kind of maturing of growth from dependence to interdependence, to a happy state of independence in learning, that a model of instruction should serve.

A Construct in Instruction: Progressive Independence in Learning

The construct, or model, of schooling that follows suggests a mode in which children—taught how to read, write, number, and speak, taught how to music, to art, to dance, to metaphor (all these are nouns masquerading as verbs)—are taught how to explore, how to inquire, and, as

boys and girls, then young men and women, are given increasing responsibility for their own learning. One may infer from the model that as
children grow, there is increasing time given to independence in learning
(synonym: self-activation or self-actualization) and a reduction in time
given over to *dependence.* That is, as the years of schooling progress
from elementary school to high school, with increasing maturity of the
learner, the teacher becomes less a guardian of the archives and becomes
more a guide to inquiry. Heuristic forms of instruction are solidly based
in understanding the past as well as the present, because the child—even
as that ever-learner the scholar—stands on the shoulders of others. It is
important to dwell on this aspect of learning—the dependence of the
learner on the past, on "masses of structurally organized knowledge,"
again to use Gagne's phrase.

A scholar, whether scientist, technicist, educationist, teacher, or
learner, does not go to the laboratory first, but to the library, or to his or
her colleagues; he or she builds on schooling and education. He or she
"stands on the shoulders of others." The past is prologue. As indicated
in the exposition of a theory of instruction, a reasonable approach to
teaching might be to provide just enough background, no more (through
homework, through talk, through books, through programed instruction,
film, computer, and the like), so that the child can uncover what is new
to him or her. It is not a useless activity to "tell" children or to have
children read what is a necessary prologue to personal or individual discovery. It is not useless for children to *know what has been learned* in
order for them to learn what is expressly new to them. The critical choice
for the teacher is to select out of the past what learners will cover for
themselves in existing archives or available instructional material so that
they will be prepared to uncover, then discover for themselves. Analysis
of a given or received past is a creative act; so is the synthesis of the past
in order to inquire into the future. If scholars stand on the shoulders of
others so that they may see farther, should not learners do likewise—at
appropriate times fitted to the tasks of inquiry or discovery?

The whims and fads, twists and turns of uncritical practice have
pushed us always to extremes. There is a mythology that gives critics
easy satisfaction. It includes the myth that structure and sequence,
whether in instructed learning or in curriculum, are rigid, inflexible, hampered by conformity, or, worse still, unresponsive to a child's needs and
interests. If anything, sequence with a carefully devised conceptual structure, a structure that sees the world whole, frees the teacher. As we shall
see, a conceptual structure does not imprison anyone who is not already
imprisoned. (If the reader is not familiar with the nature of a concept

[as compared and contrasted with an "idea"] or of conceptual ordering of curriculum, the matter is discussed on pages 152–61. A concept does not dictate the kind of experience or content; a concept is enriched by a variety of experience, intelligent and intelligible content, and analysis and synthesis. It is, rather, a topic that is fragmented, one that is rigid and confined in sequence. A topic can be "lectured"; a concept, a whole, is "sought" and perhaps "caught" in good time. One may "finish" a topic but not a concept. A concept grows, feeding on topics. In fact, a topical sequence is extremely rigid, for it is meant to be covered. Conceptual sequence allows for variety, for comparison and contrast, for exploration and discovery. It allows for problem doing and for problem solving. Thus, in a conceptual framework the concept of "empirical validity" (the validity of experiment and observation) gives the teacher scope to use whatever scientific work he or she wishes to use, but also gives scope to a comparison and contrast with "nonempirical validity" (the validity of the work of artists, musicians, poets, writers, dancers). Contrast and comparison anticipate analysis and synthesis.

Toward the Design of a Reasonable Model of Instruction

In adopting new modes of curriculum of instruction we tend to go overboard in bandwagon fashion. We go from "progressive education" to "discovery models" to "basics" to "inquiry" to "team teaching" to "turnkey systems" to "contract instruction," then "back to basics" and soon to emphasis on "duality of the brain" and "modalities," or to the "programs for the slow" and then to "programs for the gifted."

In anticipation of the coming transformation, it will be necessary to test theories of instruction and models of instruction that necessarily fit theory and practice. One such "reasonable model," which addresses not only theory but also a vast amount of successful practice, is the model offered here. It permits a variety of modes of instructed learning and a balanced combination of approaches by the teacher—didactic and heuristic, by way of example. It is intended to have one major result: *the progressive growth of the young as independent learners* able to initiate, participate, and conclude satisfactorily an activity in learning what is known or in proceeding with problem-solving processes that assist them in uncovering or discovering what they do not know. (We must assume that the problem is feasible and on the level of the maturity of the learner.) I shall call this mode of instruction the "maturing-independence model."

The model takes advantage, of course, of the powerful relationship between teacher and student. It relies on the resources of the school to initiate and take responsibility for instructed learning (that is, for teaching), but places initiative and responsibility for the activity of learning on the learner. That is, of course, an ideal for which schools that work strive—and carry out in practice. But the maturing-independence model extends the practice so that it is sequentially structured in years of instruction, and by the end of secondary school, before the "leaving time," the student is, to the degree possible, truly an independent learner—an objective to be desired, devoutly. Furthermore, as a learner increasingly takes on initiative and responsibility for personal learning and growth, it will be found that so-called problems of discipline tend to be reduced. The model *balances* contributions by the teacher and the student.

The model may be diagramed thus:

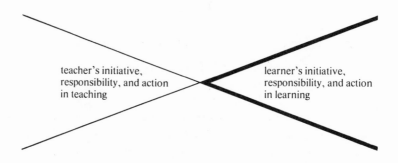

teacher's initiative, responsibility, and action in teaching

learner's initiative, responsibility, and action in learning

At the beginning it is well to note that certain students who have learned to organize their work may take on the learner's initiative and responsibility to a far greater extent than do others. Therefore, the model attends to varieties of ability and competence. "Minimum competency" is not *the* aim: varieties of moderate and maximum competency are the goal as well.

The model may be applied to any aspect of instruction employing a host of different methods or procedures; it can be fragmented into whatever time scale the teacher wishes, a few minutes, an hour, a week, a month, a semester. The essential aspect is this: at any given period in teaching, the collaborative function of teaching-learning shifts back and forth between teacher and learner. Although the teacher may, but not necessarily, utilize a lecture approach (a verbal approach) in initiating discussion in a certain area, it is possible, even likely, that the student, left to his or her own initiative, will use those modes of learning that fit personal ability and capacity (so-called modalities). These may include, in addition to language and mathematics (so-called verbal or linear-sequential approaches), a variety of spatiovisual approaches utilizing, for example, the arts and the so-called holistic approaches.

It is of critical importance to assert that a shift from instruction based mainly on the lecture to the maturing-independence model will take time—years certainly. On this aspect it is particularly important to note the discussion later in this chapter of investigations on the introduction of instructional modes different from those to which the community, a school, and its teachers are accustomed.

This is not to say that the teacher will use verbal presentation in the main, certainly not in music, art, dance, drama, crafts, industrial art, poetry, or literature (particularly in the area, for example, of metaphor). Certainly, the learner will be given relative independence in some areas where "words" are central to discussion, especially where inquiry of any kind or degree is practiced. Nevertheless, to repeat and re-emphasize, as the learner grows in maturity (over twelve years of schooling), slowly but surely the weight of time and effort—and the selection of a method of learning (including inquiry)—passes to him or her in a progressive sequence, as the following pages will emphasize.

It may be useful to set the matter forth by way of example. The following instances of a teacher's initiative dissolving into a learner's initiative were gathered from my own observations. Recall that we are gauging initiative not in terms of a teacher's thought or originality, but in terms of the time in which students are active in their own modes of learning, expression, and conduct.

A Lesson in Geography in an Elementary School

CASE 1. In a third-grade class, the teacher was introducing the nature of map making. She used a map of the city in which the children lived to "take a trip" on the map with the children. Every now and then she would ask a question. Volunteers answered correctly to receive a response of "Good." Those who answered incorrectly received a kind "No" and another was called on until an answer acceptable to the teacher was obtained.

CASE 2. In another third-grade class (of similar ability and socioeconomic grouping) in the same school, a teacher was giving the "same" lesson (that is, one with a similar objective), and was taking the class through a trip on a map of the school (which she had constructed at home). Then she asked the children each to construct (from memory) a map of their homes, labeling rooms only. She went about offering "help" (answering questions only, not giving information). Before the class was finished, she asked the children to compare the "map" they had made in class with a map to be made at home. She gave the "kids" (as she called them) questions to guide them. The next day, whoever wanted to would give a talk on his or her map. In this way she gave opportunity for differences in style or modality (in ways of learning, of presentation) and also for differences in ability.

A comparison of the teacher's initiative within the time period of the lesson and each pupil's initiative in each case follows:

CASE 1

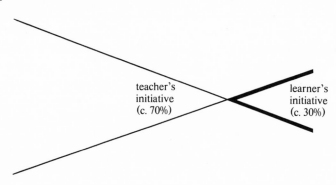

CASE 2

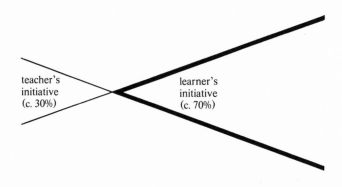

Clearly, the style in each lesson was different; in one the teacher was "dominant," in another it was the habituation of the learner as a future "independent" learner that was central. Both teachers had prepared for the lesson, but the preparation was different. The teacher in Case 1 had certainly done as much work as the teacher in Case 2. The teacher in Case 2 was a guide on the road to independence as the child matured. Both teachers, it is necessary to say, were "good" teachers, competent and compassionate. But which style is most suited to a democratic society in which the learner must eventually live independently, seeking his or her own way, yet working interdependently with others?

A Reading Lesson in an Elementary School
In another school, a teacher was "teaching reading" to her second-grade class. At least two groups of children engaged in different activities were easily discerned. (It was discovered later that there were at least four different groups.)

GROUP 1. The teacher was reading to this group. Every now and then she would ask a child to read, helping each child as the need arose.

GROUP 2. The instructed learning above was done quietly enough not to disturb different children concentrating on reading "on their own" books they had chosen in the library or brought from home. Others were reading guided by an adult, in this case a "retired" person, or volunteer (a paraprofessional). Here, equal opportunity was given for different children to achieve full potential.

GROUP 1

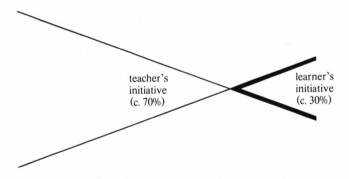

teacher's initiative (c. 70%)   learner's initiative (c. 30%)

GROUP 2

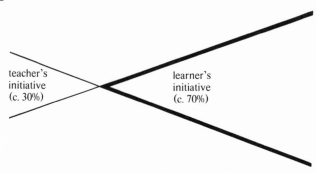

It was clear that it was the teacher's objective to bring Group 1 up to the level of Group 2.

A Junior-High-School Science Class

CASE 1. In one class a teacher was using a human skeleton to demonstrate (and talk about) the relation of one bone to another. Every now and then he would call on a student to name a bone and state its function.

CASE 2. In another class (a similar socioeconomic and ability group) the teacher sat in the back of the room as, one after another, several students using a human skeleton as a model, described the relationship of the bones in parts of the body they had selected. They had used their texts for initial study and information, after which the teacher had given each group of four students (they seemed to group themselves naturally) a bag of chicken bones and some wire and asked them to make a skeleton of a particular part.

CASE 1

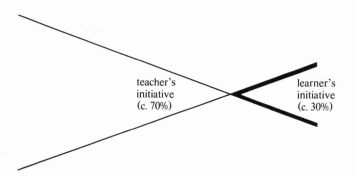

CASE 2

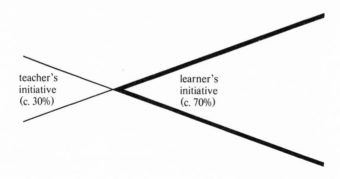

teacher's
initiative
(c. 30%)

learner's
initiative
(c. 70%)

High-School Physics

CASE 1. In one high school in a system in which there were five schools a teacher was teaching the Law of Moments. He gave an excellent lecture demonstration. Then the class went on to do an "experiment" from a laboratory manual on this law. There were some unusual questions in the laboratory manual which tested the students' ability to devise experiments.

CASE 2. In another high school the teacher (in collaboration with other teachers on the staff) used a text and laboratory manual similar to one in use in the high school in Case 1 to give the students background in experimental work on the Law of Moments. The teacher did not lecture on the information to be found in the textbook. He demonstrated the use of specialized equipment and gave cautionary advice on safety. Then students quickly did the laboratory manual's exercises, labeled "A type." Unusual questions, testing original thinking, were labeled "B type." The teachers had prepared a truly "original" series of problems (outside of text and manual) suggesting original experimentation, which were labeled "C type." The students could select B or C, or their own investigation. One investigation of the C type required considerable work on an individual basis; ingenious original investigations (true problem solving, not problem doing) were to be made by the student on his or her own time, at home, in the library, and in the laboratory. The attempt was being made to match opportunity and ability and to stimulate growth in aptitude.

CASE 1

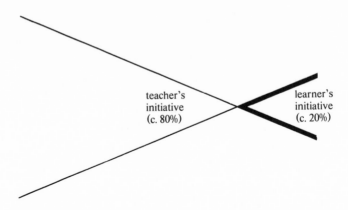

CASE 2

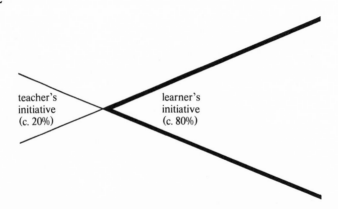

Other examples

In some instances, I observed students who had achieved an independence reaching toward an admirable maturity; they were, in effect, as independent as a school environment could permit. The teacher's initiative for these students was given over to that of adviser and mentor, not an inconsiderable function in teaching. Whether in music, art, athletics, literature, poetry, science, or mathematics, the students were truly self-activated. They had transcended schooling and were educating themselves. I have read original published poetry as well as original scientific and mathematical treatises and papers, heard original compositions in music, and seen original paintings of high caliber by these students. It may well be that certain of these were gifted students—but are not gifted students members of our schooling systems and entitled to all the privileges? In any event, these students had reached the epitome of independence in learning, within a school environment.

It will be necessary to compare the maturing-independence model of instruction with the mastery model or learning-for-mastery model. The last is often used for purposes of evaluating the progress of students in "basic" studies, that is, to assure "minimum competency." The maturing-independence model, we shall see, may be used for purposes of evaluating the progress of students in "minimum," "moderate," *and* "maximum" competency. Indeed, it is designed to encourage all students to fulfill their powers in the pursuit of excellence. Because the maturing-independence model is useful in evaluating competence and performance, it will be treated in a different context in Chapter 6.

Progression through the Schooling Years

An approach to the maturing-independence model is, in a way, utilized throughout the country at present. The following are examples. In each case, the teacher is available to assist and guide.

- In reading instruction in the classroom where children use their initiative in reading on their own
- In mathematics, where, once a teacher has introduced a new problem or theorem, the learners solve new problems on their own
- In science, where the young work in the laboratory on small group and individual problems after completing a "basic" exercise
- In art, where the young paint their own "visions"
- In athletics, where the young proceed with a series of games
- In music, where the young perform individually and in an orchestra

Other examples will occur to the reader.

The essence of the maturing-independence approach is that the *teacher's work* be followed by *independent work by students*. Through their work the young demonstrate mastery of the concept or skill introduced by the teacher. What is equally important, the young demonstrate their idiosyncratic styles, special competence, and the like. In the utilization of this model, special gifts as well as needs for remediation are readily identified, because the work of the learner demonstrates gifts and needs to the teacher. The gifted are readily identified in specific areas of instruction, as are those boys and girls immediately in need of assistance, whether it be in motivation or in remediation.

Of course, one may find ready examples of the teacher's initiative vs. learner's initiative pattern in most art, music, dance, drama, industrial art, physical education, sports, and the like. But remember that we are pressing for an instructional style that encourages the interactions of holistic activity with linear-sequentiality. In many instances this means opportunity for the child, or pupil, or student, to use his spatiovisual senses, his holistic capabilities, wherever possible. Too often when the teacher "talks," he or she "tells all." Why should a learner read when he or she is examined mainly on the "lecture" given by the teacher and the notes therefrom? The lecture, then, is a substitute for the textbook (which, if only to learn to read and contemplate, to learn to study and work on their own, the students ought to be encouraged to use). Of course, good textbooks and good lecturers do more than just "tell."

As time passes, as the learner gains in experience in the use of the maturing-independence model, as he or she becomes older and advances in "grades," or "suites," or "nongraded instruction," more and more initiative is to be allotted to the growing, maturing child. Thus the relative weight of the teacher's initiative and the learner's initiative might be graded in the progressive independence mode shown on the next four pages (always assuming the learner is readied for increasing responsibility).

In the models of teaching and instruction suggested on the following pages, the learner is given opportunity to learn in increasing interdependence and independence. The learner is, in a real sense, *learning how to learn*. The learner is thus preparing to meet an unknown world—the world of the future. The learner in learning is given opportunity to create himself, to create his or her concept of self. The teacher, then, is not merely an instructor. An instructor is only as large as his or her subject matter; a teacher is as large as life.

Ages 6–9 (Primary-School Stage)

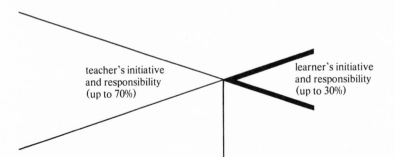

teacher's initiative
and responsibility
(up to 70%)

learner's initiative
and responsibility
(up to 30%)

In the early years, the child needs opportunity to learn the "uses of freedom," to plan his or her work, to learn how to work with others, to use resources (the advice of teachers, of libraries, of books, of equipment, of things). The teacher is the major resource at this crucial period. The major reason for the failure of individualized instruction, where it is attempted, is that the child is thrust into independence too soon; the process should be gradual—that is, progressive with growing maturity—for most children. There is always the fast, bright, or gifted child who can take more initiative earlier than most.

(About 70% of school time)

The child practices the use of freedom in small projects—particularly individual work with laboratory equipment, building models, maps, painting, music, plotting a miniature dance or play, in arts and crafts, in the beginnings of library work; "alone" at times, reading a story, doing a "problem" in numbering. The verbal-linear modes are certainly used, but ample time is given for the spatiovisual, holistic mode. Each child learns to work to full capacity and is encouraged to achieve to fullest potential. Some always do more than others, and should be encouraged to do so. We have not found situations where *all* children work to full potential at *all* times.

(About 30% of school time)

Ages 10–13 (*Intermediate-School Stage*)
(Building on the first three years)

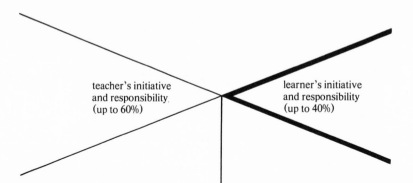

teacher's initiative and responsibility. (up to 60%)

learner's initiative and responsibility (up to 40%)

There is a reduction of time spent in teacher's guidance and/ or lecture, and an increase in time given over to individual guidance and resolution of problems in learning. Where lecture is to be used, it is selective for those areas where students cannot—because of difficulty of subject matter, because of economy of time, method, and equipment—attain the objectives desired "on their own."

(About 60% of school time)

Where the content at hand can be apprehended by the child— through individual planning, reading, problem doing, consulting, through the arts—he or she is encouraged to take increasing responsibility for learning, in collaboration with the teacher. "Homework" is part of the activity of the child; so is training in inquiry-using modes which depend on inference in linear-sequential processing and on holistic modes, particularly intuitive leaps.

(About 40% of school time)

Ages 14–16 (Junior-High-School Stage)
(Building on the first six years)

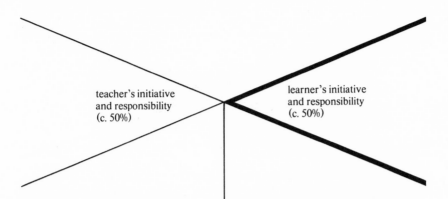

teacher's initiative
and responsibility
(c. 50%)

learner's initiative
and responsibility
(c. 50%)

This is generally the period of puberal change; the young are finding their own life style, clamoring for independence. The teacher's lecture approach is further reduced: the burden of reading, researching is increasingly placed on the learner; the teacher is increasingly a guide to learning.

Time is made available for the project approach, for greater individuation, for increase in "independent searching," for increasing opportunity for the marriage of the verbal-linear and spatiovisual holistic modes—that is, concept-seeking and values-seeking. Time is available for the development of the solid virtues of planning and adapting to changing situations. Inventiveness and intuition are given increasing play. In this period differences in approach to learning (modalities) and in special interests in different areas of achievement and competence are demonstrated, and are to be encouraged.

(About 50% of school time)

(About 50% of school time)

Ages 17–18 (High-School Stage)
(Building on the preceding ten
years)

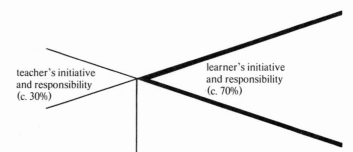

teacher's initiative
and responsibility
(c. 30%)

learner's initiative
and responsibility
(c. 70%)

There is increasing reliance on work by the learner and increasing reliance on the skills of reading, writing, numerating, on the ability to inquire, to seek out data or evidence, to use the library, to marry the work of both halves of the brain—ordered sequencing and simultaneous processing.

Increasingly the learner (increasingly mature) plans, directs, and undertakes learning within the curriculum, but the development of concepts is his or her responsibility. Once the concept has been attained, the learner may suggest a project or a problem that transcends the curriculum; individualization in pursuit of one's special abilities occurs. This is not an abdication by the teacher; it demonstrates that the learners have been taken into the teacher's confidence and understand the reasons for the institution of the curriculum at hand, as well as its utility in later life. And they have taken responsibility by exerting full effort to secure the highest achievement possible.

(Up to 30% of school time)

(Up to 70% of school time)

First Instruction in Independent Learning:
The "Parent" as Teacher

The newborn child knows little of the world in which he or she has been born. True, the baby comes prepared for existence on planet Earth: it requires a mixture of gases we call air, not pure helium; it takes milk, generally not other food; it has the devices for adapting to this planet and not another. But otherwise, the child, as organism, is helpless, and defenseless. For three years, or five, depending on wish and circumstance, the baby, literally and figuratively, is at the mercy of its environment, its parents, its family. Left unattended the baby dies. This is clear and it is true.

It follows that the foundations of schooling, and such education as is possible, are laid down at home. Schooling or education does *not* begin in school. Possibly it begins before the child is born, in the kind of uterine environment to which the child is subjected. This aside, the first teachers of the child are the parents, the grandparents, the family. And if that early schooling and education at home is faulty, the school must become a corrective institution. It seems clear that one of the most significant parts of schooling, among the most important for the future of the child, is mainly in the hands of those responsible for the early preschool development of the learner. There is mounting evidence that by ages four to six the child's brain has developed more than 50% of its learning capacity. At home, the child's mind is being prepared, or is being nurtured in preparedness. In the early years the parent, or father/mother surrogate, *is* the teacher.

The work of a host of students of child development and learning, and students of the development of adults in relation to their childhood, leads us to the inexorable and indelible conclusion that the home bears a high responsibility for the nature and excellence of the education of children. It is clear that cultural deprivation begins with deprivation at home of the kinds of behaviors necessary to succeed in our schools.

In saying this, I am not assessing the value of the culture in so-called culturally deprived homes. The cultural environment in these homes is exceedingly important and immensely worthy, and necessary to maintain, but it is *not necessarily the culture that prepares for the school as it exists.* In so stating, no defense of the American school is implied. What is implied is that every organism, human or not human, must adapt to its environment or take the consequences. And schooling is a major part of the environment of the child. Remember that school-ing is an attempt to pass on to children the customs of the community, its concepts, values, and skills.

We should not consider the early environment of the child as in-hibiting fruitful change in the future. We need a defense against ab-solutes, against dogma. That is, we do *not* know enough to suggest that the child's future is laid down in the first five years; there is no *one* proper road to development for all children, in all cultures, in all en-vironments.

What seems to be emerging from a variety of studies is this: we should not rank-order our children in the first three grades. Surely we decide too soon. Some children, children with poor environments, enter school perhaps with poor motivation (possibly because the environment does not stimulate them intellectually); they enter school behind other children in what Jerome Kagan calls "executive-cognitive" functions; that is, they do not think and act when faced with objects and events the way children with a more participatory environment do. In other words, chil-dren from impoverished environments are not yet ready for our "nor-mal" school instruction in grade one (age six). Nevertheless, with ap-propriate instruction children can and do catch up.

But it is important to distinguish between *absolute* and *relative re-tardation. Relative retardation* seems always to refer to our standard of "normal" development, that is, the middle-class child's behavior at any one point. If a child of ten cannot run as fast as a three-year-old, we might say there is retardation. But if a child of ten or eleven cannot play the piano or hockey, we should not say he or she is retarded, because these are aptitudes that can be altered by faithful instruction. Reading, numerating, and the like must be taught, that is, they must be made part of the child's effective environment and part of the child's repertory, certainly. Nonetheless, a given community should not equate children from impoverished environments with those from rich intellectual en-vironments; schools and society should not measure one child in a given environment against another from a more salutary environment (salu-tary with regard to learning). The former must be given the opportunity to catch up; the latter might move at a faster speed, or expand in other intellectual or artistic ways. Equal opportunity should not mean identi-cal exposure. In curriculum and instruction, to repeat, there is nothing so unequal as the equal treatment of unequals. In assessing the effects of the early environment, we should not confuse "love" with "instruction." Both are necessary.

Love, to say the least, is not enough. The acts of adults in the presence of the child and the environment furnished to the child in the presence and the absence of the adult are significant. We might call the activities that affect the child's nervous system (its physiology, as it were) "input." An odious word, "input," to be sure, signifying machines rather than beings. Yet it will be used here to mean what is "put before" the child, what is in the child's effective learning environment, the environment that affects behavior, intellectual and social.

The relationship of the child and the adult "vicar" (mother, father, or other adult) in the first two years is clearly important in developing linguistic competence. During the first months, a mother may spend much of her time trying to pinpoint what the child attends to. By the first year, for example, about 70% of children follow their mother's gaze. Early enough, the mother can use this physiological growth of the child to expand the intellectual environment; for example, she can point to objects and give them names.

The point of all this is that acquisition of speech is a steady accretion of experience in modeling, day by day. Speech, we are beginning to note, is not a sudden burst of achievement, but a constant groped-for response; it is a building on poor fits, or approximation upon approximation. The rewards are clear: the child's demands are met; the proper word is the key. The proper word has "power"; it brings the child what he or she wants. The proper word bends adults to his or her will. So "please" is expected to attract respectful attention, when a command or "shriek" of anger might be ignored. From the beginning the child is a member of his immediate community, the family. What the adult vicars say and do are meat for the child's development.

Here, perhaps, is a useful clue to the question What is an environment that may disadvantage the child? The weight of the evidence bears not solely on the absence of the adult vicar but on what the adult vicar does, that is, on the experiences made available to the child that in turn affect the child's nervous system.

To see "wholes" or concepts is not brought about by accident; it is brought about by many approximations, that is, by many inputs. It is not enough to hug the child and coo. Early, the child, as Gardner Murphy puts it, is engaged in "reality-seeking." The adult's input enables the child to cope with reality, approximate it, make it his or her own, in small ways, of course. But later, the early preconceptual striving, the concrete operation of distinguishing a ball from a box, will be the pedestal from which the child will distinguish ball from sphere. The foundation for developing concepts is being laid; soon enough the child will be able to articulate the word that represents the concept. But first, the

concept is "wordless." That is to say, first there may be groping, intuit-
ing, then knowing in the sense of responding in words. We are beginning
to understand that if the child does not respond in words, it does not
mean that he or she does not know in a "wordless" manner. To repeat,
caring (love) per se is not enough. The very young child (ages 0 to 3)
must also be engaged in what we have come to call "learning." Learning
to do things that are human, learning to speak, to react in human ways,
is related to learning to be human.

I want to stress the significance of the child's early environment in
determining not only the child's early *abilities* and *aptitudes* but also his
attitudes toward objects, events, and people.

For example, Eskimo children brought up in a culture that is socio-
centric (that is, one in which individuals depend on each other) are not
subject to the same kinds of "rejection" as are Western children, who are
drenched with egocentricity. An Eskimo child can be left alone for relatively long periods of time; it remains quiet. A Western child subjected
to absence of the adult caretaker generally does not react in the same
manner.

Thus, much observation and experience foster the hypothesis that
the early environment, the preschool environment, is crucial to the development of the child.

Gilbert Austin, in *Early Childhood Education,* a comparative study
of preschool education in a variety of countries—Belgium, England,
Finland, Germany, Hungary, Israel, Italy, Japan, Netherlands, Scotland,
Sweden, and the United States—concludes that "pre-school is helpful
for middle-class children and crucial for disadvantaged children. . . .
Comparing the effects of pre-school to no pre-school, the effects of preschool are significant for one or two years after the experience. . . .
The home background variables, even in pre-school children, have a
powerful effect on achievement."

In assessing the mixed effects of the Head Start program, which
was successful for some and not for others, a variety of investigators
noted the probability that certain of the "failures" (notably, failure to
maintain reading and mathematics levels) were due not only to a lack
of continuity and/or articulation between Head Start and primary school,
but also to a lack of training at home. Thus a program significantly titled
"Home Start" was initiated.

Austin concludes his study as follows: "The issue of parental in-
volvement with welfare, health and education agencies [responsible for
schooling and education] in the period of time from conception to age
9 or 12 is one of increasing importance. Research suggests that involve-

ment of the parents may be as important a factor as the help from the agencies themselves. Parents are, after all, the child's first and most important source of education. Any social policy that ignores this fact will not be as successful as it could otherwise be."

It is perhaps useful to press the point that the *parent as teacher* plays an exceedingly important role in the development of the child's *self-esteem.* Stanley Coopersmith, in *The Antecedents of Self-Esteem,* isolates four factors as significant in the kind of self-valuing we call "self-esteem." These factors are:

1. *Significance:* whether others hold the child in acceptance and affection
2. *Power:* whether the child can command attention and influence others (in his or her class and peer group)
3. *Worthiness* (*virtue*): whether the child develops standards of ethical behavior
4. *Competence:* whether the child meets demands for achievement successfully

It is worth quoting Coopersmith at length on certain attitudes and practices of the parent (as teacher) in helping the child achieve these factors, which are, in his words, "antecedents to self-esteem":

> In effect, we can conclude that the parents of children with high self-esteem are concerned and attentive toward their children, that they structure the world of their children along lines they believe to be proper and appropriate, and that they permit relatively great freedom within the structures they have established. Examination of this combination of conditions reveals some general relationships between child-rearing practices and the formation of self-esteem. The most notable of these deal with parental behavior and the consequences of the rules and regulations that parents establish for their children. These relationships indicate that *definite and enforced limits* are associated with high rather than low self-esteem; that families which establish and maintain *clearly defined limits permit greater rather than less deviation* from conventional behavior, and freer individual expression, than do families without such limits; *that families which maintain clear limits utilize less drastic forms of punishment; and that families of children with high self-esteem exert greater demands for academic performance and excellence. Taken together, these relationships indicate that, other things being equal, limits and rules are likely to have enhancing and facilitating effects and that parental performance within such limits is likely to be moderate, tolerant, and generally civilized. They suggest that parents who have definite values, who have a clear idea of what they regard as appropriate behavior, and who are able and willing to present and enforce their beliefs are more likely to*

rear children who value themselves highly. Parents who can act this way apparently have less need to treat their children harshly, and, from all indications, are viewed with greater affection and respect by their offspring.

There is, of course, an underlying question about the nature and enforcement of the limits and rules espoused by the parents of children with high esteem. Two sources of evidence lead us to believe that the limits established are reasonable, rational, and appropriate to the age of the child, and are not arbitrary and inflexible. The first basis for this belief is the consistent and marked acceptance of their offspring that these parents express. They are concerned for their welfare, are willing to exert themselves on their behalf, and are loyal sources of affection and support. They express their acceptance in a variety of ways, with expressions of interest and concern being perhaps the major underlying feature of their attitudes and behaviors. [Italics added.]

The foregoing is to say at length—and perhaps not as emphatically as it should be said—that *schooling in a place called "the school" is a continuum with education in a place called "the home."* The parent is the first teacher, and remains a teacher of the young in collaboration with school and other educational institutions. In our society, the school and the home rarely succeed without tolerable support of one another.

The Forced Congruence
between Curriculum and Instruction

An observer of the process of change in the school comes to a seemingly easy and satisfactory conclusion: curriculum, interpreted for the present as *what is to be taught,* seems susceptible to change; instruction, interpreted as *how it is to be taught,* is resistant to change.

Larry Cuban, a keen observer of efforts designed to change curriculum, writes: "The educational past is littered with the debris and wreckage of innumerable changes that were lustily embraced for short periods of time by school practitioners only to either disappear or leave a slight residue: scientific management, platoon schools, Dalton Plan, Winnetka Plan, Eight Year Study, tracking, I.Q. Tests, inquiry teaching, non-graded classes, modular scheduling, open classrooms, alternative schools and innumerable other bright ideas." Hindsight enables us to understand certain aspects of the "failure" of these innovations. Recall that an earlier analysis of certain characteristics of movements and innovations led us to the conclusion that they do not disappear, but leave (as Cuban confirms) certain "residues." It is well to repeat that the schools that have found certain innovations practicable are exemplars of effective practice which may undergird the coming renewing of schooling and education. Nonetheless, it is worth reflecting on the reasons these innovations were not embraced by the majority of the schools.

First, a theoretical underpinning—that is, a conceptualization of instruction that is intended to direct practice wherever instruction is carried on (at home, at school, through TV, or other places available in the community)—is essential to movements intended to alter instruction. Such a conceptualization was not available in the kind of systematic assertion that would define what instruction is, may be, or might be— so that a pervasive policy could be developed. Lacking a systematic assertion based on observation of practice and research (in a word, a theory), practice could not be clearly defined. The result: different principals and supervisors, different researchers, different schools engaged— honorably, to be sure—in a mélange of practice. For example:

In the 1960s many schools, elementary and secondary, embraced the remarkable innovative science curriculums supported by various foundations, particularly the federally sponsored National Science Foundation. These were to be taught through what came to be called "inquiry teaching" or "discovery teaching." Essentially, in "teaching through inquiry" the burden of learning, of investigation, of inquiry, fell on the student; the teacher was to be a guide. In effect, the "inquiry" mode of instruction recommended is similar to the maturity-independence model discussed in the preceding pages. However, numerous classroom observations made in the period 1964–1978 clearly demonstrated that the instructional model was not congruent to the practice. Thus, while the plans of instruction (curriculums) called for inquiry, the instructional model used by those who introduced the curriculums to teachers was that of the lecture. Further, the model of instruction adopted by more than 70% of the teachers using the curriculums recommending "inquiry" or "discovery" was the time-honored model of the lecturer.

These observations are now confirmed by a variety of studies made by committees of the National Science Teachers Association and the National Council for the Social Sciences, among others, as reported in a study sponsored by the National Science Foundation in 1979. Granting that certain improvements in curriculum (defined as the body of content to be taught) have been made, there are nevertheless such statements as: "Elementary school science, like that in junior and senior high schools, is taught primarily by lecture and recitation based on one textbook." With regard to the teaching of social studies and the social sciences, it says: "Experience-based curricula, despite recent professional writing about learning through participation, appear to be rare," and "More likely, however, the students' social studies classes will be strikingly similar to those that many of us experience [sic] as youngsters: Textbook assignments followed by recitation led by a teacher who, in his or her own way, likes students and tries to show concern for them— and voids [sic] controversial issues, but tries to pitch the class at the student's level."

One may find strikingly similar reports with regard to instruction in other areas. See, particularly, works by Goodlad and by Cuban.

Why, after a concerted attempt to change instruction, particularly in science, mathematics, and the social sciences, had been mounted beginning in the half-decade 1952–1957, is this? Perhaps these reasons, among others, may be adduced:

First, a theory of instruction (in a systematic assertion) that was acceptable generally and one to which practice could be referred and evaluated was not developed. Such a theory, of necessity, would stand apart from but would be considered together with a congruent theory of curriculum.

Second, there was a need for a philosophy of education that was not confused with a philosophy of schooling, which generally makes the school the major instrumentality in human development. It is time to look upon life whole and develop an environment (partly through schooling and education) that fits one to enter upon what might well be a marvelous and incomparable life.

Third, and perhaps the major reason, supervisors, administrators, teachers, and the variety of school programs generated during the period of innovation were not adequately funded to conduct the necessary training or to develop the materials needed to change instruction.

To repeat, my conclusions from observations in more than 200 classrooms are clear: *a new curriculum is relatively easy to introduce once the instructional materials are prepared* (usually in the form of textbooks, teacher's manuals, laboratory manuals, workbooks, programed instruction, films, filmstrips, records, and the like); however, *instructional modes are exceedingly difficult to alter, requiring profound changes in personal and institutional practices, that is, changes in ingrained habit.* In many cases, this habituation (the lecture, for example) is that of a lifetime. Moreover, the mode of instruction so ingrained has been effective, indeed rewarded, as the mode of choice in the plans for instruction or curriculum now to be displaced. There was a lack of congruence between the substance and structure of the curriculum espoused and the style of instruction to be utilized. Congruence does not require identity: it requires neighborliness. It requires conformity with methods proclaimed by the curriculum as being effective in changing the behavior of the learners. The "inquiry" or "discovery" curriculums in science, mathematics, and social studies placed the burden of activity on the learner, not on the teacher. Note once again that recent studies indicate that after ten to fifteen years of these curriculums the major style of instruction used by teachers adopting them (some 70%) was the lecture and the textbook. What is not, apparently, specified by the evaluators is that the objectives of the curriculums, as measured by existing tests, particularly college entrance examinations, could be, and were, effected by the lecture method as well as by the inquiry method. Furthermore, the textbooks used were developed as basic resources whether the instructional method utilized was based on the lecture, or on discovery, or on a form of "mastery learning." Indeed, the discovery approach requires more reading of varied materials than does the lecture approach, if only because in the discovery, or heuristic, approach reliance is placed on the discoveries of predecessors. The maturing-independence approach described in this chapter combines didactive and heuristic approaches.

Teaching through "inquiry," as does the maturing-independence approach, for example, puts the burden of instructed learning on students; that is, the lecture is to be steadily diminished, and in ideal circumstances reduced to a point where it is less than 50% of class time. It requires the use of additional laboratory space as well as field work, and it requires individualization of instruction—that is, students work on their own while conducting their inquiries. This is exceedingly worthwhile, but, as can be reasonably established, it requires new modes of behavior on the part of teachers who have been reinforced by the behaviors of the lecture presentation, or, conversely, it requires that teachers relinquish modes of reinforcement to which they have long been accustomed.

Nonetheless, learning the content of new and up-to-date physics, biology, chemistry, or geology would be reinforcing to teachers, particularly if they were selected as "master teachers" to attend government-sponsored institutes, as was the case in many instances. Even if this type of reinforcement was not available, learning new knowledge (new content) is generally reinforcing to teachers. But changing behaviors in instruction (performance, to be sure) is another matter, for at least two reasons. First, the performance is part of a complex of behaviors, each of which requires new contingencies of reinforcement: for example, new methods of class management, new methods of evaluating new behaviors on the part of students, including problems of discipline, new adjustments to supervisors and administrators, not to say parents, and, above all, deferred reinforcements. Second, a new body of subject matter and a new body of behaviors in instruction are to be accomplished at the same time. It is easy to understand how it was that teachers adopted a new body of subject matter (a new curriculum) but maintained an older but proved mode of instruction (lecture) and new but proved instructional materials (textbooks and laboratory manuals).

Where the inquiry mode was successful—that is, the rewards inherent in teaching remained as reinforcement—the innovative program was introduced in two steps.

1. The teachers familiarized themselves with the new subject matter. (Its satisfactory apprehension over a year or two of study was itself reinforcing.)
2. The "inquiry mode" was introduced slowly over two to four years and modified, if only at first, to fit the special physical conditions of the school, the requirements of the faculty for new but steady retraining, and the re-education of students to accept new modes of study and instructed learning, that is, to reduce their dependence on the lecture.

In other words, the educational leaders of the school and community, knowledgeable in the practical matters of administration—which in essence calls upon individuals skilled in establishing contingencies of reinforcement (satisfying and rewarding conditions) and reducing aversive contingencies (unsatisfactory conditions)—did not crush the teachers with two overwhelming tasks at the same time: changing a curriculum and simultaneously changing modes of instruction.

It seems reasonable to suggest that new and innovative curriculums and instructional modes (two different aspects of the practice of instructed learning) be fashioned in tandem but introduced in different schedules of reinforcement. In other words, while their production is in tandem, their introduction is to be in sequence: the subject matters of the curriculums to be mastered first; the modes of instruction (an overt performance) to be introduced sequentially as appropriate contingencies of reinforcement are introduced. To fail to account for contingencies of reinforcement is to put serious impediments in the way of introduction of new practices.

Effectiveness in producing change in an institution so vast in its range as a school system demands concentration on the change. Pendulation, the acknowledged enemy of improvement in schooling, intrudes easily. Nonetheless, pendulate movements will continue to exist, as they must in an open society devoted to the amelioration of social ills. The test of an effective educational system will be how it achieves a balance among countervailing, pendulating movements and innovations.

What is observable, as is noted by Cuban, and is eminently clear, is that plans of instruction hopelessly entwine different constructs and styles of instruction. Curriculum and instruction, as has been indicated, go hand in hand but are, in the final analysis, different in purpose. *What is to be taught* (curriculum) can and should be considered apart from *how it is to be taught* (instruction), but, in the end, in any new curriculum the mode of instruction should be congruent with the curriculum.

Too many innovations—individuation of instruction, team teaching, inquiry teaching, and the like—have been introduced in schools utilizing curriculums whose content (subject matter) could be disseminated by the lecture—that is, by instruction dominated by the teacher and presented by voice to a group. Thus the devices of individuation (which is concerned with curriculum whose subject matters are presumably best learned by individual activity of the learner) were introduced in the instruction of subject matters that could just as easily be disseminated by lecture. The tests devised were not calibrated sufficiently with regard to discriminating between styles of instruction, and this is necessary to determine which styles are most effective. Moreover, and most important, there is the question of whether or not there is adequate research, valid research, that demonstrates that a style of instruction affects the behavior of the individual once schooling is past. For example, does instruction through inquiry affect the young so that once graduated they base their actions on available data that are the result of their inquiry? Do the young, inquiring into the effects of smoking, or utilization of addictive drugs, and finding data reporting negative effects on growth and health, stop smoking or using addictive drugs? Do scientists use inquiry in their daily nonprofessional activity? To ask the questions is not to question the utilization of teaching through inquiry. For inquiry modes require a response, an activity on the part of the learner. Because of the response of the learner, the teacher at least learns whether what has been taught has been understood—a notable achievement in itself!

In effect, a new curriculum, to be effectively presented in a style of instruction congruent to it and therefore compatible, should concern itself with devising styles of instruction compatible with the *substance, structure,* and *style* of the subject matter *organized as content.* It will then be clear which aspects of the curriculum (assuming that effective opportunities for *response* by the student are ensured) can be effectively taught by

- The lecture—modified to ensure questions and discussion

- Individuated study—modified to ensure access by the learner to guidance by experienced learners (teachers, paraprofessionals)
- Independent study—ensuring access of the learner to guidance by experienced investigators

In short, varieties of instructional modes should introduce and unite instructional styles congruent and specific of subject matter. Compatibility of curriculum and instruction is ensured not only by congruence in curriculum and instruction, but also by congruence of administration and evaluation. That is to say, curriculum and instruction to be congruent, therefore ensuring compatibility, are required to exist in a system.

Without a system (an ecology of achievement) in which the appropriateness, compatibility, and effectiveness of plans and modes of instruction can be assessed; without a system that establishes feedback between a plan for instruction and the style of instruction utilized in accommodating it; without a system in which teachers can test the effectiveness of instructional style in relation to a curriculum—without these, an innovation in curriculum or instruction can, and probably will, founder. Teachers need to be assured—and so do administrators, supervisors, and the community—that a "new" mode of instruction does indeed effect the improvement of instruction, and therefore learning, claimed for it. It is for this reason that I have pressed forward the need for systematic assertions, compact statements of theory or design which define "new" modes of instruction, curriculum, or evaluation. Indeed I have taken the risk of formulating such a systematic assertion or theory. Advances in schooling and education deserve theories and designs compactly and systematically stated. Otherwise reference, inference, and generation of hypotheses as well as applications to instruction are easily lost.

Teachers, as do many of us, invest a life in a profession to which a good number are dedicated. Administrators, supervisors, and teachers are right in requesting assurance that what they are asked to do serves, and does not waste, time and life—surely not the waste of their time or life and surely not the waste of time or life of the young entrusted to their care. For the young are defenseless. Or they defend themselves—in a hidden agenda rehearsed covertly—by rejecting what is put before them. This need not be.

5. Regarding Curriculum

A Necessary Prologue

"Why in an institution so vulnerable to social change do classrooms seem so invulnerable to curriculum change?" So Larry Cuban, Superintendent of Schools in Arlington, Virginia, poses a central question that has plagued Boards of Education, administrators, supervisors, parents, and, as we have found, teachers as well.

The reasons are various, but we are obliged to address certain questions in curriculum design and construction which are at the base of what seems to be responsible for this incredible invulnerability to change. What we find is actually a reaction to the intolerable load with which curriculum change is burdened.

Curriculum reform (what is to be learned) is too often confused with the totality of education. In addition, instead of representing a balanced view of the culture accessible to the practices called "schooling," curriculum reform accentuates imbalance by addressing the needs of a particular group of students—for example, those displaying certain deficiencies in literacy and numeracy—at the same time ignoring options for others (say, those accomplished in literacy, in mathematics, or the gifted per se). Too often, curriculum change does not address the whole mind; it accentuates one aspect of the mind (the verbal) and ignores another, equally important (the visual and intuitive). This is another imbalance, to be sure.

But in the main, a radical curriculum innovation, however necessary, seems to introduce an imbalance in the strategy and tactics of change. Because innovation in curriculum often melds advances in knowledge (content), skills (processes), and attitudes (involving emotions), as well as newer modes of instruction and evaluation, different schedules of introduction of an innovation in curriculum and instruction into a given school seem to be justifiable. Indeed, they are required. The habits of mind needed to encompass new content (which teachers, as experienced learners, grasp with ease) are more readily changed than habits involved in instruction, for the habits serving instruction are ingrained in the nervous system by powerful reinforcements and are refractory to ready change.

Moreover, the aims of education are of larger compass than the aims of a curriculum, but curriculum *reforms* seem always to claim more than the specific curricular *aims* justify. The latter speak to schooling, and the aims of education speak to all of life. I am constrained to separate the two, and address aims of education in Chapter 7, which is concerned with initial steps in designing an educational system. We concern ourselves here with those aspects of change in curriculum that may affect the next steps in the renewing of schooling and education.

What of these next steps? Is it not time to take stock, to seek a surcease from the unacceptable pendulation that has made the schools a battleground, to seek a balance between contending forces, to cease the polemic wars? Toward this end, we may well consider the following:

• A mode of instruction based in *instructed learning,* which encourages a constructive affection, a useful collaboration, between teachers and pupils even as the young accept an increasingly mature and independent role in learning (the maturing-independence model of Chapter 4)

• A curricular mode that gives play to a balance in the varieties of knowledge, skills, and attitudes required for competent and compassionate participation in an open society (to be addressed in this chapter)

• A balance in modes of evaluation addressing the interaction of measures of achievement and the assessment of achievement resulting from efforts to reduce disadvantage and to stimulate increasingly independent work in learning (to be discussed in Chapter 6)

• And, at last, a balance in the rich futures of purposes and persons living in an open society, the promise that rests in the development of an educational system not yet in place

Recall that schooling before the industrial revolution of the late nineteenth and early twentieth centuries was limited for most to primary schooling; probably less than 10% had a secondary schooling, and a college education of whatever kind was limited to perhaps less than 2% of the population.

If one considers the effect on the schools generally and pervasively in areas other than reading, writing, and numbering, the burst of reform in curriculum noted by historians appears to have begun in the era of Horace Mann. A secondary education began to be available to "all" by the early 1900s. By the 1930s a secondary education was at least contemplated as a possibility for all the young in the range of that "capable 70%" of the school population. Yet these were, and are, still served by a curriculum forged for those who were "college-preparatory."

It is this curriculum, the college-preparatory curriculum serving the 70%, its substance, structure, and, particularly, style, that is the counterweight to all attempts at change, or reform. The college-preparatory curriculum is, in fact, the established curriculum, dominated by college entrance requirements, whether these are myth or fact. But note that establishing this college-preparatory curriculum was at one time the goal of reform in education. While the antecedents of curriculum rest in the English and German schools, its attainment was the goal of the early (1800–1860) reformers of American schooling. Free schooling, with its expression in a curriculum emphasizing the basics in the primary school and an established college-preparatory curriculum in the secondary school, was in itself a tremendous achievement, the first great accomplishment of curriculum workers in this country. It became the target of curriculum reformers in the past hundred years. It remains the mark; in fact, it is, give or take Latin and Greek, the established curriculum in this country.

We are concerned here with the design of a curriculum, not with the over-all philosophy of a school district or how the curriculums adopted by the school district serve that philosophy. The design of a curriculum per se suffers when the attempt is made to "shoehorn" the curriculum into the "over-all aims" of the school district. Moreover, the aims of schooling and/or education of a school district, as distinct from behavioral objectives, should embrace more than the aims of a curriculum in a specific content area, say, science or social studies.

It would seem that a major reform in curriculum which would serve the renewing of schooling and education would be one mounting an effort to seek a balance in the kinds of knowledges, values, and skills necessary for the next decade in the antecedent years of the postindustrial age. Pendulation in curriculum development, as said earlier, has become counterproductive.

Influences on the
Present Curriculum

Between 1890 and 1930, social reforms and reforms in schooling were in synergy once again. The poverty (by American standards) consequent on tides of immigration, the growth of the cities in response to burgeoning industrial impact, the congregation of immigrants in slums and "ghettos" was there to be corrected. Ignorance of American language and custom could be attacked readily through schooling, and the schools undertook the reform. They undertook to make the child central to schooling: the child's welfare (and not subject matter per se) would be the concern of what came to be known as "progressivism." The schools were to become not only "educationally efficient"—that is, they would prepare the young in subject matters suitable for college entrance —but also "socially efficient"—that is, they would prepare the young to become workers in industrial and clerical fields, in business and professional fields. And the schools were to prepare the young for citizenship and motherhood as well.

Nevertheless, even in the period between 1870 and 1910 schools were differentiating the curriculum, a matter worth noting. One could find "innovative" curriculums such as those in agricultural, business, industrial, printing, scientific, and college-preparatory subjects. One could find differentiation of content, of subject matter, to meet the needs of a variety of aims, a variety of abilities, and a variety of opportunities. These three objectives, relating to the aims, abilities, and opportunities of the young, were to guide subsequent curricular change. While certain educators (among them Elwood Cubberly and David Snedden) pressed for the efficiency of differentiated curriculums, other leaders in education (notably Frances Parker and John Dewey) illuminated the role of the teacher in relation to the child as learner, and curriculum as stipulating what is to be learned. But the essence of the reform that Parker and Dewey, among others, pressed was to put the child in the role of participant in the teaching-learning process, and not in the passive role of recipient. The "progressive education" movement was thus a counterthrust to the effects of the "industrial education" movement which preceded it. However, the education of the upper socioeconomic groups (the so-called elites) was still college-preparatory. The classical curriculums (college-preparatory) of the high school included not only English, history, and literature, but at least one foreign language (and

Greek and Latin where desired) and mathematics. The science curriculum was fragmentary, but it was to develop strongly after World War I. In the end, the progressive education movement did not, as far as research shows, have a lasting effect on the college-preparatory curriculum.

Curriculum reform—pressed by reformers addressing redress of grievance—has a certain style, characterized by the nature of the reform. It is at first generally *not* directed at honoring the needs of the large population of average students, but at the requirements of either the "upper ranges of intellectual ability" or the "lower levels of intellectual ability" (that is, the 20 to 30% of the young who get 75% of the failing marks). Curriculum reform seems generally to be honed to habituations that aim at further study—college, to be sure, and work other than study: a job. The question is not whether students are ever to gain entrance to college; the objective and motivation are to *aim* at entrance. In effect, our school systems succeed with the upper 70%, not with the lower 30%. The point is worth making, because recent curricular reforms in reading, numbering, writing—the so-called basics—have generally aimed at ameliorating the situation of the 30%.

A curriculum embodies, as we shall see, *nonrandom* experience, intentionally designed in a structure of concepts, values, and skills planned for both teachers and students. It is intended to transmit an *organized* content and skills to a new generation to advance their ability to cope with life and living, and possibly, where ability reaches its highest expression in an individual, to create new knowledge. Simplistically, for teachers a curriculum determines what is to be taught, and for students, what is to be learned. As has been indicated, what is taught is not a mirror of what is learned. True, teachers may have hidden agendas, often called the "hidden curriculum," which more truly are aspects of personal style reflecting their own personal experience. The curriculum is often "laid out" in the published statements of school administrations (including the Board of Education, which represents the community). These published or printed statements are reflected in the materials of instruction selected and approved for use, which are then available for a study of the intent and content of the curriculum. Often the purchased materials of instruction *become* the curriculum.

As Cuban puts it, in *Value Conflicts and Curriculum Issues:* "By the 1870's, the structure of corporate school boards, superintendents as experts, principals as administrators and teachers as all-purpose agents of society was in place. Nailed down desks, box-like classrooms off main corridors, separate grade-levels, textbooks and blackboards were familiar landmarks on the schoolkeeper's horizon. In David Tyack's felicitous phrase, it seemed as if the 'one best system' had been installed."

Note that what seems to be described is a style of administration and a style of instruction in which the teacher was dominant—notably a style of schooling. But, in fact, the substance of curriculum is implied in the term "textbook," for textbooks include subject matter comprising distillations of scholarship and research (which constitute, of course, a major component of curriculum), if not the aims of a curriculum and what it is that it professes to do for the development of the learner. As Daniel Bell tells us, "Knowledge consists of new judgments (research and scholarship) or new presentations of older judgments (textbooks and teaching)."

We may also note how the change in the goals and objectives (that is, policy) altered the style of schooling. Thus again Cuban:

> Periodically, over the last century, formal listings of goals rumbled forth from the National Education Association, White House Conferences, blue-ribbon commissions and, closer to home, Parent Teacher Association committees of the neighborhood elementary school. In 1874, a group of college presidents and school superintendents agreed that the school is "obliged to train the pupils into habits of prompt obedience to teachers and the practices of self-control in its various forms."

> In 1918, the National Education Association's Commission on Secondary Education produced seven "main objectives" for schooling. Among them were health, "worthy home membership," vocation, citizenship, "worthy use of leisure," and ethical character. Moreover, each child should develop "his personality primarily through the activities designed for the well-being of his fellow members and of society as a whole." Across the country, school systems rapidly adopted these goals.

But the reader will surely note that what is asked for is not only a change in curriculum, instruction, and administration, but a change in the objectives of a style of life as well.

Successive redefinition of what the goals should be occurred in each subsequent decade. By 1956, the White House Conference on Education looked back and concluded:

"The basic responsibility of the schools is the development of the skills of the mind, but the over-all mission has been enlarged. Schools are now asked to help each child become as good and as capable in every way as native endowment permits. The schools are asked to help children to acquire any skill or characteristic which a majority of the community deems worthwhile. The order given by the American people to the schools is grand in its simplicity; in addition to intellectual achievement, foster morality, happiness, and useful ability. . . ."

Cuban goes on to say: *"Not only do goals shift and change over time, but few formal goal statements contain sufficient clarity to guide public school administrators or board members to make policy and evaluate outcomes.* Unfocused goals mirror, in part, a lack of consensus among participants over what schools are for. Because of erratic and inconsistent entry, flow and exit of participants in making school decisions, *it is most difficult* to gain a broad, stable agreement upon what schools should do." (Italics added.)

A First Note on Meaning of Curriculum: Antecedents of a Broad, Stable Agreement

---

To some, "broad, stable agreement" will at once presume abdication of principle. Not so. There comes a time when such agreements should be *sought,* searched for, if not accomplished. As has been indicated, American schooling is at a turning point; it is becoming or seeking a mature growth; the postindustrial society is upon us; we can ill afford the luxury of internecine warfare between school and society. In the years to come, mediocrity will be insupportable. We are obliged to give each individual an opportunity to fulfill his or her powers in the pursuit of excellence: defined as the best to be achieved with whatever personal gifts and opportunities are available.

Broad, stable agreement on curriculum is possible if there is first a resolution of the question What is the curriculum?

Note the directive cited of the 1956 White House Conference on Education: "The order given by the American people to the schools is grand in its simplicity; in addition to intellectual achievement, foster morality, happiness, and useful ability. . . ."

Having participated in various White House conferences, I find such a statement of curricular objectives grand, significant, and even noble, but hardly useful—as is true of the statements of many conferences where resolutions are reached by consensus. Note that the statement embraces all aspects of *schooling* and *education,* but not those of schooling per se. In the past, society has not given the schools the superordinate powers to determine, for example, what a moral life should be, or what happiness is, can, or ought to be. These elements have generally been assumed to be the special property of the individual in the kind of *self-actualization* I have considered to be an aspect of *education,* involving as they do the individual risks undertaken in achieving a particular moral purpose and action, and of individual aspirations to the good and happy life. Once again, there is almost a blithe imposition on the schools of not only vast unfocused goals, but, indeed, responsibility for a blueprint of social advance. Granted that schools are central to the advance of society; it is also to be granted that the role of the school is not to encompass *all* of the education of the young, but to play a significant part in an ecology of achievement. Nevertheless, the building of a curriculum is consequent upon an antecedent understanding of aims or goals of schooling, and these are not static. We must face the question as we speculate later on the attributes of a boy or girl who has been graduated from an American school. First, however, we are obliged to define curriculum.

A First Note on Design of Curriculum

The world around us is full of detail—items, incidents, artifacts, expressions, objects, and myriad life forms. We seek to reduce the complexity of the clutter. The ordering of experience in search of meaning —the reduction of complexity and haphazardness of what is perceived —is at the center of the art-science we call "curriculum." We seek to cope with new experience, and, curiously, to do so we are required to order past experience. Otherwise, the world is chaotic. We seek "to know in advance," as Bruner felicitously puts it.

The mind, in essence, prepares itself to see wholes. The prepared mind has, in a sense, a mental filing system, a system prepared to know in advance, that is, to cope with new experience. For the ordered mind, the tortuous paths of unregulated thought, the melee of daily events, and the clutter that assails us daily are not resolved into a potpourri. Rather, the mind edits, selects, and connects; it patterns. It seeks patterns and it seeks wholes. If we were to set down this patterning activity of the mind, this patterning of experience, we might posit steps such as these (Bruner puts them differently):

1. The mind *sorts.* It *selects* what it attends to.
2. As we sort and select, *we reduce* complexity. As we reduce complexity, *we economize.* (The sound of a car's horn informs us of the entire car; we do not turn to see it; we jump out of the way. A single cue can save our lives.)

3. Once we attend to *the* cue, other cues assail us. *We connect* the past to the future, and the present is the connection. (In buying the ticket to a soccer game, we remember with pleasure our earlier experience with the game, with friends who have played or watched soccer with us, and at the same time summarize the forthcoming day of the game—from the beginning of the trip to the game, to the sport, to the celebration of the crowd, even to the difficulty of parking.) *We chain events.*

4. As we connect objects, events, behaviors, *we seek explanatory models* of objects, events, behaviors. We engage, in short, in concept-seeking. Indeed, concepts take the form of explanatory models. They remain with us, becoming part of the basket of behavior we carry to every new experience.

If we are scientists, we are aware of the presence of evidence, even as we speculate. If we are philosophers, we speculate, and must be aware of the canons of metaphysics and logic. If we are artists, we create form; but even if art is "free," we are not ever free of wanting form to convey meaning.

Nothing energizes the prepared mind more than incompleteness. It must complete. Rightly or wrongly, it seeks to complete. It wants to see whole.

In essence, the curriculum maker imposes, first, a structure of concepts upon the field of study, and second, a construct that enables different teachers with different knowledges, skills, and attitudes to work within a given school. Thus it is that a number of teachers are engaged in a sequence of teaching that enhances the child's growth as he or she proceeds from grade to grade, from level to level, from year to year, from teacher to teacher. With a given curriculum, the teacher has a matrix that makes instruction possible. The curriculum is the map with which both teacher and student find their way in fields that their culture, history, and individual inclinations consider important. Curriculum workers address the question What are the ends of schooling? not necessarily Who is schooled, learned, and educated?

A moment's thought on the question Who is educated? serves to show that the question is footless. The question that needs asking is: Educated to what end?

There may have been a time when the question was not asked, when it was implicit in the conduct of the individual, in his or her fitness to survive. In ancient agrarian and hunting societies, to be educated may have meant to have the capacity to use the knowledge, attitudes, and skills to survive in the natural environment. If there were a school in such a society, such would have been its superordinate objectives. But if there were no school, certainly there was an educational system. It was fitness to the ecological system itself in which the human was both producer and consumer that "educated" the individual in the uses of the environment. The reinforcements were easily perceptible. Behavior was then indeed "shaped and maintained by its consequences," to use Burrhus Skinner's magnificent phrase.

Perhaps if the word "educated" had been used, the "best educated" might have been applied to those who were "best fitted to the environment." This is a somewhat Darwinian slant, but it is not meant to be, for early in human history collaboration and competition both played their part in the survival of the tribe. This volume is not the place for educational history; it *is* the place to reflect on the part an educational system, as compared and contrasted with a schooling system, will play in the development of educated men and women. We will do this by analyzing the parts curriculum, instruction, and evaluation play in teaching and learning. And so a definition will emerge in synthesis.

At the beginning it is possible to say that what is taught (curriculum) and how it is taught (instruction) play a large part in determining who can tolerate the process of becoming educated. This is not so subtle a distinction, but it is, perhaps, subtle to connect *what is taught* with *what is known,* and *how it is taught* with *how it is known.* Perforce we incline to the perception that *what is known* and *how it is known* are interconnected, and their synergism is in part what determines *who is educated.* To belabor the point, *what is taught* is often not *what is known.*

Be that as it may, a curriculum is a choice in "knowns"; it is intended to embody what is worth knowing and worth doing. But simply to throw what adults consider worth knowing and worth doing at the young haphazardly—to make available to them experience without structure, without substance, without sequence, without systematic evaluation—is to throw them into chaos. It is to ensure failure. It is to face them, in effect, with perpetual TV, where the dials are turned by whim. Rousseau's "natural man" was in a postulated happy state, but he could not have survived in modern Western society.

To be educated may not mean to have a college education, to pass the SAT; it may mean only to have such means of self-expression and conduct as to assure one of fulfilling one's work, having the respect of one's neighbors, having one's health and the love of one's family. Perhaps this is only the ancient prescription of Freud: *Arbeit und Liebe* (work and love). But fulfillment in work may also mean to have a habitual vision of greatness, and the respect of one's neighbors may also mean to have the attitudes and skills worthy of fulfilling relationships in family, at work, and in society. It is to say that the term "curriculum" is not to be used loosely, to be bandied about, or to be treated gently. A curriculum is thus a dovetail with the objectives of society. As a first assumption, we might say (modifying Bruner somewhat*) that a curriculum is perhaps a compact delivery system of the culture (and of its subcultures, certainly), embodying its fondest and finest hopes, dreams, and, in the vernacular of education, its most respected objectives and behaviors. It will be important for us to determine whether this assumption holds.

To repeat: a curriculum, to be effective, has structure; it has substance; it has style; it survives systematic evaluation; it survives within a system—an ecology of achievement. To understand curriculum is to respect structure. To recall one of Piaget's paradigms: teaching and learning were significant because, in effect, the "teacher created situations in which children discover structure." To understand curriculum is not only to understand its structure, but to understand the substance of the culture accepted by the community.

It is self-evident that the states of knowledge and skills undergirding a vigorous culture such as ours are in a constant process of reinvention. The function of scholarship in a self-examining society is always to create and disseminate a meaningful world—that is, one in which students of the culture constantly alter the constructs of what is to be known. In turn, these constructs are the antecedents that qualify decisions determining the education of the young. Thus, in an open society the states of intimacy and freedom change constantly, not only in their constraints, but also in their redefinition. It is self-evident, then, that considerations and propositions attending to what is to be taught (curriculum) to the young, and how it is to be taught (instruction), need redefinition in each generation.

Nevertheless, there are certain constants defining the nature of curriculum and instruction to which we can and should repair. Education is a dialogue with and of the culture, the substance of the culture with the mind. And curriculum is in a respectable view a compact delivery system of the culture. A curriculum is to be compact because to deal effectively with the culture means to invent devices to reduce its complexity. To roll the entire culture upon the young all at once and

---

* Bruner notes that curriculum may be considered a "compact delivery system of the culture."

without preparation is to crush them. A curriculum is a delivery system because it is, in fact, prepared for delivery to the young in a particular setting—the school. Curriculums prepared for delivery by TV are no different; their place of delivery is different. As we shall see, the failure of education through TV is its failure to distinguish between the special nature of a compact delivery system prepared for the schools and that for TV. The two are different not only in the melding of the structure and substance required, but also in the settings involving different methodologies, that is, different styles. A curriculum reflects the culture; if a curriculum outstrips the culture it is essentially not suited for the schools. The obstacles to its introduction are enormous; often it is merely ignored. But—and this is important—such a curriculum may well be suitable for purposes of *education* outside the school, where experimentation with purpose and the future are permissible and risk is acceptable and possible.

On Design of a Curriculum:
Reduction of Complexity in Constructs

In examining the multiple reasons schooling fails, Philip H. Phenix, Professor of Philosophy at Teachers College of Columbia University, reminds us that "human intelligence is too rare and precious a quantity to squander on a haphazard program of instruction." This point is clear: a curriculum is expected to have substance and content, a structure, scope, sequence, and objectives. At best, it has a style that embraces the usually flexible, usually confident mode of enterprising learners, all learners, whether "gifted" or "average" or "slow."

A curriculum comprises a series of progressive steps in development. Or if the notion of continuous progress seems too deterministic, then let us say that, as learning proceeds, the elements that make up the growth that characterizes learning exist in a kind of cognitive and affective counterpoint, each resonating or extending the other. Curriculum must have structure, for a curriculum is a plan for learning. To foster instructed learning, to consider *what is to be taught,* is to ask how we shall order what is to be taught; it is to ask, *What is worth knowing?* After all, a school or any place where education is carried on is a place where teachers meet learners. They do not meet by chance: they meet, in intent and in effect, to teach and to learn.

An individual's learning may be random or it may be consciously ordered; the individual learns under either condition. But random learning within the plan of schooling runs the risk of being inconsequential or haphazard and inefficient. Ordered learning, on the other hand, can become a strait-jacket. Inconsequential, haphazard, or strait-jacketed instruction can be avoided. A school is in the main an environment for instructed learning and therefore for organized experience. The effective curriculum and effective instruction must draw heavily on the child's previous experience. The curriculum is not, under any circumstances, *prescriptive.* It is *perspective:* it opens up a view of human knowledge, values, and skills. A curriculum imposes discipline because it presumes to create a plan or a structure for seeking, recognizing, valuing experience, and coping with new experience.

Creating a curriculum, however beneficent it may be, is an awesome task. In thinking of curriculum, one asks, What kind of a world do we want for children? This is a terrible question, for it forces us to face the ideal. This world that we seek in the mills of education is not chaotic; it allows both freedom and order. It has relevance; it has structure, which preserves unity within diversity.

The prime purposes of planning a curriculum are not solely to meet the needs of the young for understanding and growth. There is also the reduction of complexity. From the chaos of experience we all try to redact experience in the search for meaning. We must. It is not the whole world that is experience. We see selectively, of course: we sort out what we see. Curriculum is not an unnatural imposition on the child; constructed rightly, it helps him to select what is meaningful and useful to him in his life. If a curriculum does not reduce complexity, it is too cumbersome for the school and for the learner; it is an obstacle to instruction. But life itself as curriculum, as what is to be known, offers no such reduction. The meanings of its random experience are forever undulating in simplicity and complexity.

Schooling is another matter. Schooling and education both turn upon experiences in search of meaning. A school, however, is a careful design for the search for meaning. It has a certain identifiable structure, certain sequences in experiences parallel to the maturation of its students, and an administration designed to undertake continuous assessment of these experiences as they affect maturation. The school is an environment that children come upon. It should not be alien and confusing; to the contrary, it should become a place that children understand. A proper school does not remain a constricted environment. A proper school makes the world a child's home.

The school is, of course, a social institution. The community (a coalition of families and other groups) has invented an institution whose main purpose is to reduce the complexity of experience, to reduce randomness; to develop, if you will, compact forms for the delivery of experience—classrooms, laboratories, books, computers, films, and the like. A school's curriculum is obliged to use orderly and harmonious methods because, socially, people who are allied as nations or otherwise want to be able to assume that they share certain experience. Beyond this, the school gives the child practice in planning his own experience. To plan one's own experience is a uniquely human act. In planning a curriculum, one recognizes that the child is first an organism not yet fully equipped to meet the world on its own terms. The child grows in personhood only as he or she combines a unique freedom in planning experiences within the social necessities of order.

Yet the child cannot examine all behavior, all environments, all experience. An attempt to understand or deal with all experience is, in fact, a contradiction of life, inasmuch as time and energy in one's lifetime are limited. Total experience is impossible. Faced with vast stimuli, especially in a world of television, the child is forced to construct a world with which he or she can cope practicably. Children learn quickly to survive the onslaught of stimuli and other impressions. They reduce the multitudinous facets of experience into constructs; these are concepts and values. Or they ignore them till they mature sufficiently (in age and experience) to order the stimuli and impressions into concepts or "wholes." A baby's apparently neutral sound "ma ma" becomes invested with meaning and feelings. That is, it becomes a construct. How soon, too, the random sound "pa pa" becomes invested with meaning. But how different from "mama" is "papa," in the meaning it elicits, the behavior it motivates, the feelings it inspires. To be sure, both words are constructs that help the young child to order his world. In turn, the world's constructs, its values and behavior-ordering myths, have impact upon the child. Each newborn child is an alien. It is the world's constructs, its concepts and values, that are devised and taught so that the alien becomes the citizen.

What constructs, what concepts and values, determine the structure of the curriculum? Structure may be defined as a practicable form of interrelated constructs. Interrelated constructs we may recognize as wholes, or concepts. The structure of a particular curriculum—science, health, mathematics, history, music, or the visual arts—has at least three characteristics:

1. It is a body of concepts that will be useful for anyone to recognize the elements and details of the subject matter.

2. The concepts control the procedures (or modes of inquiry) by which what is known is discovered and verified.

3. The concepts (and the modes) extend themselves as learning proceeds: concepts lead to other concepts and to still other concepts. Learning subsumes itself and is, theoretically, never ended. The known leads to the unknown.

All scholars know that they begin with the known before they probe the unknown. Then, when they have probed the unknown successfully, the unknowns become knowns. These knowns then become the basic concepts for a probe into newer unknowns. One of the major obstacles in the institution of curriculums is basing the inquiry (the "discovery") activities of children in problems, without affording them the background to understand the objects and events with which they are to work.

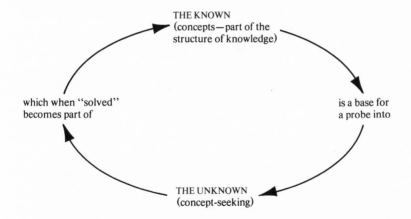

Knowledge is organic: it grows. In the social sciences, for example, there are such major concepts (often called "conceptual schemes") as interaction between social groups, market choices in an economy, and resolution of international conflict. Subsidiary and lesser concepts exist, of course. In social interaction there are subsumed the concepts of group, family, community, leadership, citizenship, and the like. In market economies there is a range of subsidiary concepts, such as gross national product, balance of trade, cost of production of goods and services, and currency. These concepts can be thought of as a shorthand of conceptual language: they are the sentences of conceptual grammar. Thus the concepts of price, goods, and services are linked in the concept statement "The price of goods and services in an otherwise unregulated market depends on supply and demand." Such a statement is, for common purposes, generally "true." In the sciences there are major concepts (or conceptual themes): life, matter, energy, interdependence, and continuity. In the humanities there are truth, beauty, justice, love, and faith. These are stated in terms that the teacher grasps immediately; the child's comprehension and language are, of course, different.

Gerald Holton, a physicist who is a student of the structure of science, writes of science, in *Introduction to Concepts and Theories in Physical Science,* thus: "First of all there are the *concepts or constructs,* like velocity, mass, chemical element, etc.—the main ideas which in the particular sciences are as vocabulary. . . . Second, there are the relationships between the concepts (we have called these relations or relationships concept-statements) . . . These relations may be simple factual observations . . . or may be general summaries of fact called laws, principles, and so forth. . . ."

Concepts govern our view of the present. Fritz Stern, in discussing the nature of inquiry in the humanities in *The Varieties of History,* suggests: "In the last analysis what will shape a particular history is the historian's concept of the past, whether or not he has formulated it, whether or not he is fully conscious of it. These conceptions, compounded of tradition and temperament, govern the unity of history."

In probing the philosophy of education in an article in *Educational Forum,* Phenix remarks: "It is commonly assumed that abstract thinking is difficult and complicated. This assumption betrays a misunderstanding of what abstraction is. Analytic abstraction is a way of thinking which aims at ease of comprehension and reduction in complexity. For this reason all learning—all growth in understanding—takes place through the use of simplified concepts."

But concepts are not only the building stones of understanding, or, more simply, of communication. When men share fundamental values and recognize concepts in common, the organization of society becomes possible. Indeed, social discourse cannot take place without a common heritage of concepts. For example, in one school an elementary orchestra was preparing for rehearsal. The conductor, an older high-school student, asked the pianist to sound an *A.* The girl sounded the note:

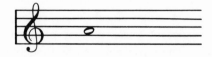

Now this is *A,* but it is not the letter *a.* Why? The operations of the orchestra took place within an established environment; that is, within an established or agreed-upon set of concepts and values. If, in a different environment, say a lesson in some area of linguistics, a child was asked to "sound" the grapheme *a,* what would happen? The setting of a given environment (music room or language class) calls forth a stimulus. The stimulus follows a familiar or habitual track of association. A curriculum reduces obstacles in understanding if it builds upon the habitual tracks of association, making new associations and new habitual tracks possible.

Put in ordinary terms, a concept is a mental filing system for quickly sorting experience. A concept isolates from the rest of experience the common attributes that are characteristic of objects, events, and behaviors. There are more than 4 billion men and women. And yet when the term "man" is used, it is edited, as it were; the concept *man* embraces the 4 billion or more discrete men and women. Perhaps we have never been to Afghanistan, or seen a Riff, or a Kurd, or a native of the Kalahari. But we can take all their common attributes and conceptualize them as *man.* And so, too, we can conceptualize *woman, girl, boy, baby,* in all the countries of the world. We have come to "know" the general traits of mankind by visiting mankind conceptually. The informed mind quickly sorts experience.

Possession of a concept eases learning, but it also coerces thought. When we say Giovanni "reads a book," we are not assailed by images of the child Giovanni reading a piece of candy, a tablet, or runic stones. We have a clear image of what he is doing. But we know nothing of the kind of book. The sentence "he reads a book" coerces us into thinking that it is a "right" experience; in many societies, books are respected, even revered, as repositories of valuable information or art. Yet the fact may be that the actual book in hand is reprehensible for some reason. Similarly, if we grow up in a society in which disease is believed to be caught from evil spirits, then we will not look for the microbe.

Of course a concept can be developed out of random experience or from insufficient experience. Most concepts that deal with the inferiority or superiority of a given "race" are of this sort—for instance, the misconceptions inherent in the category of Hitler's Nordic superman. Misconceptions also exist about the "musicality" of Italians as a nationality, about Irish "truculence," Scottish "penny-pinching," French "logic," Oriental "patience," Latin "hot-bloodedness," and the like. To repeat, a concept can be "wrong." A concept, to be correct, must seek its support in valid data or valid experience. Science generally draws its "truth" out of an empirical validity. There is, however, a nonempirical validity in art, music, literature, dance, and drama, which depends on psychological and cognitive qualities that are relative, the qualities that make up esthetics and criticism.

There are also what may be called "natural and spontaneous concepts."

Natural and Spontaneous Concepts

It should be clear that concepts are constantly in a state of renewal. How the mind forms is not yet known. Indeed, the awesome and marvelous activity of the mind in seeing whole is one of the beneficent human traits; understanding its process would be to understand, in effect, how the human became pre-eminent in the environment. Nevertheless, we begin to see its origin in children as they put, so we say, "two and two together."

Early on, a child will form the concepts "cold" and "hot" from concrete experiences with cold objects (ice, snow, cold water) and with hot (boiling water, steam, radiators, hot electric light bulbs), but he or she will not be able to relate cold and heat conceptually to the movement of molecules—not yet. We term such concepts, which do not come out of formal study, "natural spontaneous concepts."

So a child "knows" (synonym: has formed natural spontaneous concepts) many things relating to friendship, justice, love, gravity, rules, force, motion, and the like. For example, he or she says, "I like you"; "It is not fair"; "All things fall to the ground"; "You have to wash"; "You have to brush your teeth."

A child "knows" where to stand to push another just so on a swing, without knowing what is involved—the relationship between the square root of the length of the rope and the retrograde motion of the earth. So, too, an adult, and in good time a child, determines the weather by looking out the window and noting how others are dressed, whether they carry umbrellas, wear parkas and galoshes, without determining temperature, moisture, wind velocity. Children form natural spontaneous concepts; teachers and parents can build upon these to develop concepts more systematically derived, that is, derived on the basis of investigation, experiment, reading.

It is also clear that children develop natural spontaneous concepts at different rates, and that the subject matter as well as the content of these natural spontaneous concepts is different in different children, different cultures, different motivations, different gifts and opportunities.

There need be no pressing effort to develop systematically stated, non-randomly organized concepts early on, say in preschool. The elementary grades are soon enough.

All disciplines have concepts that are particular to them. Atom, ion, gene, magnetism call to mind the sound and smells of science. Vote, government, nation, group, race, region, economy are associated with social science. Poem, symphony, color, tone, ballet, song, picture, drama indicate a departure from science, social science, and mathematics, for they belong to the world of the humanities.

The school is the environment that reduces random encounters and complexity. It reduces complexity through the constructs (the concepts and values) it assembles into curriculum. The curriculum, having reduced the complexity of experience, in turn reduces complexity of instruction. A notable yield of this process is a stability in instruction and in schooling situations, a stability that does not preclude the variety necessary to the teaching of a variety of children.

There is a myth in educational theory that gives critics of modern education an easy satisfaction. It is the myth that structure is rigid and inflexible and is hampered by conformity, and, worst of all, unresponsive to a child's needs and interests. Not so! If anything, sequence with a conceptual structure frees the teacher; it does not imprison anyone who is already independent. Teaching a concept does not indicate a specific experience or a mode of instruction. A concept opens up a variety of experience, of intelligible content; it leads to analysis and synthesis. It is not concepts but encyclopedic "topics" that tend to be rigid and confined in sequence. A topic can be "lectured"; a concept is "sought" and perhaps "caught" in good time. One can "finish" a topic; a concept grows. In fact, in teaching, a *topical sequence* is extremely rigid, for it states inflexibly the body of knowledge that is meant to be "covered." A *conceptual sequence,* on the contrary, allows for variety, for comparison and contrast, for exploration and discovery. It depends on problem-posing that varies within the idiosyncratic modes of inquiry.

The Power of Conceptual Structures: Coping with New Experience; Seeing "Wholes"

Concepts are stable intellectual currency; they keep their value even in foreign fields. One reason is obvious: we need some means by which to gain and give knowledge. Recall that a concept is a mental construct, isolating from experience the *common attributes* that identify objects and events. Thus the concept "teacher," once formed, is apart from specific relation to the image of Signor Casalini or Mr. Nimwahli or Mrs. James, but it categorizes a host of teachers. A concept is flexible; it will hold an incredible variety of facts. The concept "candy" exists, as candy in all forms exists: chocolate creams, fudge, rock candy, bars, drops, and so on. The concept exists in the mind; the objects (sensations and images) exist in the experience. Experience forms the raw material of the concept. A new object bought in a candy store which is wrapped in metal foil and resembles a bar of chocolate is easily categorized as candy; it is not assumed to be a rock, a bird, or a body. Its common attributes, its consistent stimuli (foil, shape, odor) form a consistent response—candy.

Possession of a concept eases learning. Possession of a concept almost automatically applies past experience to present events, or immediately perceived objects, or stated "problems." Yet when a concept is developed out of experience that is not tested by scientific inquiry, or if it is developed out of a "random" experience that bears no definition of its source or its intent, then such a concept generally becomes a stereotype of human behavior. A concept can be "wrong," judged by the principles of a humane society.

The school structure, whether it consists of graded or nongraded classes, depends on the time-binding nature of events, growth, and the relationship between teachers. The grading system, in schooling, was invented in order that what is learned before is strengthened by what comes after. This is to say, the teacher in the fifth grade builds on what was *taught* and presumably *learned* in the fourth grade. For the most part, both biological and instructional experiences and goals seem to be bound by time: walking occurs before running, the kindergarten is entered before college, puberty precedes childbearing. Concepts in teaching and learning are also bound by time. A child can cope with the concept of gravity earlier than he can with the concept of ego. Even so, he or she has an early experience with both. The child's goals in learning seem to adjudicate themselves in a typical order: the simple to the complex, the concrete to the abstract, the familiar to the unfamiliar. Evidence seems to indicate that children are able to observe very early in life. Somewhat later, children are able to categorize. Still later, the child seeks to undertake the design of experiment, and then only with great difficulty. Skills in observation seem to precede skills in experimentation, if only because (stated somewhat simplistically) observation *finds* a fact and experiment *makes* a fact.

Teachers are no less subject to time-binding. They need to communicate with each other. Within a school organization, they are, after all, guides to the same children, who pass from one of them to another in a sequential, chronological parade. They pass on to each other a child who carries an increment of physical and mental growth. This growth needs, for several reasons, to be measured; and thus teachers appraise the child.

Concepts have stability. New nations, as they are created, may develop as "new data" (economic tables, population figures, and so on), but the concept of nation remains. Within a child's schooling in the past generation, Africa exploded into nationhood. It can be argued that the "old facts" about Africa that were taught the child are no longer tenable, and no longer can serve the child, but the concept of nationhood still serves the child in his attempts to understand his culture and to live successfully in it.

Let us postulate a child entering the first grade and being subjected for the next eight or ten or twelve years to a "fact"-oriented, topic-centered course of social studies. At the current rate of creation and generation of knowledge, perhaps little that he or she learned will be sufficient merely as "fact" by the time of leaving school. The child's school life would, in a sense, have been "wasted." Let us postulate another child, one taking part in a curriculum based on concepts. Eight or ten or twelve years later, schooling behind, the data will still have changed: nations may have agreed on a uniform code for defining territorial waters; the United States may count fifty-four states; Canada might have become a less unified nation and become a commonwealth of provinces; the power of oil-producing countries to control the energy market may have been reduced; a new technology may be burgeoning so that we become less interested in "outer space" than in "inner space." Nevertheless, for the child emerging from schooling that is based on concepts, the terms "nation," "scarcity," "man," "interaction," "norms," "values," "family," "interdependence," "community," "environment," "time," "rules," "law," "role" will be conceptually his or hers, and they can be applied to a host of tactical details, however often they change or proliferate. The child can use these concepts to explain the creation of new nations, the new cycles of art and popular culture, the new modes of behavior he or she meets in certain groups. Concepts are the envelopes for "unplaced" objects and events. A concept enables us to know basic stimuli and standard responses in advance. Simply, the possession of the concept "heat" enables us to know in advance the searing effect of boiling water.

Concept-forming and the Duality
of the Mind

Because time is short, both in a person's lifetime and in the period of his schooling, we may ask which patterns of concepts and skills are worth the time that is given over to schooling. Surely the patterns of concepts and skills we call "language" are essential. Similarly, are not science and mathematics vitally important in our modern technology? Yet do we then need only scientists and engineers in our society? To ask the questions is to pose the answer: No.

Even a casual glance at a day in the life of *Homo faber* (technological man and woman) shows how much we depend on music, art, dance, drama, and graphic experience (whether TV, theater, museums, or libraries). Hobby or avocation is important, almost as important as the job. We recognize that hobbies are a way in which we, consciously but not harmfully, gain relief from our professional and perhaps even civic responsibilities. Does this mean that science, mathematics, and logic are the main uses of the mind, and that, conversely, esthetics are a lesser use? Recent researches on the function of the brain may clarify our reflection on these matters.

It is becoming ever clearer that in addition to their functions in perception, in interpreting, and in motor control, the right and left brains have certain specialized functions. The left brain, for example, is adept in processing verbal-linear modes. It seems to be the repository of learning capacity for language and mathematics. The right brain is specialized in the spatiovisual, holistic modes, and it would seem to function strongly in painting, sculpture, dance, and other skills that depend on nonverbal cognition. (Our description here of the duality of the mind refers to right-handed individuals. For left-handed individuals the situation is more complex.)

A representation of the brain with a dual function is expressed in the diagram on the opposite page (adapted from Joseph E. Bogen):

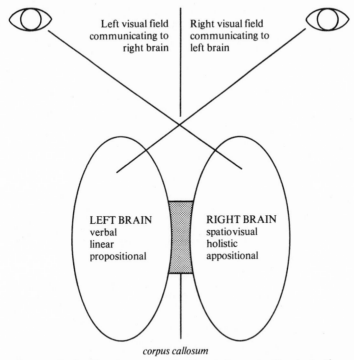

corpus callosum
(communicating fibers between cerebral hemispheres, the "two brains")

The neurosurgeon Joseph Bogen has been one of the pioneers in split-brain surgery. He notes, in the *UCLA Educator,* that "our schools are left-brained," which is to say that we prize and put a social premium on verbal-linear skills. Our standards are set for those who are proficient in these skills. But how can we measure *educationally* one kind of brain function against another? These questions intrude: Is the IQ a measure of only the left brain? Does it measure but one-half of our potential?

Michael Gazzaniga, whose split-brain research furthered our understanding of the dual function of the mind, in the same journal says:

Indeed, one of the intriguing possibilities deriving from split-brain research is the possibility that man can be explicitly specialized in a variety of aspects of mental life: superiority in the visual-spatial area—while the reverse may also hold true. If this proves correct, it may well follow that a particular child might be able to solve a problem using verbal symbols with greater ease than using visual-spatial ones, while another child might be better off solving the same problem using visual-spatial relations.

The motivational aspect of this observation, of course, cannot be over-emphasized. When a child's talents lie in visual-spatial relations and (s)he is being forced into a curriculum that emphasizes the verbal articulatory modes of solving a conceptual problem, this child will encounter enormous frustration and difficulty which may well result in hostility toward the teacher and worse, toward the learning process itself. If the teacher were to be made aware that the child is specialized in visual-spatial skills and the same conceptual problem is introduced, both the discouragement and the subsequent hostility might be avoided if the child is allowed to use his special talents. Conversely, the child with high verbal skills may quite frequently be unable to visualize the spatial aspect of an assigned task; in this case also, far better results could be obtained if (s)he is not forced into academic areas for which (s)he is not naturally equipped.

And Bogen comments: "Since education is effective only in so far as it affects the working of the brain, we can see that an elementary school program narrowly restricted to reading, writing, and arithmetic will educate mainly one hemisphere, leaving half of an individual's high-level potential unschooled."

We are accustomed to hear, these days, of the "culturally disadvantaged"—those persons whose propositional potential has remained underdeveloped for lack of relevant exposure. There is likely a parallel lack of appositional development in persons whose only education consists of the three R's. That is, just as the left-hemisphere potential for propositionizing may be underdeveloped, so, too, should we expect that right-hemisphere capacities can suffer neglect.

Merle Wittrock, emphasizing the need for spatiovisual as well as verbal-linear presentation, tells us, in the *UCLA Educator:*

At UCLA several experiments were conducted to determine if kinetic molecular theory could be taught to kindergarteners and primary-school children using pictures, concrete examples, and simple verbal text to introduce and explain the concepts of molecules in motion, states of matter, and changes in states of matter. Several hundred original colored drawings prepared by artists were used to represent molecules, gases, liquids, solids, evaporation, and condensation. After two to four weeks of instruction, two-thirds of the children in one study (Wittrock, 1963) successfully answered most of the questions about the comprehension and recall of the concepts. These concepts were previously thought to be too complicated for children below Piaget's symbolic (age eleven) or concrete (age seven) levels of intellectual development.

Perhaps in our urgent determination to secure scientists, technicians, mathematicians, lawyers, and teachers for our social progress, we have emphasized the verbal mode of learning and expression and have neglected the spatiovisual. We begin to suspect that many children may lead from the spatiovisual to the verbal, and that others may lead from the verbal-linear to the spatiovisual. Is it possible that for "failed" children an approach to teaching and learning that stresses the spatiovisual, the holistic, the patterning skills can be intelligently combined in instructed learning with the verbal-linear? Would such a combination "save" them from failure? Is idiosyncracy in learning, then, more than supposition? Indeed it is. To build a significant curriculum it is necessary to encompass the activity of both the linear-sequential and holistic modes of mind.

The implications of this work for a curriculum are significant. It is dangerous to assume, however, that one mode of learning, one modality, is more important than the other. To survive in the modern world, proficiency in the verbal modes is required. Granting that, the knowledges, skills, and values that are imbedded in the spatiovisual, holistic modes are also clearly essential in modern schooling and education. Furthermore, in the world of work they play a critical part. For example, spatiovisual, holistic modes characterize part of the enterprise of engineers, gardeners, pilots of airplanes and boats, gymnasts, football, soccer, and basketball players, surgeons, architects—the list is endless. The writer's art rests in good part on metaphor, and metaphor is a spatiovisual, holistic mode.

On Design of a Curriculum: Organization of Domains of Experience, in Balance

The world about us seems random, but the substance of scholarship is a search for the nonrandomization of events—that is, a search for nonrandom regular structures in the universe. This search, too, is the substance of curriculum. Such searches, the thrust of intellection, have for purposes of schooling concerned themselves with domains of experience, or "realms of meaning," as Phenix calls them. In stressing that *meaning* is not the sole property of *reason,* Phenix, in his book *The Realms of Meaning,* goes on to say in reference to the usage of the term "meaning": "This term is intended to express the full range of connotations of reason or mind. Thus there are different meanings contained in activities of organic adjustment, in perception, in artistic creation, in self-awareness, in purposive decision, in moral judgment, in the consciousness of time, and in the activity of worship. *All the distinctive human functions are varieties of meaning,* and all of them together—along with others that might be described—comprise the life of meaning, which is the essence of the life of man." (Italics added.)

It is reasonably clear that such meanings as we make our own are based on experience. Indeed, Einstein defined a science as a form of endeavor as "experience in search of meaning." Further, the meanings, rules, logics, principles, theories, hypotheses, explanations seem to be resolved—if they are ever clarified—in the systematic assertions, the orderings, the cognitive structures we know as concepts. In order to understand the conduct of an individual human life it is necessary to seek to understand the complex of meanings that individual accepts as precious. Not to press the point, students of human behavior, including the psychotherapist Viktor Frankel, insist that worthwhile human existence is found in the meanings that are at the basis of life and that the basic cause of "human deterioration" is loss of meaning. Erich Fromm ascribes destructiveness of the human personality to "meaninglessness," and Theodore Hesburgh asks us to consider our enemies to be meaninglessness, inhumanity, ignorance, and stupidity (meaning wanting in understanding). In fact, an individual's self-expression and conduct are clarified when ambiguities in meaning are clarified. What does he mean? What is meant by her act? These are questions that are prelude to perplexity, to uncertainty, and often to distress.

A curriculum appropriate to the life of individuals in a democracy is an antidote to meaninglessness. A curriculum establishes its faith in the possibility of making meanings clear; it serves understanding. A curriculum serves to clarify understanding of human nature and the nature of the world in which we live.

Our stress on Einstein's definition of science as "experience in search of meaning" was not a mere exercise in developing a relationship. Curriculums are indeed domains of experience, and the curriculum of a school or educational system comprises those domains of experience (courses, subjects, disciplines) that the school accepts as worthy of the individual and the culture. The curriculum is a systematic interpretation of the individual's search for fulfillment in society, and thus the specialists who develop the curriculum select those domains of experience—in search of meaning—that enable the young to fulfill their powers in the pursuit of excellence. The domains of experience fitted to competent utilization in a school or educational institution are reductions in complexity. For a domain of experience—a course, a discipline—cannot include all experiences if only because curriculum in a school is time-bound in inexorable hours, semesters, and years.

A curriculum, then, is predominantly a plan for instruction and not primarily a plan of instruction. It comprises a body of content and skills intended to be taught, and if the curriculum is responsibly prepared and is seriously considered as affecting significantly the life of the learner—as indeed it should—then it follows that the *responsibility for instruction in the significant elements of the curriculum is not discretionary.* A curriculum suggests sequences of development of understanding (cognitive structure), hence suggesting sequence in instruction. It is in these elements that curriculum and instruction are related, but the particular method of instruction involves matters other than consideration of curriculum, that is, structure and substance. To emphasize once again, a distinction between *what* is to be taught and *how* it is to be taught has value not only as an exercise in distinguishing content from method, but also in the emphasis that content is in its own right important. The sloppiness inherent in certain thrusts in instruction is that too often content is not considered important. Curiously, as we shall see, curriculum describes *competence* as compared and contrasted with *performance,* an outcome of effective instruction. This may have a certain relevance for competency testing. But this distinction, too often ignored, is more profitably discussed in the context of evaluation, if only to emphasize that although they are interrelated, they are different, and this will be done in Chapter 6.

Substance in Curriculum: Domains of Experience

Domains of experience each have a particular organization of concepts, values, and skills. Each has a style of presentation, of thinking. Painting has a different style, structure, and substance from music, and these in turn are different from the inherent substance, structure, and style of the sciences, the social sciences, and economics. Nevertheless, there is some agreement on the coherence of various disciplines, or domains of experience. Their coherence is based on the manner in which understanding in the domain is achieved. Phenix has made a contribution to definition of the curriculum by his penetrating analysis of these "realms of meaning":

Symbolics	Ethics	Synoptics
Empirics	Esthetics	Synoetics

Symbolics embraces spoken and written language and mathematics, in the domain of discursive symbols. But symbols are also nondiscursive, that is, holistic. For example, there is a vocabulary of signals, "body language," consisting of gestures and expressions, that we must master in order to read. Symbolics, then, is concerned with both discursive and nondiscursive areas.

Empirics consists essentially of those areas that involve inquiry of the type requiring evidence and experiment, the self-correction of confirmation by one's peers—in brief, verified knowledge, or evidence. Empirics embraces the physical sciences, biological sciences, psychology, and social sciences (note: not social studies).

Esthetics as a domain of experience is concerned with particular forms of expression, rather than with the general forms implied in the term "symbolics"—although symbols are indeed used in the area of esthetics. Not only are the forms of expression particular, but the execution is particular to an individual. For example, within esthetics are included literature, music, the visual arts, and the arts of movement, including dance, gymnastics, and the like. Without belaboring the point, work in these areas speaks for itself; it is not generalized; it relates to an individual, or to specific and special groups of individuals (say, Indian dance).

Ethics embraces the domain of morals. Simply, what is considered right and wrong, what one ought or ought not to do in relation to a system of conduct, is at the heart of the area of morals.

Synoptics derives from synopsis, implying the summative or integrating functions of knowledge. History, philosophy, and religion embody disciplines that seek "world views" in understanding, either by re-creating the past (history), by reinterpretation of understandings of the ways of human nature and the universe (philosophy), or, in religion, probing an individual's "ultimate concerns," to use Paul Tillich's phrase.

Synoetics is a domain concerned with personal knowledge. The other areas require certain elements of objectivity; synoetics, Phenix argues, requires subjectivity and insight. Personal knowledge is the goal, and, of course, personal relations are unique. It is in this way that synoetics is concerned with uniqueness, with interpersonal relations, including the varieties of love and affection. And possibly for this reason, synoetic aspects of the curriculum or the realms that address personal knowledge have been considered too hazardous for inclusion in the school curriculum. But personal knowledge—the varieties of love and affection, the realm of personhood—is eminently the concern of education. Synoetics also includes the realm of work, for without work an individual tends to lose character.

Note that if we consider schooling as presently organized, certain of these domains of experience (or realms of meaning), as part of the formal curriculum, are excluded. For example, synoetics generally. In synoptics, religion and philosophy are generally excluded. The nondiscursive elements of symbolics have little emphasis. Ethics, as we shall see, is part of a hidden agenda—that is, teachers often "approve" in nondiscursive ways the behavior they find acceptable. But ethics per se is not part of the formal curriculum in schooling. In emphasis, the entire area of esthetics (excluding athletics) is given less than 5% of curricular time. In other words, the domains of experience necessary to the education of the individual exceed those available (and even permissible) in the schooling of an individual. A schooling system does not—perhaps it cannot—achieve a balance in the treatment of the realms of knowledge and meaning. The reasons seem obvious: the limited time given to schooling, the immaturity of the young, the legal imperatives of church and state, the conflict of personal values and values of society, of personal and community desires and objectives. But an educational system *can* achieve a balance—and should.

The stability and balance of curricular practice require a careful consideration of the extent to which the schools can attend to the realms of meaning Phenix has delineated. What domains of experience within the realms of meaning lie within the responsibility of schooling? Which, within the large area of education? For example, schooling is concerned with symbolics; that is, with spoken and written language, with discursive symbols. But the nondiscursive (except in courses limited to "drama" and to a small number of students) is rarely given attention. Again by way of example, in the area of empirics, science is studied more or less extensively by all in the schools. But we have yet to see the greater number of students perform a true experiment, in the scientist's sense of a probe into the unknown, without the restriction of time that a curricular plan usually imposes. Moreover, true "experimentation," or the search for confirmable hypothesis, verified knowledge, in the social sciences is strictly limited. Are these, then, not to be within the domain of school experience? Or, for that matter, freshman and sophomore collegiate experience?

To take another example, the area of esthetics, excluding, perhaps, literature and poetry, but specifically referring to formal instruction in music, dance, drama, painting, and ceramics, is limited perhaps to less than 5% of the elementary- and secondary-school curriculum.

In the area of synoptics, although history is taught, philosophy and religion, however defined, are generally disregarded. A study of the relation of the individual to the universe—properly the study of philosophy —is not out of place. A study of religious beliefs in the variety of religions is not forbidden by constitutional imperative; only the teaching of one religion, exclusive of others, is under such constraint.

With regard to synoetics, that domain so earnestly the interest of the young (particularly the adolescent) is as yet given little consideration. Yet without a self-concept, without the personal knowledge so essential to development of the healthy personality, the integrative functions of knowledge, values, and skills lack a matrix. The young are concerned with understanding elements of truth, beauty, justice, love, and faith—as are we all. And they are concerned with being prepared to get and keep a job, and with advance in the skills of the career that is theirs.

Obstacles to the kind of stability we seek—that is, a state of dynamic equilibrium characteristic of an open society in which balance is sought in the areas of the mind (symbolics, empirics, synoptics, esthetics, ethics, and synoetics)—will continue to arise until an analysis of balance in the curriculum takes place. This is not to suggest that schools are to be "forced" to sample each. It is to suggest that a considerable number of curriculums in areas of knowledge, skills, and values devised for schooling ought to be available for study by the schools so that choice may be exercised. Stable offerings in the schools are hardly achievable if the curriculums are not available and sufficient time for mature consideration of choices is not a matter of conscious practice.

We may nevertheless, as a first approximation, define the "essentials" as embracing a curriculum representative of essential elements in the areas of the symbolic, synoptic, empirical, ethical, esthetic, and synoetic. The term "essential" is not a quibble, nor is it an elliptical bypass of the term "basic." What is basic, or essential, is not to be defined as the present prejudice of different individuals or groups. In the renewing of schooling and education, what is essential, or basic, and is therefore the property of schooling or education, or both, should come out of the mature deliberation of a society facing a turning point, as our society presently is. In the end, the dynamics of practice based on the best practice may well take hold. We have time for reflection and invention; the human is not about to disappear.

Obstacles to Effective Introduction
of Curriculum: Pendulation

It is useful to offer the reader some titles from the Table of Contents of *The Bulletin of the National Association of Secondary-School Principals* of April 1953, almost thirty years ago:

"How Can We Develop Better Reading Skills and Habits in Junior and Senior High School Students?" (Caspar C. Clark and Mrs. Z. L. Serriver)

"What Provisions Should be Made for an Instructional Program in Basic Skills for Youth in the Junior and Senior High School?" (William liam H. Dunn and O. I. Schmaelzle)

"How Can the School Program Contribute to a Better Appreciation and Acceptance of Moral and Spiritual Values?" (Everett B. Chaffe and Wilson H. Ivins)

"How Should We Provide for the Slow Learner?" (Varian M. Shea and Meriven A. Lewis)

"What Improvements Should be Made in Professional Standards for Principals?" (Harold R. Olson and Donald F. Stone)

"How Can We Recruit Better Candidates for Teaching?" (Lawrence V. Jordan and Ralph F. Evans)

"How Can the School Meet the 'Attacks' on Education?" (R. L. McConnel and Carl L. McDonald)

I have selected these at random, but a list of the topics would represent a list selected for a meeting in the 1980s. There was concern for the improvement of

citizenship education

conservation education

evaluation

audio-visual materials, including television

supervision

in-service education

training of teachers

In other words, problems of curriculum, instruction, evaluation, and administration—and "attacks on education."

Why do these continue to be the stable topics of meetings of school people? One reason is that they are areas constantly being improved. Another is that these might be said to be "problems," which are the energy behind the pendulum. But to my mind, the problems they pose are not codified in successive researches. This lack of codification of theory and practice in continuing research resulting in systematic assertions is an obstacle to the building of successful practice in schooling and education. In schooling, we do not follow the principles of scientific inquiry, attempting to codify what is known in theory—however unsatisfactory the theory for a given period—in the knowledge that theory directs thought and research. Research is by one definition the creation of generalizable knowledge, but there is little generalizable knowledge upon which schooling and education can build. To re-emphasize, it seems that one of the essentials of the renewing of schooling and education will be to formulate brief systematic assertions in the form of theory or hypothesis summarizing past achievements and, further, systematic assertions that will act as theory or models to direct thought and research.

Over the past thirty years, I have studied curriculum in its various aspects. I have spent much of my professional life in the development of curriculum for this country and for countries over the world. To assist in this work, of necessity I have searched for systematic assertions (theories and concepts) dealing with the nature of curriculum and coming out of the researches of scholars concerned with curriculum. I have studied more than 2,000 curriculums used in various schools and school systems. What I found, in essence, is a certain adherence to the concept of the "realms of meaning," but variously these "realms of meanings" are translated into

- curriculum areas (English, social studies, science, mathematics)
- courses of study (arithmetic, biology, economics, algebra)
- fields of study (foreign language, literature, conversation, political science)
- requirements for graduation (years of study in a given curricular area and a standard of achievement in the area)

While the potency of a brief systematic assertion—a theory, if you will, as a model to think with—in directing thought and practice is well understood, there is a notable lack of curriculum theory in a systematic assertion which limits its field of operation. There are, of course, many excellent studies and analyses of curriculum. These are, in effect, theories of schooling and education, and not curriculum per se. For example, as late as 1977 the Association for Supervision and Curriculum Development published its volume *Curriculum Theory,* edited by Molnar and Zahoric. It reviewed a variety of models, including the splendid models of Tyler, Taba, Goodlad—all highly respected workers in the field—among others. But it did not provide a systematic assertion of a theory of curriculum.

Possibly the reader will question the need in an essay of this nature to engage in discussions that may be considered overly specific. Nonetheless, the renewing of schooling and education will not proceed unless definitions of essential functions of schooling and education are clarified; and this requires formulation of theory which delimits a given field so that relevant examination and study are feasible. Otherwise schooling, for example, a microcosm, becomes as large as the macrocosm. Otherwise, curriculum, a relevant field within schooling and education, may become synonymous with both. As indeed it threatens to become—if it is not already larger than its scope.

Essentially, what is widely acceptable as curriculum theory is the substance of Ralph Tyler's model, expounded in his *Basic Principles of Curriculum and Instruction*. He emphasizes four basic questions:

1. What educational purposes should the school seek to attain?
2. What educational experiences can be provided that are likely to attain these purposes?
3. How can these educational experiences be effectively organized?
4. How can we determine whether these purposes are being attained?

Tyler believes that these questions "must be answered in developing any curriculum and plan of instruction." The model, taken generally from Tyler's work, and congruent with his questions is this:

1. Specifying of aims and objectives
2. Selection of content and learning experiences
3. Organization of learning experiences
4. Evaluation of attainment of objectives

John Goodlad would place greater emphasis on the "values" of curriculum workers. James McDonald, writing in *Confronting Curriculum Reform,* insists that questions such as "what is the good society, what is the good life, and what is a good person" are implicit in the curriculum question. Further, the "moral question" of how to relate to others or how best to live together is clearly a critical part of curriculum. As an aside it may be noted that he also states: "Curriculum as a field of inquiry, and curriculum theory in particular, have been said to be moribund."

I agree with Tyler's model, which embraces education (more than schooling) and perforce embodies instruction and evaluation as well. Certainly Goodlad's call for emphasis on "values," and McDonald's insistence on "moral questions" are central to the development of the individual through schooling and education. But it is not to quibble if I question whether these areas in schooling and education are to be assigned to the school curriculum solely.

Profound knowledge of what constitutes "the good society, the good life, the good person" is indeed the necessary qualification, among others, of curriculum workers, teachers, administrators, parents, Board of Education members, experts in tests and measurements, and, indeed, all citizens who live in an open society. I would argue that these are aims of schooling and education and constitute the major aims of the enterprise. Curriculum is a part of the whole but it is often discussed as if it were the whole of schooling, although Goodlad, Johnson, and McDonald, among others, would separate the consideration of instruction from that of curriculum building. Of course, they assert the interdependence of the two in the classroom.

A *specific* curriculum, or specific mode of instruction, or specific mode of evaluation should serve specific aims of schooling and education. The general overarching aims of education (which, of course, include schooling) are discussed in Chapter 7, and not as the aims of a specific curriculum per se. Specific curriculums would adopt and adapt certain of these aims—not all. The processes of developing aims of schooling and education and those of the aims of a curriculum are different aspects of the processes of schooling and education, and require different modes of scholarship and research in their statement, design, and eventual construction. In effect, a theory of curriculum is general and, like a general theory of instruction, should fit any country, any population, and *any* situation in schooling—a public function. The *aims* of schooling and education, however, should fit a *particular* society or culture. For example, curriculums in Iran, the Soviet Union, and the United States are different because the aims and objectives of schooling and education of the society and, if you will, the culture are different. However, the theory that directs the development of the *structure* of a curriculum per se could and should direct the work of curriculum makers in any society or culture.

Perhaps one reason curriculum as a field may be moribund is that curriculum, as a field, has often been loaded with the entire burden of the aims and objectives of schooling—not only the knowledges, values, and skills that are to become the repertory of student and teacher, but also the aims of schooling, its administration, its instruction and evaluation. In short, under these conditions, a clear definition of curriculum, and, therefore, theory is impossible. In the absence of a theory that states what constitutes a curriculum per se, theory-dependent observations of what functions a given curriculum does accomplish are difficult to make. If curriculum is equated with all of schooling, and/or all of education, the evaluation of a curriculum becomes difficult if not impossible. Specifically, evaluation becomes impossible because too many variables have been introduced—for example, those affecting social aims, aims of scholarship and inquiry within a given domain of experience, aims of administration, of instruction, of evaluation, each a different distinct field comprising the curriculum.

McDonald argues that "a specific failure or irresponsibility of curriculum developers is a failure to distinguish between curriculum and instruction, or if you wish to distinguish two distinct realms of relevant operations." So, too, Mauritz Johnson, in his *Intentionality in Education,* limits the responsibilities of the curriculum by considering it as consisting of a structured series of intended learning outcomes.

This view is also held by other workers (including John Goodlad and Harry Broudy) but not by, among others, Daniel and Laurel Tanner, who, in *Curriculum Development,* define curriculum (tentatively as they state) as "the planned and guided learning experiences and intended learning outcomes, formulated through the systematic reconstruction of knowledge and experience, under the auspices of the school, for the learner's continuous and willful growth in personal-social competence."

The definition is an excellent one—but it encompasses schooling and education, and is not limited to the field of curriculum. What we need first is a theory that explains *what happens* when a curriculum is developed, and not *what ought to happen.* We need to describe what *is* (based on observation) and not what *ought to be.* We may, of course, enthusiastically embrace the latter as all-important to the renewing of schooling and education.

Point Counterpoint: The Pervasive Forces of Style in Relation to Curriculum Theory and Practice

---

As it is commonly represented, curriculum is concerned mainly with *what* is to be taught; instruction, with *how* the curriculum is to be taught. But reformers of curriculum are not content to alter what is taught—that is, to introduce a new realm of meaning, a new domain of experience, or simply a "new" subject, or redirect its point of view. Generally, reformers of curriculum muddy the waters of logic and effectiveness of curriculum work by elaborating definitions of curriculum that are, in essence, theories of schooling or education and may variously include new styles in the management of the new curriculum, as well as new modes of instruction. In addition, there are sometimes newer modes of administration. These may be new styles in the administration of pupil placement; for example, pupils in the first three grades are no longer to be taught grade by grade, but in "suites" in which the three grades are taught together. Or self-pacing is introduced—that is, pupils may proceed at their own pace in "learning" the subject matters (the domains of experience) of the curriculum. Or there is a new style of presentation— that is, the subject matter is presented on TV or by machine-assisted instruction, or through individuation of instruction, which, to be honorable, requires not simply self-pacing, but diagnosis of abilities as well as the accommodation of the curriculum to the needs of individual learners. There is, however, an inherent dilemma in these necessary attempts to alter curriculum and at the same time to alter instruction and administration as they relate to the new curriculum.

The thrust of curricular movements almost always makes correction for application of particular elements of the culture—and not for a necessary balance in realms of meaning, which would reflect the culture entire. And this characteristic style of response by curricular movements to crises in schooling militates against, first, the full reflection of the culture by the school, and second, the uses of curricular method as an instrument of educational policy, rather than as a special instrument of schooling. In other words, a narrow modification of the curriculum in response to a particular crisis may upset the ecological educational balance characteristic of a healthy ecology of achievement. A useful analogy is this: a healthy forest is in ecological balance; a forest fire destroys this balance, killing vegetation and animals (birds, mammals, reptiles). To put out the fire is a first step; but then quickly to reintroduce only one element—say, the deer—may help the deer to flourish, but not for long. For the deer require a balance in plant growth. Similarly, to carry the analogy so far and no farther, to reintroduce the "basics" quickly and thoroughly impoverishes other aspects of schooling —namely, instruction in the sciences, in the kind of mathematics particular to the sciences, in the arts and crafts, in attention to the gifted, indeed, to the wide variety of abilities. It would be as inappropriate to turn the attention of the school to programs for the gifted, or to sciences and mathematics (as was done in the 1957–1967 curricular movement in "correction" to life-adjustment). When a balance in the domains of the culture represented in schooling or education is upset, it is the culture that may suffer. Application of curricular poultices is ineffective; balance is all. *The history of curricular reform is a history of redress of imbalance.*

The elements of pervasive strategies in the area of curriculum seem to be these five.

1. *A curriculum (as it is developed by curriculum workers) is composed of domains of experience present in the culture, and acceptable for purposes of schooling and/or education.*

Domains of experience comprise areas of intellection, of attitude, of feeling, of values, of skill—in short, experience—which the culture has developed and which individuals encompass in such studies as literature, poetry, science, painting, dance, social science, mathematics. Certainly these may be segmented into their components—the sciences into physics, chemistry, biology, geology—and these segmented in turn—physics into mechanics, optics, thermodynamics, solid-state physics; the social sciences into history, sociology, anthropology, economics. The segments can be general or particular. Domains of experience are, in effect, subsets of Phenix's six realms of meaning. These six realms embrace knowledge, attitudes, and skills that are characteristic and are an essential of modern life, not necessarily to, for example, the liberal, or the conservative, or the humanist, or the fundamentalist view, but to life entire. The realms of meaning are at once the elements of the kind of intellection, of values and attitudes, of feeling, of skills, one would like to see in the possession of an educated person.

Consideration of these realms as a base for the practical building of a curriculum might form a base, also, for substantial broad, general agreement. Consideration of a set of "givens" does not mean acceptance, but it does wonderfully concentrate discussion and the uses of time. In any event, Phenix's six realms are intimate to our culture. Their consideration should at least bring to the attention of curriculum builders the unnecessary pendulations in emphasis to which schools and public are subjected. For example, at one time or another public discussion whirls around these "oughts": there ought never to be a disregard of reading, numbering, language, in any period of life; in a techno-electronic society there ought never to be a disregard of the mathematics and science necessary to maintain a technologic society; in a "global village" there ought never to be disregard of a "foreign" language, or of a second language; in a society where life spans are constantly expanding, there ought never to be a disregard of the body, of health, of diet; and, put last for emphasis, in a society in which music, art, literature, poetry, dance, sport, and drama are the ingredients of the "good life," there ought never to be a disregard of the elements of our culture that stimulate the life of the emotions (or feelings), those elements that give the individual his or her self-concept.

Under whatever guise, serious consideration of *all* the realms of meaning will reduce pendulation and stimulate a dialogue on which to base a search for a broad, stable agreement. At least it will be a search for balance—a dynamic equilibrium, to be sure.

2. *Once the domains of experience are selected, compatible orders of concepts, values, and skills within the domains are selected.*

To exaggerate the case to make the point, it does not serve the uses of effective organization for instructed learning to group as compatible, within the domain of experience of, say, economics, such concepts as the atom, supply and demand, the nature of the poem, the legislative process. These concepts are, on the face of it, incompatible, even in a carelessly contrived conversation. The possible ineffectiveness of TV, where the sequence of presentation is at the mercy of the viewer, is a result of the mixing of incompatible orders of concepts, values, and skills. The TV dial is used to fit interest rather than sequential, disciplined, instructed learning. But it does serve to have in hand a library—a reserve, if you will—of concepts, past and present, and in development or in the process of invention, so that curriculum revision with regard to new demands is not cataclysmic or of crisis proportions. The purpose of such a library is not to impose stability; it is to serve the purposes of stable, purposive search and to minimize effort at reinvention of what exists, or what exists in a form ready for reference. In the postindustrial years, such a library, continuously replenished, might be the base for the "software" computers devour.

3. *It is almost self-evident that the ordering of the concepts, values, and skills within a curriculum is to be sequential and not random.*

Nonrandomized ordering, day by day, week by week, year by year, is necessary to a plan for instructed learning. Indeed, in a program of instructed learning the school imposes attention, connection, and pattern on the learner so that he or she may know in advance. In self-activated learning (a characteristic of education), which is not necessarily curricular in nature, the learner imposes on himself or herself attention, connection, and patterning. Thus, if the learner imposes a discipline on random experience, he or she weans from the random experience in life a nonrandom ordering resulting from reflection on experience. Essentially, such discipline comes out of increasing ability to order concepts, values, and skills and to utilize them in further experience.

4. *A curriculum used in an institution devoted to schooling serves instructed learning and not learning at random.*

Nonrandom ordering is not necessarily an ordering in logical sequence; it is a psychological and logical patterning in which a sound curriculum is achieved. That is, the concrete precedes the general and integrative, which are sequenced on the concrete, and the precedence and sequence follow each other in a "spiral" or "ladder" year by year. Concepts, values, and skills are thus seeded early, emphasized later (even in later years) at a given time, and reviewed in new contexts and applications contingent on the growth of the individual. Thus, a child may begin a "study" of rhythm with Patchen (essentially, clapping), later with the rhythm of a march, of drums, then of 4/4 notation, and so on. One begins a study of electricity by switching on a light; later one may examine a battery, then a circuit, then Ohm's law—almost certainly not the reverse. Piagetian sequences in the "logic of the child" are, to certain purposes, but not all, a useful guide. Piagetian sequences in instruction may not be useful, for example, in programs for gifted children.

5.   *To determine the effectiveness of a curriculum, one determines whether the instructed learning based on the curriculum is directed toward changing the behavior of individual learners.*

Aims should state clear-cut goals—aims, but not behavioral objectives. (Behavioral objectives constitute the language of instruction, not the curriculum.) Nevertheless, if a curriculum is developed in the area of reading, the aim can, and should, qualify the nature of the change of behavior; for example, improvement in skills of reading correlated with the aims of the curriculum. But these skills and the changes in behavior expected should be delineated as goals (not as discrete knowledges, or attitudes, or skills to be evaluated, because, again, these are the objectives of instruction).

What of values or attitudes? In my view, even casual examination will show that no curriculum is free of values, whether they be the values by way of example, of democracy, of trust, of justice, of patriotism, of thrift, of courtesy—the list is endless. But values are caught as well as taught; caught through the behavior of parents, teachers, members of society acting as models; taught directly through the content selected for study in the social studies, the sciences, literature, poetry, art, sports, music—again by way of example. Certainly a form of truth is taught in the empirical sciences; a form of justice in teaching the customs and laws of Western society.

However this may be, curriculums that deal directly and substantially with the values and attitudes that are, of necessity, part of an open society are difficult to find. My experience is that such curriculums are open to attack and indeed are subjected to it.

Values are transmitted, whether or not they are consciously a part of the elements of the curriculum. Values play a part in the stated curriculum—they are put in written form as policy—and in the hidden curriculum, the unstated behavior of the family, the school, the church, the media, and the community.

Let us now proceed to a systematic assertion of a theory of curriculum. A theory does not rest outside its environment or ecology; it rests within an ecology of achievement, in which certain elements, such as the following, are interconnected in a web (not a thread or line) of causation and correlation:

- The culture (a repository of realms of meaning and domains of experience)
- The school or educational institution (selecting the domains of experience fitting its objectives)
- Specialists in curriculum (students of the practical psychology of selecting and ordering concepts, values, and skills)
- Specialists in instruction (students of the modes of instructed learning)
- Teachers (masters of the art-science of instructed learning)
- Specialists in evaluation (students of the modes of evaluation that determine the effectiveness of instructed learning)
- The community (a cadre of individuals, physically outside the school but intimately connected with the institution of policy in the school)

In Chapter 4, I noted my failure to find a systematic assertion of a theory of instruction. A search for the systematic assertion of a theory of curriculum has also resulted in failure. So has Cuban's.

Our observations then of what *happens* as a curriculum is designed and fashioned in the various societies and cultures (therefore, an attempt at a factual rather than a normative theory) can be summed up as follows: *In the design of a curriculum, a reduction of complexity is imposed on domains of experience by reconciling compatible orders of concepts, values, and skills interpreted as essential to the development of learners in a given culture; in turn, nonrandom ordering is imposed on these compatible orders so as to increase the effectiveness of instructed learning described in aims directed at securing changes in behavior affecting individual learners.*

In effect, this statement describes what curriculum workers *do*, not what they ought to do.

None of the statements on curriculum theory readily accessible is in the form of a systematic assertion of the brevity a theory "in use" should assume. Theoretical models prominently in use treat, not only curriculum development, but also instruction, evaluation, and administration, and often specific philosophies of education. They confuse the strategy and tactics of one area with those of other areas. Therefore, present models of curriculum include, as McDonald asserts, different "distinct realms of relevant operations."

Perhaps of parallel importance is a distinction that needs to be made and is breached in practice. The kind of intellection and discipline that characterize curriculum workers is not necessarily that possessed by excellent teachers, excellent administrators, or excellent managers. Curriculum workers must see the work whole; theirs is a skill of the architect, a holistic skill in which detail is subdued by a vision of the whole. Theirs is also an ability to proceed in an indomitable manner to reduce the complexity of a huge domain of knowledge to accommodate the minds that will deal with it—that is, to envision congruently the field of knowledge and the child's development.

Curriculum workers proceed not only to lay out the sequence of a field in congruence with that development, but also to fix eyes unswervingly on the objectives of growth in instructed learning as well as those of child development. The effectiveness of the experienced curriculum worker is different from that of the experienced teacher, who must, for example, bring to bear qualities of immediate accommodation (that is, must accommodate emotion as well as intellection), and thus considerable flexibility, in dealing with varieties of response in the classroom. The attitudes and skills of the curriculum workers are different from those of the administrator, who must bring together people, places, and money in the interests of the smooth running of the complex of people who make the curriculum work—Board of Education members, parents, teachers, the young—all in the fixed architecture of the school. An analogy—always unsatisfactory—is the distinction between the finest of blueprints of a spaceship (the designer's work), the work of the engineers who will build the model, and the work of the artisans who will create a spaceship that will go into orbit and stay there. This is not to say, of course, that experienced curriculum workers may not, or should not, come out of the ranks of teachers, supervisors, administrators.

In the renewing of schooling and education, not only curriculum theory but also the meaning of theory needs wide and enthusiastic discussion. In our search for the pragmatic and the practical, the field of theory in schooling and education has been treated with considerable mildness, if not ignored. But theory is the most practical of all things, directing, as it does, what one thinks and how one thinks about it. Curriculums and theories of curriculum do not define what is good, but are concerned with the goods attainable through schooling.

A Certain Obduracy to Change

Plans for instruction, or changes in curriculum, seem to retain an obduracy to change. Or, if they do seem to change, the pendulation so characteristic of educational practice neutralizes the change. Cuban puts it this way:

At least one tentative statement can be made with a fair degree of confidence on curriculum reform penetrating classroom life: while substantive changes have occurred in what courses students take, the style and content of instructional materials and instructional ideology, there seems to have been stubborn continuity to what happened in classrooms over the last century that seems resistant to the intentions of those changes. This is not to crudely say that what happened in teachers' classrooms in 1870 is exactly the same as a century later; that is silly! It is to say that there seems to be a puzzling structural continuity between classrooms a century apart. It suggests a question: Why in an institution so vulnerable to social change do classrooms seem so invulnerable to decades of curriculum change?

As I see it, the "puzzling structural continuity between classrooms a century apart" is not due to a failure of innovation in curriculum, or instructional materials, or even instructional ideology (philosophy, to be sure). The innovations take hold and work in those cases where an ecology of achievement is established. Recall that ecology requires, first, a cohesion in the pervasive policy that orchestrates people (in the school and in the community), ideas (modes of curriculum and styles instruction), funds, and the management of people, as well as a focus on the places where these are brought together. Second, a close correspondence is required in the substance and structure of a curriculum, as a plan of instruction, with the modes of administration and instruction deemed necessary for the most effective instructed learning. Effective instructed learning implies systematic evaluation of management, of funding, of administration, of curriculum, of instruction—all these with constructive affection. Otherwise policy may not be pervasive; it may not even be, as has been suggested, honored.

Further, the introduction of a new curriculum usually requires corresponding changes in instruction and administration, as well as evaluation. To repeat, in another context, when a new curriculum is found to fail, it is usually because the correlative changes in instruction and administration have not kept pace. But remember that this is not to say that correlation means that changes in habits of instruction can be changed as quickly as the fashioning of the substance and structure of a curriculum. It is also probable that too often administrative procedures outstrip the institution of new instructional and curricular modes, causing unnecessary pressures on staff and pupils.

Much of the friction between innovation in curriculum and instruction seems to be the failure to define clearly the functions of each in schooling. This is partly, as has been noted, the result of a failure to develop theories that define and direct practice in each area. Remember that a useful theory nourishes stability in practice and reduces pendulation. However, generally speaking, instability and pendulation in curriculum are often the result of a failure to develop a policy in which the various factors operating in an ecology of achievement are patiently brought to bear on each other over sufficient time. It is well to repeat that the various aspects of a coordinated policy of instructed learning (philosophy, curriculum, instruction, evaluation, and administration) require different strategies and periods for successful introduction. As has been indicated, curriculum (as a body of knowledge) is most easily embraced; instruction (as a change in habituation in instructed learning) is most difficult, and takes considerably longer to encompass than does a body of knowledge. And a change in philosophy takes even longer.

Cuban's use of the term "curriculum" has reference also to the mode by which a curriculum is introduced into the classroom: through *instruction*. It is well to recall that a teacher's method and manner of instruction is the strongest of habituations. Thus the failure, even given appropriate innovative methodology, to apply the necessary energies (time and funds, patience and affection) to the modification of instruction so that teachers are enabled to change their own behavior, their own style, is a strong deterrent to educational innovation, particularly in curriculum. Teachers have pride in their ability and they do not lightly throw over their past, their beliefs in what should be taught (curriculum). However, their convictions on how the curriculum should be taught (styles of instruction), which up to the moment of its introduction have been found effective, remain invincibly obdurate.

This last paragraph is a response, in part at least, to Cuban's question Why in an institution so vulnerable to social change do classrooms seem so invulnerable to curriculum change? There are at least two reasons: the absence of a systematic assertion of curriculum theory, and the fact that a curriculum that does not call for a change in instructional mode is readily accepted, but a curriculum that requires a radical change in instructional mode, administration, and philosophy as well has rough going.

Is our culture, then, reflected in the schools? Culture is a way of life; it is not only representative of what people know, but what they do. What they do (overt as compared with covert behavior) comes not only out of knowledge and skills, but also out of the values that are prized. Thus Bruner's assumption that a curriculum is a compact delivery system of society should be modified to mean that it is a system acceptable to a given community's special interpretation of its own particular aims. And these in turn rest on the interpretation by an interested and active group (often a minority in number) of citizens within the community of the role of the school in keeping pace with innovation.

Schooling traditionally brings the "immature" to the point of a certain maturity called "graduation." Schooling, then, whatever a utopian view might envision, is at this point part of a restricted sequence in life and living—that related to a community's view of what is appropriate to the capacity of the gradually maturing minds of the students, and to its own view of the maturing of the community proper. Education, however, is as large as life, and lifelong, resting in individual choice, not necessarily influenced by the approval of the community—its majority vote, as it were. The curriculum of the school is characteristically the choice of the active members of the community interested in schooling, enlarged or limited by their view of purpose—that is, whether the community is concerned with schooling (a narrow sequence in years) or with education (a full sequence of a life span). In a real sense, a new curriculum may be introduced by an active minority of citizens within a community. This minority may or may not be in accord with the majority view of the aims of the school or the educational facility.

My observations over the past thirty years assure me that there *are* schools and school systems that have incorporated aspects of the innovations in curriculum and instruction that are, first, supported by valid research, and, second, have proved practicable within the conditions of schooling. These are the school systems for which the factors that comprise an ecology of achievement exist; this ecology I consider essential to advancement of curriculum and instruction. I consider to be inopportune statements of curriculum policy that embrace all schools and school systems, as if there were a single school or educational system in the United States. There is not.

Indeed, a renewing of American schooling and education which is in the making, may see the development of a schooling system within an *educational system* composed of a plurality of interests, as compared and contrasted with a *schooling system,* under a single governing entity.

With regard to curriculum, the following developments should be antecedent to the renewing of schooling and education. These may not occur in the sequence suggested, for the elements, suggested here in whatever sequence they occur, are part of one major interdependent thrust—an ecology, to be sure.

1. A recognition that it is no longer feasible to accept the kind of pendulation of curricular movements that oscillate attention to the needs of one population of learners, then to another, then back again. Pendulation is an obstacle to the forward movement of a society. So we have oscillated between attention to "intellection" and "attitudes," to the "gifted" and "disadvantaged," to "college" and "career (vocational)" preparation, to the "basics" and whatever it is we consider "not basic." We have the resources, in minds and money, to look at curriculum whole, as we should.

2. A recognition that an education fitted to a society considered among the foremost (if not *the* foremost) of those on the globe today can afford its young a balanced curriculum, balanced in its attention to the knowledges, skills, and values requisite to modern life and living in one of the most fortunate of social and political environments—namely, the United States. The balance is to be sought in the kinds of experience that can be made available to the young through fruitful plans for instruction: in a word, curriculum. The kind of balance we seek is a balance in the realms of meaning and domains of experience elucidated in this chapter. Imbalance in curriculum is an obstacle to the growth of the young, who need to see the world whole.

3. While it is singularly important to avail all young of equal access to balanced curricular offerings, it is no longer fruitful to consider that all can traverse periods and areas of personal development or somewhat similar areas of knowledge, skills, and values at the same rate. There are various swaths of excellence; not all can excel in all undertakings. Thus we may acknowledge difference in the rate of achievement without confusing it necessarily with defects in intelligence. To ask all learners to advance in the acquisition of knowledge at the same rate is to create an obstacle for those who are slower or more deliberate learners, or those who are gifted in a given domain of experience.

4. Schooling being what it is (not only development but also preparation for further development), attention to all modes of learning (modalities, to be sure) is provident without assuming that one modality is superior to another. However, the world as it is con-

ceived is a whole; the effort in curricular development should aim at seeing wholes, not parts, the latter being encompassed within the whole. To create a curriculum not based on wholes is to impose a view of parts; and such a view is an obstacle to a world view.

5. Experience in schooling and education (both), being a preparation for participation in both interdependence and independence within society, should concern itself with the knowledges, skills, and attitudes (values, if you will) that fit one for participation in society both as an individual and for contribution to the group. We should not set aside the fact that prudent, social behavior is the cement of a society. Curriculum is concerned not only with intellectual achievement, but also with physical, esthetic, and ethical constraints. The "basics" are thus embedded in the development of knowledges and skills required to attain and hold a job and also in the conduct that attains and holds respect. We are required to accommodate self-expression and conduct both, and these are marks of the educated. To teach a body of knowledge and impose values not explicitly a part of the curriculum is to impose a "hidden curriculum"—values that are dissonant with those intended by those responsible for schooling. An educational system, as compared and contrasted with a schooling system, permits an examination and a clarification of values that are not always appropriate to the school.

6. The transformation of one aspect of schooling occurs not by wishing it to be so, but by attending, as has been indicated, to what is to be taught—namely, curriculum. But attending to changes in curriculum without attending to change in instruction, evaluation, and the administration required to make them effective results precisely in the kind of failures of curricular innovation noted by a great number of observers, among them Goodlad, Cuban, and Silberman. While the development of the substance and structure of a curriculum and the modes of instruction and evaluation that are congruent to it is essential, it is an error in intellection and logic to ask teachers to become expert in both a new curriculum and a new mode of instruction simultaneously—a considerable error in administrative practice. As indicated, of necessity but doubtlessly ad nauseum, this error in practice has indeed been one of the major reasons innovations in curriculum and instruction have foundered. They are two hands on the same body, and one knows what confusion can occur if one does not distinguish, first, between right and left hands, and, second, between their usage in a common collaborative function.

The nub of it is that teaching is a performing art based on the art-science of the psychologies of human development, curriculum, instruction, and evaluation. Too often it is not so considered. A painter does not change a successful style easily, if ever; a musician is characterized by performance; a writer is known by his or her style. The successful performance in teaching has a noble end: growth in learning and growth in personality leading to a balanced maturity in the young. A teacher engaged in the constant endeavor to change behavior of the young perforce changes as well year by year.

Teaching is its own cause and effect; it enhances the lives of teacher and pupil—and parent—and eventually the community. We reduce the rewards of teaching (and these are not, in the main, financial) at our peril. Teachers value themselves as we value them. So do the young.

6. Regarding Evaluation

A Necessary Prologue

Most of us feel uneasy when we are tested or measured against a standard. The young in our schools feel this no less than their parents.

This chapter, too, is devoted to seeking a balance in practice to secure a measure of the plurality of a pupil's abilities and aptitudes. The balance is not sought through the sole use of tests. The art-science of testing is not at its zenith, but then, neither are the arts of curriculum, instruction, and administration. Instead, the balance is sought through the use of the full range of valid tests available and balanced against a mode of instruction reflected in the maturity-independence model described in Chapter 4. Through this type of instruction, what is appropriately a test of achievement through work can be sought.

I posit, in short, that a form of curriculum and instruction centered in work that demands satisfactory achievement (competence and performance both) is prelude to satisfactory performance on achievement tests. One may test to determine levels of achievement and performance and thus discover the level of an individual's competence or incompetence, advantage or disadvantage but, in the end, the purpose of schooling is to ameliorate disadvantage and make provision for growth in excellence in those knowledges, values, and skills an open society prizes.

What of IQ? Perhaps at this point it is best to note that it is discussed, but that it is precarious to discuss so tendentious an area within the brief scope of a prologue. Suffice it to say that the American mode is "fairness," and fairness in testing is being and will be pursued.

We know these things: all of us learn; we learn in different ways;

we learn at different rates; we learn both common and different things. So do the young. All of us prosper when we receive careful and constructive attention to our gifts, our opportunities, and our destinations. So do the young. In work and in activities outside of work we are constantly being tested. So are the young. What we seek always are fair tests. What we seek for the young are tests that will enable us to determine whether they are learning in accord with their capacities, in accord with their opportunities, in accord with their destinations, in accord with the principles of equality and equity of opportunity.

In attempting to develop devices of continuous and fair evaluation, we have set ourselves a large task, but it is only one of the great tasks we have undertaken and will be required to improve in the coming transformation of schooling. If we can muster the resources of the nation to meet the requirements of its needs for energy, if we can, and will, muster our energies to enter the postindustrial era, we must also muster our thinking to consider the requirements of our major resource: the young who will maintain, sustain, and invent new elements of our culture. Let us turn, then, to the questions of evaluation of "success" and the obstacles to evaluation of "success in school."

On Assessing Achievement
in Schooling

In a way, each of us is constantly being compared to others. That is, we are being measured against some standard. Sometimes the measurement is a casual appraisal, as happens when we meet a stranger; at other times it is calculated but nevertheless informal, as in an interview; at still other times it is formal, as in a written or practical test. A practical test seems fair: it assesses our performance in a way definitely related to the thing to be achieved—a driving test for the driver-to-be, a typing test for the typist-to-be, a test in programing a computer, in welding a seam. Generally, one does not quarrel with a practical test. A practical test predicts the probable achievement of an individual on the job or one applying for a job. Of course, once on the job other factors may enter into the conditions necessary to keep the job—small factors of punctuality, large factors of personality, of ability to get on with others, and so on.

As Western society became increasingly industrialized, it became increasingly necessary to develop sources of manpower for industry (mechanized manufacturing and mechanized agribusiness). History is clear on this point: home and school furnished the manpower necessary. Simplistically, home and society furnished predictable personnel (an incredibly impersonal and unappealing term) for factory, farm, and office. Personnel consisted of people (not machines) with the basic skills—the skills to read, write, and number—to help make the United States the paragon of industrial power, the giant of technology. Training for a specific job was, in effect, done on the job. Though the schools took on the tasks of industrial and agricultural education, soon corporate industrial society and the unions surpassed them in technical education and took to themselves the tasks of training workers.

The demand for manpower required indices to measure the adaptation of the child to schooling—that is, to the special kind of excellence to be required of him or her. And measurements of the child's success in school and, curiously, predictions of success in the environment we know as society seemed to be codified in achievement tests.

The meaning of the term "environment" needs to be extended. It does not suffice to say that environment means all that is around us—air, water, light, heat, fumes, houses, automobiles, people, animals, plants, and the like. The environment *within* us is all-important. Breathe in carbon monoxide from the exhaust of an automobile or sulfur dioxide from the smokestack (an exhaust, indeed) of a manufacturing plant and these gases become part of the environment of our cells, as does unpolluted fresh air. Noxious gases limit the function of our cells. Drugs, too, whether beneficent or harmful, food, air, and water we take in become part of our internal environment. Modern men and women are now generally considered to have Strontium-90 in their bones, DDT in their fat, mercury in their nerves, asbestos in their lungs, carbon monoxide in their blood, Iodine-131 in their thyroid. In older times, bacteria lurked in the environment and played their part in the deterioration of bodies; today, it is the physical and chemical deteriorators that play a crucial part. Ipso facto, this is not to say that today's environment is worse than that of the 1840s. The average life span in the 1840s was some forty years; nowadays insurance companies will bet on a life span of seventy-two years or more.* In the past thirty years, many childhood diseases have been eliminated, though mainly for those individuals who by accident are born in the Western world. In the underdeveloped countries (or less-developed countries) the average life span still hovers around a murderous thirty-five to forty years.

---

* The "average life span" is, of course, a measure of those surviving diseases. The actual life span has not yet been determined; some specialists in geriatrics estimate it to be over 100 years.

Environment, then, comprises all the factors (people and things) that affect the functioning of our bodies; it includes all the microscopic molecules outside the body and within the body. The strand of DNA, packed into the microscopic nucleus of each cell making up our genes is itself a complex of molecules. A boy or girl may have considerable capacity and ability, but a drug habit will reduce this capacity and ability in the practical evaluation that school and society make: the completion of work. It is not that the young under the influence of drugs lose intelligence; they lose desire, energy, or motivation to complete a task.

Genes, or complexes of that life chemical DNA (chemical shorthand for Deoxyribonucleic acid), are the root substances of our existence. Some say that what we are is in our DNA. The great majority of geneticists agree that, generally, the interaction of DNA with a specific environment makes us what we are. It seems now as if we can alter DNA a bit, and the environment a lot.

What is not in the mind (the environment of the intellect) is certainly not in one's intellectual capacity or in one's attitude, that is, behavior. This, generally speaking, is true, even though all "truth" composed by the mind is generalization. We are born, normally, with the capacity to breathe, to make blood circulate, to excrete—that is, with the capacity to record the environment. In other words, the child has inborn capacities—reflex actions such as heartbeat, swallowing, blinking, and the ability to see, hear, smell, tell by touch. The seven openings to the environment bring in the stimulus of a flood of things, of ideas, of people and their personality, of new tasks and new ideas. The "whole" child soon interprets their meaning. Simplistically, it requires a certain amount of "intelligence," of intellection, if you will, to interpret the stimuli that assault us, particularly those given in word or number.

On Measures of Achievement:
Tests and Self-Tests

Few disagree that it is important to assess the abilities of pupils. At least we can then determine how best to serve them.

A common type of test of scholastic aptitude—that is, a test that "predicts" learning capacity—is one commonly called an "intelligence test." This is an unfortunate name. How much mischief would have been avoided, or undone, if these intelligence tests had been named "tests of general scholastic aptitude," as Cronbach suggests! It is true that intelligence tests reasonably predict a child's aptitude in tasks central to our present modes of schooling, to our present curriculums and their modes of instruction. Their use in assisting the growth of a child has been documented. It is their use in assessing a child's gifts and destiny that is in question. Nevertheless, it is conceivable to use the intelligence test as a test of general scholastic aptitude. In the elementary school, for example, a teacher might use the test *initially* to establish reasonable goals for pupils in subject matters appropriate to the elementary school.

Let us for the moment consider intelligence tests as useful for appraising a child's present, or current, readiness to cope with the tasks imposed by the school. The tests are generally verbal and numerical in character; they are centered in linear-sequential, mainly verbal and numerical, subject matters, as is the learning environment of the school. The tests, then, may well be prognostic of success in verbal and numerical ability—for example, in reading, spelling, and arithmetic.

Yet the notion of intelligence tests is an obstacle to the notion of the need for continuous evaluation: the need to determine whether a child is working to full potential and thus to determine how instruction may be modified to be of greatest help to the individual. Consider first the use of achievement tests in reading, arithmetic, spelling, and the like. Few people object to measuring the level of attainment of a pupil in English or Spanish, in reading ability, in arithmetic, in history, or in science. If the acquisition of these knowledges and whatever skills are necessary to attain them is accepted as a goal of schooling, it seems sensible to determine where the child stands at a given point in his or her schooling. Then a teacher may plan modes of instructed learning to increase the child's repertory of knowledge and skills in the area measured. Focusing for a moment on the general theory of instruction discussed in Chapter 4, we will remember that if a teacher's instructed learning cannot elicit a response from a given pupil, it may well be that the child's prior background (for background, read environment) has not given him or her the oportunities desired, or the teacher's instruction may be at too difficult a level, or range. On the other hand, if the child's response is readily and easily given—that is, the child has had a rich *educational* background—then that particular instruction at that time may be a waste of time. The advantages or disadvantages a child brings to a given task of learning need to be assessed, and that assessment is the proper goal of achievement tests.

It is essential that the interpretation of scores or performance of any particular test taken on any particular day should not be used to generalize about the genetic base ("natural endowment" or "innate ability") of the child or his or her potential success in society past the period of schooling. There is sufficient evidence that economic success is not necessarily related to "success" on achievement tests. An inference warranted by an achievement test is simply this: a child scoring in the upper percentiles of, say, an achievement test in arithmetic will tend to do better in the kind of arithmetic that is the subject matter of the test than a child scoring in the lower percentiles. Achievement tests can and do assist the teacher in developing programs of instructed learning (curriculums) and modes of instructed learning (instruction) appropriate to the child's present level of achievement as shown by the achievement tests. When we adopt a mode of continuous evaluation—similar, perhaps, to the maturity-independence model of instruction discussed in Chapter 4—we will be assured that achievement tests, although necessary, are not the only tools of evaluation.

Standardized achievement tests are developed by trial on children in the schools of the nation. If the test is properly constructed, the population on which the achievement test is itself tested for validity will comport itself in accordance with that group's present achievement in school. Those who are doing well in school will do well on the test sample of the achievement test. Those who are not doing well in the established programs of instruction (curriculum) and with the modes of instruction (instructed learning) in the school will not do well. That is, the test is a norm-referenced test. If a random sample of the population (which would include learners at all levels of achievement) takes the test, the scores will range along a bell-shaped curve. The characteristics of such a curve are that there will be some scores at the bottom and some at the top, but most will be in the middle. A test, and, as a matter of fact, a test item, will be discarded if *all* the pupils taking the test scored at the top or at the bottom or in the middle. The tests afford us rankings of any group of children, at any grade level, at any age. They tell us who may do well at that grade, at that age. They do not tell us how the child will do as an adult, or how much he or she really knows.

A Measure Misunderstood

It is well to recall that, essentially, modern intelligence tests measure capabilities as found and defined by modern schooling—that is to say, in curriculum and instruction. In other words, modern intelligence tests measure the capacities that schools emphasize, and IQ is thus a factor that predicts success in most modern schools. IQ, as a score, is in this way a predictor of what the community now wants the schools to do: instruct children in the knowledges (concepts) and values and skills mostly in the linear-verbal mode. The IQ test is, then, mainly a measure of knowledge secured by linear-verbal ordered sequencing, now thought by some to be a postulated quality of left hemisphere brain activity (in right-handed people, however). The score is not balanced by a test of the knowledge in the domain of simultaneous processing in the arts—in dance, music, or painting, for example—the postulated dominant quality of the right hemisphere.

IQ tests do not necessarily measure the quality labeled "intuition" and the ability to invent "new ideas" and generate "new knowledge"— traits of the creative. E. Paul Torrance reports, in *Guiding Creative Talent,* that in most of the groups he studied in certain schools, "almost 70% of the most creatives [*sic*] would have been eliminated if a 'gifted' group was being selected on the basis of the intelligence test or Miller Analogies" [another type of test of cognitive abilities]. J. W. Getzels and P. W. Jackson have confirmed this by similar findings. And, using a method of self-selection, I have found that gifted (synonym: highly creative) students who later became productive scientists were also to be found among students with IQs below 130, the usual cutoff point for selection of students for "gifted/talented" programs in a good number of school systems in the United States. This is not to deny the fact, as L. M. Terman and M. H. Oden found among more than 1,500 young selected on the basis of high IQ (top 1% of the population), that a good number achieve in a manner expected of gifted individuals. The IQ test does seem to measure certain aspects of ability that yield good achievement in later life—given a decent early schooling and education (that is, family and neighborhood), luck, health, and opportunity.

Whatever the assumptions underlying the interpretations of the IQ test as a measure of intelligence, the assumptions most likely to assure bitter controversy are these:

• Differences in IQ determine how well different individuals are likely to do in school

• Differences in IQ in different individuals determine the likelihood of economic success

• IQ, in a quantity not yet assessed, is genetically determined—that is, it is "unchangeable"

Present evidence concerning the inheritance of intelligence shows that the factor "intelligence" is complexly multifactorial—that is, a host of genetic and environmental factors are involved. Although the IQ test does generally predict performance in the range of activities required of a child in present school programs, it does not necessarily tell us of a child's prospects as an adult. Samuel Bowles and Herbert Gintis, among others, have shown that social class (social status at birth) and amount of education play a far greater role than IQ in explaining adult economic success. Their data demonstrate that persons with IQ scores in the 90th percentile (top 10%) are only 1.5 times as likely to place in the 90th percentile in job status and wealth as compared with persons whose IQ scores are in the lowest 10%. Put another way, social status and amount of education (*not* only schooling) are factors more useful than IQ in predicting economic success.

Recall Lee Cronbach has suggested that the IQ test be called a test of "general scholastic aptitude." Indeed, such tests as those designed to determine intelligence quotients are measures of what the community prizes at present: success in school, intellectual achievement, and achievement in cognitive skills, to be sure. Recall that the school is precisely an environment designed to ameliorate past environments, as well as one in which instructed learning hastens the acquisition of knowledge and skills. Still, were the efficacy of the IQ test demonstrated to be infallible and unchangeable, I believe that, our society being what it is, equality and equity of opportunity designed to hasten equality of educational achievement would still be prized, and sought, in our schools in an effort to overturn any index of inequality.

Creativity (inventiveness, innovation, intuition, originality) may, it is now thought, well reside in a combined activity of simultaneous processing (so-called right-brain activity) and linear-verbal processing (so-called left-brain activity). We must therefore consider the schools' overwhelming, inexorable need for developing a curriculum and mode of instruction aimed at developing the abilities and aptitudes of the whole person—that is, the human as both ordered sequencer and simultaneous processor; the human able to see whole and be whole. Although there are some decent tests of predominantly right-brained activity (tests of spatiovisual and musical ability), these tests are rarely used for all individuals. In sum, what we have is a decent test of an individual's ability (mainly verbal and numerical ability) but hardly one of "total intelligence." It is nonetheless true that some items testing a capacity for wordless spatiovisual abilities are included in the tests.

It is probably true that tests purporting to test a child's "intelligence" at six months of age have little relationship to that person's IQ at age eighteen. On the other hand, IQ tests given between the ages of five and seven predict reasonably well the IQ at age eighteen, although there is some 20% variance. Further, IQ tests given in the preadolescent period (ages eleven, twelve, thirteen) predict with an even higher degree of accuracy the IQ at age eighteen. In other words, there is relatively high constancy of IQ between the ages of twelve (sixth grade) and eighteen (at graduation from high school). Thus IQ tests given just at elementary-school leaving age predict IQ scores obtained at age eighteen. This is significant. It is to say that once a child achieves a certain degree of success in the activities central to the school, his or her scores on tests whose items are derived from the contents of knowledge, values, and skills characteristic of schooling are predictive of success in further schooling. IQ tests given at age twelve also predict with a high degree of dependability success in academic areas in high school and college. As Erness and Nathan Brody put it:

On theoretical and on logical grounds it is unattractive to assume that the intelligence is constant during the growth period. That is, the structure of intellectual abilities is probably different at different ages. An individual may develop new ways of attacking problems and new intellectual strategies as he becomes older. These lead to qualitative changes in intelligence as a function of age. Note that we do not measure intelligence at different ages with the same items. In this respect, intelligence is not like height, which can invariably be measured by the same procedure and invariably refers to the same thing.

For this and other reasons, but mainly the inconstancy of IQ in the early and elementary years (ages one to ten), evaluation in the elementary years should be based not only on achievement tests, but also on a practical test: the direct observation of the child's work taking place in an excellent school environment, an environment of excellence in curriculum, instruction, and evaluation. Direct observation could and should be based on a continuous evaluation of a child's work in instructed learning through devices similar perhaps to the maturing-independence unit mentioned in Chapter 4. This is not to exclude the advisory function of achievement and aptitude tests, which will and should be given as a matter of practice, but it is to make the child's work per se central to an assessment of achievement.

It is not necessary to defend achievement testing. Achievement tests properly used furnish useful information. It is to say that there appears to be a "closed" circle of curriculum, instruction, and testing. The last tests the former, and the former two prepare for the last. In other words, through the use of instruction by a device such as the maturing-independence model (or something similar), we may conceivably measure the "plurality of human mental abilities," particularly those abilities that critics of intelligence tests indicate are not part of the repertory of the tests.

Sheldon White, a psychologist with a considerable interest in early childhood education, observes that it is "simply not true that society rests on one order of human excellence, or that schools should be in the business of promoting one kind of excellence." Nonetheless, certain of White's additional points require attention here, especially on the need for plural tests of human mental abilities.

Considering all the problems with intelligence testing, it is tempting to argue that we ought to throw the tests out as illogical and mischievous. It seems possible to do that. The Soviet Union officially banned all intelligence testing in 1936, and, so far as I know, it has gotten along without it ever since. But we might have problems doing that. Intelligence tests moved into usage because of difficult and real problems that bureaucracies had in their basic business of categorizing people. Suppose we were to throw out the tests and put the decisions they serve entirely in the hands of human judgment and estimation? What problems would arise from human bias, carelessness, and incompetence? How intense and how hurtful would be the problems of conscience and politics that afflict the decision maker who holds the power to help or hurt a child by choosing whether the child will go to a special class, receive extra remedial help, or qualify for higher education or a job? These are the problems now eased by the science-plus-magic of intelligence testing. The problems attendant on categorizing people are endemic in bureaucracies. On the one hand, we have national commissions deploring and viewing with alarm the problems of labeling children; and on the other hand, we have commissions calling for more widespread diagnosis of early handicaps (as though we could find true positives without false positives, or as though we could diagnose without labeling).

I believe we must imagine that the reform of intelligence testing can be accomplished by the widespread adoption of plural tests of human mental abilities. Those giving mental tests have for some time recognized that human test performance tends not to be uniform but, in part at least, seems to be broken up, so that clusters of items tend to go upward and downward together in groups, setting themselves apart as incorrelating entities. This kind of observation has brought forth various proposals that a plurality of human mental abilities exist—such things as verbal ability, spatial ability, reasoning, numerical ability, idea fluency, mechanical knowledge and skill, and so forth. Some relief might come from this body of pluralized mental testing.

But, as White suggests, different students of measurement and testing do not agree on the number and kinds of diverse abilities a human repertory includes. For this and other reasons not necessary for this argument, let us move forward with the notion of *work* as an additional, but highly equitable, measure of ability—not just one piece of work, but work over the years of elementary schooling (eight years). Of course, this is not a new point of view. The apprentice methods utilized by the guilds of medieval Europe were based on assessments of an individual's work. Effective modern unions include a schedule by which apprentices achieve skills through units of work designed by a master artisan. The mode of instruction in the arts, whether cultural or industrial, has been based on a maturing-independence approach. In various sports, those who achieve the kind of competence necessary to make the team are those who have been adjudged best in their *work,* achieving competence in certain concepts, values, and skills. Most teams have a second squad or bench which is not up to the level of the first; but the judgment is also based on work done. Clearly, assessment of work done is the criterion in the arts and in athletics by which a student is advanced. Thus a freshman can play on the same team with seniors. In short, in the arts and athletics, administration of curriculum and instruction is devised around a maturing-independence approach in which a pupil is indeed judged on the basis of work completed.

We must consider a kind of self-assessment as well as assessment by a teacher from observing the continuing and developing work of the child. This, added to the inventory of devices that assess children on the basis of prior history (say, intelligence and achievement tests), would offer a more complete assessment of the plurality of abilities a child possesses. The maturing-independence unit offers, in a sense, an assessment of developing aptitude compared and contrasted with developed aptitude, which is measured by aptitude and achievement tests. It offers opportunity to identify and approve learning based on a plurality of abilities.

Clearly students and teachers alike are each an exception to the "norms" of society and of "biology." Studies ranging from biology to sociology show that each of us is quite complex, an indescribable amalgam of factors. Each person's genetic lineage is enough to distinguish him or her from all others. Yet the situation is still more complex: at birth an individual biological entity enters a particular home, in a particular area, and enters one major socialization process—societal, economic, political, religious—and is, generally, fixed in one language group.

The accidents of life, too, determine our nature. No two people encounter the same set of experiences, social opportunities, and obstacles.

If the Chevrolet automobile company can announce its ability to assemble more than 4 billion cars, each one unique, each one a shade different from the next, then what of the almost infinite variety of the human species?

We teach unique individuals. But at present we tend to teach them in groups, that is, in classes. We are forced—even as we believe that each individual is of moral worth—to teach the individual within the group. And too often the individual is lost in a larger statistic. So the burden of learning, in a real sense, is placed on the group. Teachers tend to be bound by the pace of the group. In accepting maturing-independence units as a useful approach, we would place the burden of learning on the individual. In such a situation, teachers would be bound by the progress of individuals and the assessment of progress on individual work. The normal curve of distribution would not hide individual achievement. Naturally, in teaching individuals a teacher requires the monitoring assistance of paraprofessionals, but this is not onerous or, even in the short run, expensive.

To repeat, no two people learn in exactly the same manner. Moreover, no single person learns, remembers, or expresses in one mode all the time. People differ from each other in personality, in capacity to attend and to retain, and in cognitive preference. A person may well change as his or her career develops, and may even alter markedly throughout one day, as his or her biological rhythms merge and go out of phase. So we are different waking, working, resting, playing, sleeping. We are different in our learning capacity. And this difference should be accommodated in the next transformation of our schools.

On a Certain Controversy in Evaluation

Arthur Jensen titles a paper in the *Harvard Educational Review* "How Much Can We Boost IQ and Scholastic Achievement?" His answer is: "Not much." The reason he suggests is that IQ differences are, in the main, inherited. On the other hand, Richard Lewontin, in an article in *The Sciences,* states bluntly, and so would most biologists, that "it is totally incorrect to equate terms such as 'inherited' or 'genetic' with a term such as 'unchangeable.' " It is indeed possible to change scholastic achievement by the utilization of different modes of instruction (for example, the maturing-independence unit). It will not be known until different modes of instruction, as well as improved programs of instruction, have been instituted in proper experimental procedures over a durable period. Lewontin goes on to point out the fallacy. In summary:

Certain inherited disorders can be treated and corrected as easily (or with as much difficulty) as those arising from environmental difficulties and accidents, before and after birth. For example, Wilson's disease is characterized by early death due to the steady degeneration of nervous and other tissues. This disease is hereditary; the genes that are responsible cause the sufferer to retain too much copper in the body. But a simple drug removes the copper from the body, and the degeneration is prevented. There are numerous other instances to set aside the notion that *heredity* means *unchangeable*. The factors for height are inherited, but a felicitous environment (good food, good living conditions) does increase height. Witness the Nisei and Isei. Increasing or reducing one's weight is possible. It is also possible to increase IQ scores, although not extensively. As our expertness in dealing with DNA proceeds, we may be able to "change" various aspects of heredity.

It is worthwhile to quote Lewontin on an important matter of experimental technique:

The study of genetics is the study of relatives. If genes influence a trait, then closer relatives should resemble each other, on the average, more than distant relatives. This study of relatives presents no problem in experimental organisms, where related individuals can be placed randomly in different environments. In the human species, the problem is to distinguish similarities that arise from environmental correlations, since close relatives tend to share environments as well as genes. Any estimate of heritability will then be upwardly biased by an unknown amount, unless the relatives being compared have been randomized across environments. That is, we must place children of the same biological parents with adopting parents who will represent a random sample of the population with respect to various socioeconomic variables that might influence intelligence.

Despite this elementary consideration, the first lesson in any course in biometrical genetics, the great bulk of estimates of heritability of IQ come from a comparison of relatives raised together in the same family. Thus, these estimates are completely useless. Although this kind of error is so elementary that no student in an animal breeding course could make it without being called to account, behavioral geneticists continue to publish such estimates of heritability in the leading journals of their field with the approval of the editors and referees who are their colleagues.

But gross experimental errors are only a part of the story. Realizing the importance of adoption studies, those who have attempted to estimate heritability of IQ from published studies of identical twins raised apart and together have relied heavily on four such studies. The largest of the four studies comparing twins raised apart and together was the series carried out by Cyril Burt and his colleagues; the Burt studies are a major source of the 80 percent heritability of IQ so often quoted. It now appears, however, that Burt's "data" are not part of the corpus of science at all, but of science fiction. In 1973, Kamin, addressing the American Psychological Association, showed so conclusively that Burt had cooked his data in at least two ways that Jensen was forced to conclude that they could not be relied upon. (*Behavior Genetics*, 4:1-28, 1974.) Kamin has since published his brilliant detective work as *The Science and Politics of IQ*.

There is a view that is perhaps simpler. It defines a time-honored ethic bred in the bone of American social and political thought: Every individual of whatever origin is entitled to equal opportunity and, what is more, access to a variety of opportunities, as well as special opportunity to reduce disadvantage or to fulfill special abilities, talents, and gifts. In other words, each and every American is to be given the justice that is his or her right in being born American: the right to the liberty to secure equal opportunity compatible with the right of others to secure similar liberties. Assume, *against the evidence, by the way,* that each individual is indeed only and solely what he or she inherits. Then the only fair way of demonstrating that the future is biologically determined is to give every individual a fair chance to achieve to full capacity, to develop to full potential in an educational environment designed for that purpose. Then, after a suitable time (several generations are not out of the question), it could best be determined to what levels a given individual has achieved, and how this has been accomplished. After many years, we will know further whether IQ can be altered or whether it is a fixed quantity. This is only fair. And in a democracy that is the richest and most powerful, and the hope of the world, it is a patent and potent objective to conduct this *experiment in justice*.

The schooling and educational systems, about to be renewed and transformed, are the places for the second chance. That is to say, children culturally deprived should be given the opportunity to make up for the deficit. They should not be treated as if they were not impaired by the deficit. Children impoverished, debilitated, without decent food, physiologically unfortunate, culturally deprived, children who develop more slowly, for whatever reason, should *not* be forced to go at the same pace, at least at the beginning, as those who leap through a race, a subject, a thought. Recall the postulate: In curriculum and instruction there is nothing so unequal as the equal treatment of unequals.

With this frame of reference we may proceed to probe the nature of evaluations of "success," "moderate success," and "failure" in schooling. For success in schooling, or lack of it, tends to label us as "gifted," "bright," "average," "failing," or whatever terms are used to describe "success" and "failure" in schooling.

Achievement in a Schooling System (within an Educational System): Schools without Failure

---

It is clear that schools form the environment in which ability and aptitude are enhanced and also assessed by many measures. In the elementary school not only is there a record of achievement of the child in a variety of subject matters and in a variety of social situations, but there are also scores on standardized tests (reading, arithmetic) in addition to tests of overall scholastic aptitude (intelligence tests). I have pressed the view that even if a definition of intelligence were agreed upon, even if its multifactorial make-up were agreed upon, and even if it were demonstrated to be a sure measure of intelligence, the fact that the measure is not considered finally and inevitably a measure of innate ability (a genotype, that is), but that environmental factors intervene, would lead us to defer the use of the measure as a *final* and *fixed* index of intelligence. Even if the extent and effect of the intervention of the environment is not yet finally and inevitably demonstrable, still the only course left to an American school is to assure and institute practice to enable the best possible schooling to be made available to all individuals, regardless of race, creed, or prior condition. To repeat a thesis stated in other terms, the assumption fits the American ideal, now law, of equal educational opportunity for equal educational achievement, and permits a cherished objective not yet realized, and perhaps not yet accepted: that a judgment of an individual's capacity to learn shall be made after an environment optimal for learning has been made available to each and all.

The particular assumption that success in schooling (with standards and practices particular to the constructive affection under which teaching and learning are effective) is a gauge of the individual's effectiveness in the marketplace, where economic success is often the result of competitive activity and standards of behavior to which the young may not be accustomed, has too long stood in the way of a clear determination of what schooling can and should do. Schooling is but *one* important factor in the interplay of multiple factors that compose the total educational opportunity of the individual, which altogether constitute an ecology of achievement. The achievement of the individual in school—described in a variety of judgments coming out of a variety of tests, of judgments by teachers, parents, the community, and arising, in no small part, out of the self-concept of the individual—is but one pattern in the mosaic being fashioned in the coming transformation of the schools.

I have observed certain "school systems without failure." That is, by far and large the young in these school systems did not consider themselves oppressed or rejected, nor have their parents come to the conclusion that these schools were "systems of rejection." The responsibility for achievement was borne by the school, by parents, by the community (in an ecology of achievement) in those areas assigned to the school. However, it is not my desire to describe schools that are fortunate in their community, but schools that are possible and feasible. Accordingly, let us consider the conditions under which a school may perhaps be considered a "school without failure"—that is, a school that attends to the fulfillment of the capacities of its students and frees them for maximum effort and achievement, given the constraints of society and community. This school is an amalgam of practices that exist. Indeed, there are schools in which the practices to be described exist, and which, if not unsettled by another surge of social unrest and the demand that a "new" social reform be pressed through the schools, are well on their way to achieving that stable ecology of achievement that assures the achievement of its pupils within the wide swath of excellence in which we are required to live.

Conditions and terms need, of course, to be defined. This is best done within the context of the practices of the school systems observed. A good number of these schools, with adjustment of practice here and there, are approaching the point where they can, if they would, become school systems. We should examine not only the external structure of such schools, but also their infrastructure (plans of instruction, modes of instructed learning), to discover a concept of substance, structure, and style coalescing to free the capacity of the individual. I have in mind particular school systems in the Northeast, Mid-Atlantic, Southeast, Mid-Northwest, Southwest, Northwest.

We may then construct a schooling system that is part of an educational system, in which practices that are effective in teaching and learning are so organized that it is indeed possible to have "schools without failure," and in which practices (including special schools or new organizations within present schools) designed to assess learning (tests, measurement, reports of work) are organized to assist in the fulfillment of individual promise. In other words, schooling in elementary and secondary school is to be considered as the initial environment of choice (outside, of course, of family, religious institutions, and the like), and thus the daily business (work, if you will) and commitment of the young as a significant part of the first period of life, as well as a preparation for life as an adult in an open society. True, such a society is one in which all the young are to be afforded a generous measure of justice, but are nevertheless to be required to achieve to capacity, however varied, and to make their special contribution to the society that, in turn, serves them.

This schooling system will be concerned not only with the elements of teaching and learning that can be readily assessed or measured, but also with that which is not necessarily measurable. Assessment is more than measure. Further, a school system fit for the future should, as a system, have the architecture for the nurture of varying capacity. To repeat, not all the young can learn all things at the same rate. There are differences in learning capacity. Yet all the young are to be given equal opportunity for equal achievement, though this does not mean an environment in which the young lose individuality. It also must mean difference in achievement in various areas—that is, difference, not *sameness,* of level in mastery of concepts, values, and skills.

Maturing-Independence Units, as a Form of Assessment

Elsewhere we have had occasion to dwell on the simplism in thought, in objectives, and in actions of a community, indeed of society, which separates the thought and objectives and actions of its schools from that of society. For instance, a good case could be made for assessing the decline of test scores (particularly SATs) by looking at certain flaws in the goals and motivations of social action, crippled in part by a "creeping hedonism," particularly in recent years, but this would serve no useful end because what would be said would be in the realm of guesswork and certainly would incite useless polemic. Reports on the reason for the decline of SATs have not been based on hard evidence, to say the least. The purpose of this book is not to assess blame; there is plenty of that around. Its purpose is to ask that we fix our eyes firmly on the transformation in schooling about to come and set about preparing the ground. Band-Aids will simply not do, nor will a search for scapegoats.

One of the Band-Aids in use is "minimum competency testing." The term itself is abhorrent because it sets bounds on teachers, on new pupils, on the spirit of an open and freedom-loving society which has always reached for the noblest of aims. By its use we are again treating a symptom and using a wide brush to paint over problems that affect schools and society. The symptom is a number (unascertained but in all probability a small number) of high-school graduates who are deficient in arithmetic, reading, and writing. But the uproar, particularly in the press, has been so loud that the movement toward minimum competency testing is beginning to affect schooling for all. There is, for example, a movement for "competency based education," which should, of course, be called "competency based schooling." Minimum competency testing and "competency based testing" are part of the movement. Moreover, there is already a countermovement burgeoning. It is a movement to resuscitate *"education* for the gifted and talented" (once again, pendulation; once again, a forgetting that talent, giftedness, advantage, and disadvantage begin with nurture in the home).

Perhaps minimum competency testing and competency based education will work, though it is doubtful. In the works advocating the movement little attention to the long-term development of an ecology of achievement is found; it is the current crisis that is to be ameliorated by ad-hoc solutions. What is more discouraging is that there is the same grimness that was so characteristic of the innovation of "programed instruction." Indeed, part of the movement toward competency based *schooling* involves the utilization of "mastery learning" (also called "learning for mastery" or "LFM") through "mastery units." Mastery units (not to be confused with the maturing-independence model proposed in Chapter 4) are, apparently, a modified form of the "bit-by-bit" instruction that characterized programed instruction. Success in a mastery unit is followed by immediate positive or negative reinforcement. The units I have seen and the practices in mastery learning as I have observed them have not rid themselves of the obsessive boredom that characterized the materials developed for programed instruction. This view is well stated in the title of an article by Charles Glickman in *Educational Leadership:* "Mastery Learning Stifles Individuality." Mastery learning as described by J. H. Block and articulated by Benjamin Bloom may be useful in achieving minimum competency. So might programed instruction. On the other hand, there are more eclectic views of the mastery approach and competency based education—for example, those of

Kay Pomerance Torshen. As she suggests, in *The Mastery Approach,* competency-based education is

an approach to instruction that aims to teach each student the basic knowledge, skills, attitudes, and values essential to competence. This approach begins by identifying the outcomes most important for students to attain. Then instructional programs appropriate for helping each student acquire the learning most relevant for him are designed. Each student in a class can learn from the same instruction, or varied types of instruction can be employed, depending upon the needs and preferences of the students, and the resources available. Performance is evaluated by measuring whether the student reached each of the outcomes defined as essential for him.

The practices Torshen describes are remarkably like the quest for individualization of instruction that Goodlad and Robert Anderson and J. Lloyd Trump and Dorsey Bayham, and William Georgiades, among others, have advocated and described in detail. Perhaps it is not a digression to comment that these workers are concerned not only with competence in teaching and learning but also with the joy of teaching and learning. The newer writings advocating mastery make learning a grim task, or so it seems. On the other hand, in *Individually Guided Elementary Education,* Herbert Klausmeir, Richard Rassmiller, and Mary Saily have re-emphasized a more provident attention to the personality as well as to the "mastery learning" of children. In any event, there is increasing good evidence from experience that active participation in learning (by the learner, of course) does not reduce competence in basic skills. Indeed, participation in learning requires ready and active utilization of skills in reading, writing, and arithmetic, and of skills that enhance personality. The maturing-independence model suggested here is "new" (if it is new at all) in two senses:

1. It stresses as a necessary practice the gradual progression of independence in learning from the home through the secondary school as the learner matures.
2. It is to be considered seriously as a model for the transformation of schooling and as a device to be used in combination with testing in the evaluation of children.

It has its roots in the work of a considerable number of people, but it is also rooted in experience. Whatever independence one gains in life is the result of maturity in thought and action, that is, in learning resulting from schooling and education both.

A Point of View: Instruction in a School System within an Educational System

The essence of the maturing-independence mode is that the initiative of the teacher and the student are so related that although the teacher may initiate the work, the student's initiative is not only to demonstrate mastery of the minimum but to assure that maximum competence can also be measured along the entire range of capacity. In demonstrating mastery in a given maturing-independence unit the student permits evaluation of success in instructed learning. In incorporating individuality in the mode of learning, the student demonstrates special talents or giftedness, or, at the least, style, approach, technique, individual ability. Let us recall the mode of instruction fitted to an acceptable theory:

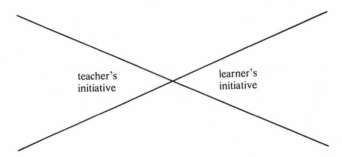

Remember that the teacher's initiative can be in any suitable form —lecture, assignment, project, film, work of art, TV program, whatever furnishes a suitable background for the student's work. Similarly, the student's "response," to demonstrate capacity, can be in any suitable form of work—presentation to the class, paper, poem, story, film, work of art. Certainly the student's response through work in an English or social-science class will be different from that in an art, music, or machine-shop class, and different still from that in a science, mathematics, or drafting class. Thus we may stipulate the central virtue of continuous evaluation: the student's *demonstrated work in learning throughout the year—and throughout schooling.*

In general, as described by Goodlad, Anderson, Georgiades, and other practitioners, the maturing-independence mode, called variously "continuous progress," "individualized instruction," and the like, affords the continuous evaluation central to an appraisal of a student's work. There are a sufficient number of accounts of the method in practice to show that it is no more expensive, no more demanding than a normal schedule of five classes and other teaching duties, each with thirty to thirty-six students.

Where I have observed the method at work, the school utilized its teachers (as well as aides from the community) and its instructional material in a manner such as the following:

After one or more (but no more than three) presentation-discussions of one hour each by a teacher particularly skilled in lecturing to three classes grouped for this purpose (ninety to a hundred students, three teachers, two paraprofessionals), each student is given an outline of the unit (a maturing-independence unit on, say, "The Structure of the Federal Government"). As part of the unit there are directions and questions to guide study, references and directions to guide development of a presentation in a written report or orally, with the help of visual aids. Also available are a schedule for the completion of the work (ten schooldays) and schedules for films, filmstrips, and conferences with individual teachers. Of course, the student may ask for additional conferences. The outline of the unit and directions to guide study are sometimes called a Learning Activity Package (LAP) or Independent Study Design (ISD). In the unit on study of government, students are asked to consider such aspects as, for example, the relationship of executive, legislative, and judicial branches in national and local government; powers given to the federal government and to the states; the relationship of the citizen to government; the method of passage of laws, statutes, and amendments. The student is required to read not only from assigned texts but also from a variety of references in the library. Certain field trips are required.

Within the unit (a device of instructed learning, to be sure) the learning activities of the student are related to A, B, and C levels, delineating levels of the probe: Level A requires study of primary documents and field trips; B, at least three references outside the basic text and a field trip; and C, study of at least two references outside the text. All maturing-independence units require a written report, answers to an "open test," using all the references available, and, finally, an "oral" test with a selected teacher. The oral test is given in an interesting way: the student selects at least three questions on cards from a file based on the questions in the open test. In other words, the student may study for the test and is free to discuss the answers with the teacher. Based on the oral examination and the report, the student is given a tentative grade: 5 = excellent, 4 = good, 3 = passing, 2 = inadequate, 1 = failing. Depending on his or her satisfaction or dissatisfaction with the tentative grade, the student may ask for a "make-up" oral examination or expand his or her report to suit. No student is permitted grades of 1 or 2 on any of the levels, and only a 4 or 5 on the A level. Thus "mastery" of a minimum is assured. But note that maximum capacities are encouraged. In one school, students were required to do at least two A-level units and were limited to four C-level units over the year's work. Maturing-independence units in science, for example, were based on minimum activities in the laboratory and offered an "original" project or investigation for A-level performance. Gifted students could literally advance at "lightning speed," as one of the students put it.

Maturing-independence units have a healthy function—aside from their benefits in instructed learning. First, teacher, pupil, and parent have a self-demonstrable way to determine how well the young are learning and at what rate. Second, the program of instruction itself is constantly and consistently being evaluated in a convincing manner: Do the young (different in ability and aptitude) learn what has been projected and in the manner postulated? Third, the evaluation is continuous and not subject to the hiatus necessarily a part of a schoolwide testing program. Fourth, tests (which are part of a continuous program of evaluation) themselves are not the sole or final or major evaluation, but are part of a program to determine efficiency in instructed learning. Nor are the tests challengeable as being "culturally biased," because they are to be used in consonance with the units as one more tool in validation of effectiveness in instructed learning, or in diagnosis. The fact that the tests are given as a matter of course is a healthy practice in itself; students become accustomed to them even if they are never quite comfortable with them.

The work of J. Lloyd Trump is particularly useful in describing a type of schooling similar to the one discussed here. There are also many accounts of continuous progress using the kind of learning packages (or independent study units) described here. But all are based on the type of instruction used in the maturing-independence mode we have discussed in Chapter 4. The lecture method per se is *not* central to these schools. In addition, there is IDEA (pioneered by John Goodlad), an organization concerned with innovating and describing the work of schools that utilize units of instruction as well as types of instruction adapted to small groups and individual students.

What of "failing students"? Will there be any? There should be none if appropriate provisions are made in early and subsequent years. After all, "failure" should mean that the student is working to capacity but cannot "succeed." In the kind of instruction suggested, the maturing-independence unit is at the level of the student's capacity, and a bit more demanding as the student undertakes succeeding years of work. Provisions are thus being made and continually revised to meet varying capacity. How will provisions for varying capacity be assured in the schooling system suggested in Chapter 3.

Architecture for the Nurture of Varying Capacity: A Schooling System within an Educational System

It is necessary to begin this discussion with the secondary school, to shed light on means and ends, if only because in the secondary school the ends are perceptible in terms of a limited number of years, three or four, available for their achievement. Also, the tactic is thus permitted of shedding light on obstacles, of working backward to beginnings, from outcomes to objectives, from practice to theory. It permits light to be shed on structure as well as architecture, on schedules, rates of progress, and the like. Several observers of educational practice have insisted that the fragments of a fine educational system are lying about waiting to be put together, as has been said before. Here we will be concerned with melding these splendidly contrived fragments of a schooling system into an architectural whole.

In Chapter 3 the structure of our secondary school was planned to consist of three distinct articulating segments:

Intermediate or transitional school (a junior school)

Secondary or preparatory school (a senior school)

Apprentice or intern school (after the senior school)

None of the schools would require a specific number of years of attendance. The leaving age for a boy or girl attending the first two schools would depend on his or her progress and the consent of parents and certain designated members of the staff. A student could conceivably leave in two years, or four, or stay even five or six, spending some time in a program of work (gainful employment) in an establishment outside the school. However, the secondary school is to be scheduled for a four-quarter year (including summer): three quarters would be scheduled for all students; the fourth would be optional. It is necessary to say that a quarter-system year is not a "grade" or a "semester"; students progress on the basis of work accomplished, not on the basis of attendance. In short, progress is on the basis of work continuously evaluated (in maturing-independence units) and not on periods of time where all students are kept to the same schedule and similar rates of achievement. This is not new, having been advocated by a number of students of schooling, particularly Goodlad and Anderson, and in recent years by advocates of individualized instruction, particularly Georgiades.

Participation in the apprentice or intern school would be optional. A small staff would serve to place and guide the students. The staff might well include retired members of the community selected for their capacity in working with the young—retired teachers, physicians, artists, homemakers, nurses, carpenters, plumbers, gardeners, by way of example. The student's time would be spent in a durable form of special service (with financial remuneration) to the community—say, assisting in the teaching of other students at all levels, particularly in reading and mathematics, but not necessarily in these areas only. Some might assist in special programs for the "gifted" or the "slow." Some could "run" the audio-visual schedule of the school, including TV. Others could assist in hospitals, in conservation tasks, in community-service tasks of all sorts.

Recall that the sequence of transitional to preparatory school is also devised to detect, treat, and reduce or eliminate disadvantage. In the transitional or intermediate school (junior school), the elementary-school record and the variety of abilities and capacities of the young are reviewed by teachers, parents, and guidance workers trained in psychological services, test and measurement, social services, career opportunities, and employment services. At all times during the intermediate-school years the students take part in conferences appraising their abilities. It is perhaps the last opportunity for special remediation of disability or inadequacy in reading or mathematics, or, for that matter, in other areas of instructed learning. Indeed, the fourth quarter of the year in an all-year transitional school may be used for additional work in remediation. It is in the years of the transitional school that special tutorial work by specially equipped young men and women in the apprentice or intern school is made available. It is in these three years that the special psychological and social services are brought into play. For example, it may be essential to assist in job placement for members of the family; special study facilities may be necessary; there may be a drug problem or a health problem. Students with study problems (drug-induced) or personality problems leading to drug addiction cannot generally be expected to do well on SATs. The transitional school is there to eliminate blocks to future achievements—those blocks that have not been eliminated in the earlier years.

The preparatory or secondary school (senior school) is to be a comprehensive school, or is to be part of a schooling system that is comprehensive in its objectives. Like many unified high schools, a comprehensive high school or comprehensive school system makes provision for different destinations, that is, career opportunities—an academic stream leading to college entrance, a commercial stream leading to secretarial and clerical careers, and an industrial stream leading to work in industry and to apprenticeships in trades (automotive, electrical, machine, carpentry, food service, construction, and the like). There are streams preparatory to community colleges and work leading to careers, for example, in computer programing, dental and medical technology, police and social-service work. All possible opportunities within the scope of schooling addressed to the realization of potential, present and future, are available. Where feasible, work-study programs are to be developed, with the student spending one-half or one-third of the time at work, the rest in complementing schoolwork.

Thus appropirate placement—agreed upon by parent, young, and school staff—practices in remediation and advancement, and wide opportunities in the comprehensive schools (transitional and preparatory) should reduce failure to a minimum. Moreover, the use of the maturing-independence unit—that is, the need to complete it to satisfaction before advancing to the next unit—should assure the best performance possible.

There are additional facilities for the young whose growth and development require special opportunity. On this point, special emphasis needs to be placed on the social services of the school—on the professional service staff (working within the school) and on the apprentice- or intern-school students assisted and guided by a competent staff of paraprofessionals drawn from the retired cadres of the community.

Granted that all teachers have taken work in the psychological and social aspects of schooling and education. Granted they are aware of the often severe problems of growth and development of the young at whatever stage—particularly pre- and post-puberal development, particularly those problems troubling adolescents. Nonetheless, the professional service staff is to consist not only of specially qualified teachers, but also of specialists trained in the diagnosis and treatment of those special problems that only specialists can address. These specialists are particularly capable in psychological and social testing and diagnosis of learning disabilities and behavioral maladjustment. They are able to bring in experts where necessary or refer the young to them for treatment. Moreover, in these days of freedom of movement in and out of large comprehensive senior schools, a trained security staff with responsibility for maintaining safety against unwarranted intrusion may be required.

The apprentice or intern school (consisting of the graduates of the senior school) needs further consideration at this point. The benefits of such a school to the individual and the community need hardly be emphasized. Aside from encountering directly many of the problems faced by the community and assisting in their solution, aside from the healthy practice of participation in the kind of community service that is the privilege of all citizens in an open society, aside from experience in the real work of the community, aside from remuneration (nominal, to be sure, but related to minimum wage scales), the young would use skills decidedly relevant, in good part, to their future careers. A partial list of the tasks they could take on speaks to their relevance:

- Assist in the care of children in preschool and Head Start programs
- Assist in the teaching of reading and arithmetic in the primary school
- Assist in remediation work in the intermediate, junior, and senior school
- Act as special tutors at home for the disabled or those requiring remediation
- Act as "big brothers" or "sisters"
- Function as laboratory assistants in the science laboratories of the school
- Function as aids in research laboratories, in commercial and university laboratories, in hospitals, in local government, in conservation projects
- Serve in task forces in conservation or in the armed forces

In one sense, through these schools, community services as well as school services will be enhanced and enlarged. In another sense, the self-concept of young men and women doing exceedingly worthwhile work in the community will be enhanced and enlarged. The question is: Is this not a waste of time? Some will certainly think it is and consider that young men and women ought to be about their business of making their place in a world of work, or in preparation for work, in apprenticeship for work, at the university, or the like. I would plead for making available to the young a year of "moratorium," as Erik Erickson calls it. A year, that is, of taking stock, a year of relative surcease from the pressure of steady scholastic achievement, a year of service to others, a year of selflessness, of life-affirming activity, of *giving*—and of experience generally lacking in schooling. With regard to the criticism that this would be a year "wasted" in terms of life span, I repeat that the latter, on the average, is increasing with the elimination of childhood diseases and with an understanding of the place of diet, rest, and exercise. However, the value of such a year of special service might well be determined by making it optional, as suggested. Might it become obligatory? First, its value would have to be demonstrated.

The curriculum of the transitional and preparatory schools should consist of the balance proposed in Chapter 5, a balance in six curriculum areas. In sum, it would be a balanced template of the culture, preparing the young for participation in home, community, state, country, and world; balanced in the areas of science, technology and the humanities, in literacy, not only in word and number, but in self-concept, in conduct fit for life in an open society.

Would all the young fit into this pattern of junior and senior schooling? Probably not. There are the gifted, for example. Within the comprehensive school there is no difficulty developing the special programs for these unusual young men and women with their splendid gifts. The special requirements of the gifted—those off the normal curves of distribution—are often ignored on the assumption that they can care for themselves, supply their own intellectual and emotional diet, as it were. The evidence is otherwise. In a sense, the gifted are handicapped (in a program requiring a certain conformity with procedure) by their own idiosyncratic, innovative, and unusual modes of learning.

Having looked at the geography, as it were, of the transitional and preparatory schools in order to acquaint ourselves with the destiny of the young child, let us now attend to the early years.

Achievement within an Educational System: The Early Years

For the early years, as in the transitional and preparatory years, there are four essential ingredients of whatever curricular and instructional modes are to be used.

1. It is not too difficult to rid ourselves of the notion that all children can, and do, learn at similar rates and that they can therefore be, or should be, put in grades progressing at the same rate. Further, we need to rid ourselves of the notion that the young coming to

school are at similar stages in learning. The incredible notion that somehow children are prepared to proceed at the same rate is useful in serving what may appear to be (but actually are not) efficient administrative modes—efficient for the apparent physical progress of children in a school, perhaps, but not for their mental and emotional progress. In such cases, it is usual for the "slow" child—one who learns slowly—to fall far behind the "fast" child— one who learns rapidly—although they appear to be in the same grade. (The difference in rates may not be due to innate ability, but to familiarity with the material studied, prior training at home, or a multiple of such factors.) It is nevertheless necessary to acknowledge that children do learn at different rates. We will need to rid ourselves of the notion that reading, writing, or computing rapidly is necessarily better than reading, writing, or computing slowly. It is the comprehension and accuracy, not speed, that are of the essence. We will need, in other words, to make provision for a *constant* in schooling procedure: administration of programs accounting for and serving differences in rate of learning.

Further, we should find it relatively easy to rid ourselves of the notion that all can learn the same subject matters equally well. We know this; the assumption is basic to our present modes of instruction. But the use of different modes of instruction may upset this notion. (For example, "slow" children can use calculators to add or subtract or divide with reasonable speed.) All of us who have taken piano or violin lessons know that differences in achievement exist. So, too, some children cannot learn algebra, or the calculus as well as others, or draw or paint with a skill "equal" to that of others.

In short, we will have to change our estimates of "success" and "failure" and learn to adjust to estimates of differentiated abilities on a scale of abilities. We will need to acquire habits of acceptance of those who are not at the highest levels on the scale of abilities. This will be difficult but necessary if we are to reach the next step in the transformation of schooling: the building of an educational system. It should go without saying that all children (perhaps almost all) would like to achieve at the highest levels, if only to please their parents and teachers.

2. There is need to introduce a form of instruction in which the child is taught the kinds of behavior that may be defined as "self-activated learning," that is, behavior that emphasizes freedom in initiating and completing learning. In effect, the self-activating

model or maturing-independence unit is at the base of instruction in the kinds of freedoms necessary to initiate and complete learning. In accommodating to the maturing-independence mode of teaching and learning, the child assumes greater and greater responsibility. The error is often made, in programs designed for individuation of instruction, of freeing the child for individual work too quickly. Where I have observed programs in which individuation is forced into the graded system—that is, the child is required to move with the group at his or her own pace—there has been consistent failure, accompanied by frustration of teachers, pupils, parents, administration, and community. Programs based in the mode known as "self-pacing" are, in a way, different from those based in individualized instruction, although individualized instruction accommodates self-pacing. Individualized instruction permits the use of the model of instructed learning called here the maturing-independence model. The individual moves at his or her own pace but also uses methods and subject matters particularly aligned to his or her own personal choice, with the guidance of teachers and paraprofessionals, of course. On the other hand, in self-pacing the individual does indeed move at his or her own pace but does not necessarily encompass new or advanced subject matters. In the elementary school, in the primary grades particularly, teachers are accustomed to permit work at a pace dictated by the maturity of different groups of children. Certainly in lessons in art and music each child completes a "work" (a learning task, if you will) at his or her own rate.

3.   While the utilization of maturing-independence units does not of itself eliminate grade placement, advancement by grades may not be a useful practice. A certain number of such units may be designated for each quarter, but a certain number are to be required for minimum competency in an area, say, skill in addition of a given number of digits. However, in the most beneficial programs a sufficient number of maturing-independence units are available for a variety of abilities. The simplest model to comprehend is in music: some children with ability in music may be playing a Beethoven minuet while others are still at "Frère Jacques." But all are achieving a measure of both competence and performance.

In a number of schools, I have observed an organization of *suites,* not grades, where children of different ages work together at certain times, the older "assisting" the younger in certain learning tasks; at other times, similar age groups working in advanced study or gifted children working alone or in groups; at all times, adults (teachers, paraprofessionals, high-school students) serving as guides and presenters.

4. The program of instruction is comprised of cognitive and holistic spatiovisual areas of instruction. Reading, writing, arithmetic, science, social science, literature, poetry, painting, music, movement (dance), crafts, and athletics are combined in such a way that "play" and "study," linear-sequenced activity and simultaneous processing, are appealingly designed to give children surcease from concentrates (huge doses) of linear-sequentiality or the spatio-visual. There is increasing evidence that the "freedom" of activity, mental and physical, that is characteristic of activity in literature, poetry, art, music, dance—the arts and humanities—acts synergistically to advance learning in the linear-sequential areas.

On a Gap in Schooling:
An Obstacle to Satisfactory Achievement

It has become increasingly clear that it is no longer feasible to consign schooling to the years from entrance into kindergarten at age five and elementary school at age six to continuous schooling until graduation at age seventeen or eighteen. Research summarized by Gilbert Austin has shown that the years before formal schooling (beginning at age five or six) are when the deficiencies caused by disadvantage occur. We must consider in greater detail the feasibility of certain "new" divisions as essential parts of a complete schooling system within an educational system about to be developed. One of these, the apprentice or intern school, has already been discussed. Certain of the young in this school, who have taken the option of joining the school at the point of their leaving age in the preparatory school, would be equipped to assist teachers and young children in the elementary school.

The elements to be placed in a formal organization of schooling are:

• Home school: a period of schooling, from birth to three years, under control of the parent-as-teacher (with assistance where desired)

• Preschool: devised for three- to five-year-olds under the guidance of specially trained teachers. Parents would act as paraprofessionals.

• Kindergarten: conceivably this period might meld with the preschool as the latter takes shape

- Primary school: for ages six through nine, based on a gradually introduced maturing-independence approach
- Intermediate school: for ages ten through twelve, based on a maturing-independence approach
- Transitional school: a junior school for ages thirteen through fourteen, also based on a maturing-independence approach
- Preparatory school: a senior school, based on a maturing-independence approach for ages fourteen through, perhaps, seventeen (leaving age optional)
- Apprentice or intern school: one year of service after leaving the preparatory school

To say that the home environment is a significant part of the education of the young is to say nothing new; to insist that the *home* and the *school* should be collaborative in the education of the young is supportable, but nothing new; to claim that the parent *is* a teacher and should act as such reflects the needs of a newer position on the part of most teachers, and the community generally. The parent is the *first* teacher of the child—and, in a sense, the home is a "school." A school system cannot function without the parent as part of the system; an educational system cannot function without the parent as teacher. A parent is in fact a teacher who changes the behavior of the young. Part of that behavior is preparatory to satisfactory achievement in schooling.

Burrhus F. Skinner, whose recent interpretations describe the concept of reward as reinforcement, would press the view that we are all the products of an environment where appropriate and inappropriate reinforcements surround us. In *Walden II* he has proposed that a new society could be organized and its children educated using the elements of reinforcement—positive reinforcement (reward) and aversive reinforcement (withdrawal of reward, or administering some useful sort of "punishment") being used judiciously to develop the behavior wanted. Recall that essentially Skinner proposes that behavior is shaped and maintained by its consequences, that is, by its satisfactory or unsatisfactory outcomes. Thus both satisfaction and dissatisfaction (commonly and simplistically called "reward" and "punishment") act to shape behavior.

The point to be made here is that parents, knowingly or not, use these principles with the young child. While it has been demonstrated that appropriate reinforcement (both positive and aversive) can speed up the acquisition of required behavior in table manners, toilet training, even early usage of language, one may also interpret the early behavior of the child in imitating the behavior of parents and siblings as a form of conditioning or reinforcement. It is argued that the child has, after all, associated "food" and "comfort" and "care" with parents and siblings, and indeed has been conditioned by them with rewards for appropriate behavior. For example, the child is "fussed over," "fondled," or fed with "goodies" whenever it demonstrates desirable behavior—walking, answering to a name, speaking, using new words, demonstrating some talent, and so on. In any event, it is clear that parents, siblings, and relatives have a demonstrable effect on the behavior of the young child. That is to say what is obvious: the home environment is the early *educational* environment of the child. Parents, siblings, and relatives are the first teachers. And some would say that machines are also part of the early home schooling environment: TV, radio, phonograph, pianos, and other instruments.

One example bears comment. In recent years, much has been said of the need for a standard in English usage and speech. How could it be otherwise? But this is not to say that the young child, whose pattern of English usage is certainly not yet his or her own but learned from others, should be penalized for performance. In our concern for valid evaluation of competence, we need at times to distinguish between *competence* and *performance*. Competence is generally judged by performance, but the relationship is not a simple one. The child who says "I knowed it" is not grammatically correct; the performance is properly judged to be poor. Perhaps it is the pattern of language of the early environment in which the child developed. But, in fact, use of the form "knowed" indicates a certain competence, that is, possession of a basic knowledge of the structure of the past tense: to the verb "know" add "ed." Put another way, the child's intellectual processes are competent and he or she has a concept of "language," but not yet of irregular verbs.

A case in point is that of the bilingual child, not yet equipped in English. A decent policy, recently articulated by various pronouncements, is that in this country it is well for a bilingual child deficient in English to receive instruction in his or her native language (say, Spanish) until a reasonable *competence* and *performance* is achieved in English. Then further instruction in the native language ought to be reduced —except possibly for purposes of remediation. Reasonably this might also be done for those who are skilled in what has been called "Black English." American English, after all, is the language of the nation.

In any event, our schools—indeed, as many of us do—emphasize performance, and poor performance is seen as a sign of incompetence, that is, poor intellectual process. Perhaps we may consider the early performance of the child to be a result of an educational environment "reinforced" by accepted behavior, whether intellectual, emotional, or in the amenities. A reinforcing environment is the home, to be sure.

But to say that reinforcement is the method of choice in inducing all forms of behavior is to go beyond the evidence, possibly even beyond conjecture. What is not explained (scientists would say "not yet") is inventive or idiosyncratic behavior in the very young child. Almost immediately (even in the infant) one may observe differences in personality, differences in what is learned and how it is learned. One may observe the remarkable learning activity of the "gifted" and "talented" in language, mathematics, music, art, even in social talents (the outgoing, charming child, or withdrawn, reclusive behavior). For example, one finds early expression of talent in music in children born of parents without such talent, intellectual prodigies in homes without prodigies. However this is explained in this time of incomplete knowledge, the environment at home must at least be conducive to the exercise of talent. Simply, while we can explain a good deal of the early behavior of the child on the basis of conditioning, our knowledge falls short of explaining generation of language, the learning and ordering of concepts —whether in language, mathematics, science, or social science—on the basis of reinforcement psychology. One needs to bring in the principles and concepts of the cognitive psychologist to explain the nature of more complex learning—say, of cardination, ordination, factoring, quadratic equations, writing a poem, or inventing a hypothesis and empirical experiment—even on an elementary level. The explication of the complexities of learning is not within the purview of this book. It is, however, within the scope of this book to suggest that the early teaching and learning environment in the home is of paramount importance within the construct of an educational system, and even of a schooling system. If the base for successful learning is not a property of the child early in life—the first three years, in fact—the child is indeed "disadvantaged" as compared with children who are blessed with such an environment. Indeed, to be disadvantaged where early schooling is concerned means precisely this: the early environment of the home has not been conducive to the most advantageous development of the child, physically, intellectually, emotionally, and socially.

The Home School: The Parent as Teacher

Where the home environment has been egregiously disadvantaged, the school may not be able to make up the loss. In that case, the school becomes a corrective institution, given over to constant remediation. In colloquial language, the child "falls behind," and, in fact, unless a type of individualized instruction (remediation) is instituted, the child may remain behind until he or she perforce drops out. To say this is undesirable is to use language that does not convey the desperation of the "drop out." Generally, he or she remains disadvantaged throughout life, and there is enough persuasive data to suggest that these dropouts may become the "mix" in which crime flourishes. The expense to society in time and energy, not to say money, of housing and feeding recidivist criminals is enormous, far outstripping the sums required to develop modified curriculums and programs of instruction.

Perhaps enough has been said to indicate that in the coming development of an educational system designed to secure the participation of all its citizens in the advancement of an open society, the home is to become an integral part. And its educational environment should be one to advance successful learning; in short, as there are to be schools without "failure," so, too, the home. At least the following educational activities need to be secured, all on a voluntary basis. If they are shown to be useful, there will be willing participation.

Education in parenthood (called "parenting") needs to be advanced first. This is desirable if only because we need to dispel the view that motherhood or fatherhood is natural. Recall that love is simply not enough. Perhaps the knowledge and skills required might follow these lines, under the rubric of coursework titled "The Parent as Teacher":

• Home Environment: first nine months as fetus
• Home Environment: first years (especially detection of physical disability—hearing, vision, motor action, or other)
• Development: including biology, psychology, nutrition, habit formation, the function of play, and formal teaching in learning
• Learning: teaching with constructive affection—the nature of positive and aversive reinforcement; the nature of concept formation in cognitive learning
• Learning Abilities: in relation to linear-sequential and simultaneous processing
• Learning Disabilities

The curricular and instructional base of such a program would be subject to the kind of overall planning proposed in the last sections of this chapter.

Information somewhat along these lines, prerequisite to an understanding of the child's development, could be made available in the following ways—and *should* (or is the word "must"?) be available to all parents who desire it to avoid disadvantage in their children. The information might be given under these conditions:

- In the regular program of the secondary school (before graduation) as required work
- In the evening in the local school to working parents in the community
- By means of educational television, to keep the information up to date for the community. There are such TV programs now, and they may soon be available also in disc, cassette, or Telex form. Eventually, cable TV, which permits questions and responses by the watcher, will, or at least should, be introduced.
- By means of books and self-appraisals, in programed instruction or in tests. Not all parents can attend classes or find the precise time to watch TV. But books can be used as reference in response to a given problem. After all, books are distillative; they synthesize a field's essential knowledge and disclose its unresolved issues. Even as school and TV programs are "free," so, too, the community should make books and magazines on "parenting" available.
- Through trained visiting teachers, certain of them drawn from the ranks of retired and retrained teachers

One or more of these sources of information ought to be available to all who want it. For new residents in the community, community services should be prepared to give information not only on the social services available, but also on the educational programs available to parents—and children.

In a word, the entire educational services of the community, home, school, church, synagogue, social services, play facilities, TV, among others, are to unite to ensure that the child's early home environment be advantageous to the child's development. Disadvantage should thus be neutralized early. It is not sufficient to give a course to adults, and have done with it.

In an educational system that values each child, the parents who are its teachers, and the home that is the educational environment, provision should be made for individual differences. Parents should not ever fall into the error of thinking that all children can and do learn the same way or can advance at the same rate. For this and other reasons, regular sessions for parents, perhaps one evening a week, ought to be available to present the nature of a program for a home school for the infant one to three years of age. It might be possible to have three sessions on alternate evenings in a school or on TV for information and discussion in three areas: Teaching and Learning: The First Year; Teaching and Learning: The Second Year; Teaching and Learning: The Third Year.

Of course, these areas are related to a chronological sequence (suitable to TV presentation) dependent on the convenience of the viewer. But it is also possible, for example, to organize the information on the basis of areas such as "The Cognitive Development of the Child: The First Years" or "The Kinesthetic-Muscular Development of the Child: The First Years," and so on. For each of these courses, adequate materials—books, films, filmstrips, realia—need to be made available. The books—as are books for children at school—ought to be made available without charge. However, TV programs should be developed on public and commercial stations to enrich the work given at the local school. TV can bring to view experts not otherwise available. But TV— as it is now doing sporadically—should, as part of an educational system, bring suitable programs *regularly* to children and to parents. Even now TV programs are watched by children two and three years old, who remain transfixed before the screen. From the moment of birth the child is a learner. A program developed for these early years might well be on the road to eliminating disadvantage in learning ability.

Schooling within an Educational System: "School" before School, the Preschool

It is fair to state that, all in all, schooling and educational practice have been based on the assumption that somehow the infant and young child fared best when "brought up" in the home, or a home. Years ago, Friedrich Froebel and Maria Montessori, to mention but two of a host, understood that a child's development began early, that children could not be treated like adults. The purpose of these schools, and other preschool environments was similar: to foster the development of the preschool child. Now the conditions of our society, which foster equal opportunity, not only for minorities, but for the sexes as well, have found an inevitable consequence: the working mother seeking proper care for her young. Generally speaking, grandparents no longer live with the family and are no longer available for "baby-sitting"; thus the need for "day care." The day-care school and the preschool are recent phenomena, resulting from economic conditions and from demonstrations out of research that the young preschool child from one to five years of age is active not only physically but also mentally. We must consider then that a child between ages one and five is undergoing rapid and basic development of linear-sequential and simultaneous processing as well as physical development. Mind and body are no longer to be separated.

Development of preschool and day-care centers is proceeding rapidly; a growth from a population of 50,000 in 1967 to approximately 4 million in 1980. As is to be expected, some of the day-care centers are baby-sitting devices, and certain preschools may not as yet have useful programs, but the movement is at its inception. It constitutes the single most important development that could well serve to eliminate certain learning disabilities caused by environment. As Austin has indicated, the preschool is essential to the "disadvantaged."

The massive efforts undertaken by programs such as Head Start have been criticized because the first programs were not as productive as they might have been—that is, the gains resulting from Head Start were not sustained in the first years of schooling. However, various studies have indicated that the failure to *articulate* Head Start, kindergarten, and the first grades may have been responsible. Head Start programs that may be considered to be successful as determined by reasonable assessment had these characteristics:

• The program ministered to children in *small groups* (three to five children). Their selection was based on assessments to determine rate of development in both cognition and spatiovisual perception.

• Participation of parents in the program was secured where possible.

• Paraprofessionals to assist the teaching staff were available. They acted as assistant teachers as well as attending to rote learning—drill, practice, supervision of play, feeding, exercise, rest, and the like, especially for ages three to five.

It is in this last feature that the young men and women in the apprentice or intern schools would be useful. Not only would they serve as assistant teachers, but also they would be involved in and perhaps learn certain aspects of "parenting." It is here that retired men and women, too, would be of considerable help.

It is here also that TV programs designed for day care and preschool could be of considerable importance, and not only the excellent programs now directed at children at home—"Sesame Street," "Electric Company," "Infinity" (a mathematics program), "Ding-Dong School," and the like. These programs are pioneer efforts of considerable importance, though they fail in an essential aspect, of which their creators were aware and would have given much to ensure: the absence of a device for securing the "response" of the child. In the preschool period it is essential to monitor the kind of group that will be attending to TV or films, for it is obvious that children of different ages may respond differently. (In the home, films that teach "language" and "number" to siblings of widely different ages and development may be ineffective for the younger viewer, if only because one viewer may respond and "rob" the other of the feedback of the "correct" or "incorrect" response.) This aside, it is probable that TV cassettes, or discs, designed with great care to teach a concept or skill to children at different levels of development, aptitude, or capacity for three-to-five-minute viewing, depending on the age of the group, would be of considerable effectiveness. This assumes that an adult (preschool teacher, trained parent, paraprofessional, or intern-school student) would be able to conduct a "discussion" in a preschool after the "viewing" of the audio-visual device, and could show the segment as often as is needed to fulfill the objective of the lessons. A program of TV lessons, on cassette, disc, or cable TV, should be especially beneficial in the preschool period, or at home where parents or grandparents or a trained sitter is available. Naturally, every TV production would be accompanied by a "teacher's guide," explicating modes of securing response and modes of evaluating the response.

The field of preparation of instructional materials—books designed for children and comprising a series of three or four lessons aimed at a single objective with accompanying evaluative devices—is as yet unexplored and undeveloped. The manufacture of children's toys is a burgeoning industry, but their optimum adaptation for utilization in instruction is not yet employed.

The Possible Impact
of a Preschool Program

The dimensions of a full preschool program, including a home school, need careful planning, for, after all, it will compass a considerable and diverse population. The benefits of a soundly developed preschool system as part of an educational system can hardly be questioned. Among these are:

• The *gradual amelioration of disadvantage.* I emphasize *gradual* amelioration because of the impatience with which the early disappointing results of Head Start were greeted. To undo the adverse effects of disadvantages takes time—steady and purposeful effort—if only because the growth of the community should be commensurate with the growth of the children. In other words, the effective environment of the school needs to be reflected in the home and the community. Further, the program requires a sequence or consequence: the skills the young acquire at home need to be built on in a primary school designed for the purpose.

• The *detection of variation in learning ability.* Aside from attempts at remediation (which will of course be beneficial), there will be opportunity to detect physical impairments and learning disabilities such as dyslexia and hyperactivity. As important will be the recognition of learning ability in its various forms. Indications of high artistic, musical, verbal, and numerical ability—giftedness—are subject to detection. A variety of tests are available, but surer instruments need development. The surest instrument, in my view, is observation by trained teachers in a curriculum that gives opportunity to all in a program of instruction where the learner can progressively exercise initiative and independence.

• The *development of a cadre of paraprofessionals.* The opportunity for a population of retired individuals not usefully employed, trained in a variety of ways—as nurses, teachers, social workers, cooks, experienced caretakers of children—to serve in the preschool is of considerable value in itself. The opportunity for the competent secondary-school student in the intern schools to assist in teaching and caring for the young assures a continuing supply of paraprofessionals and offers experience to future parents and teachers. It also brings the community into the school, a valuable exchange in itself.

Naturally, the most important benefit is the probable one of enhancing the learning environment of the preschool child and reducing in good part the "failures" of children now due to an inadequate learning environment prior to kindergarten and primary school.

A rich preschool environment, at home and in a school, will do much to spare a community the ugly spectacle of waste. It is not that every child will reach a desired level of competence. It is, rather, that every child will have equal opportunity to reach his or her level of competence and compassion. And an advance toward that goal is indeed a measure of success. With regard to the education of infants and young children, we may advance slowly and surely to homes and communities without failure, insofar as the early care and education of children are concerned. And homes and communities that assure children an opportunity to advance to their highest level of achievement in body and mind are themselves not disadvantaged.

Schooling: Is It a Life Sample?

The educational system discussed here is one in which aims are carried out, but differentially realized in each child, each girl and boy, if only because abilities and disabilities are variable. Nevertheless, the extent to which the aims are carried out is known. They are to be evaluated at each step in the progress of education, because disadvantage is to be remediated up to the hilt.

For example, at the end of the preschool period, the rate of advance of each child is at least noted, so that further observation can determine whether the abilities and disabilities of the child have been identified and clarified. In no way should final judgments be made on the future of each child, although judgments may have been made on the kind of program that will advance the child to the fullest extent. In effect, no judgment on the future of any child need be made until the elementary period of a child's education has been completed. Recall that there are to be four distinct periods within an educational system, each of them to be evaluated: the home school, preschool, primary school, and intermediate school—a period of twelve years. The elementary years are periods of opportunity and constructive affection in appraisal and prescription of programs. The elementary years are, to be sure, the years when parents, the community and its services, the school, and a variety of experts have been at the service of each child. In an open society dependent on the contributions of all its people and determined to avoid the catastrophes, small and large, that even a single self-destructive personality can and does generate, we can and should do no less. The elementary school and the secondary school will build on the foundations of both preschools: the home school and the preschool.

Assuming that proper nutrition, rest, and other health measures are constantly under assessment, the child's mental and emotional development is to be under constant assessment as well. Measurements of weight, height, blood pressure, hearing, sight, and the like are assessments. There is generally little objection to these; they are, in the sense of the term, "objective." We expect children to gain in weight and height as evidence of development. Similarly, assessment of progress in learning is a form of constant assessment. Some children will progress slowly, some rapidly, as the case may be. Slow learners might learn more if they were permitted to learn at their own rate (after all, some first-rate scientists read slowly, pondering meaning as they read). Slow progress is not "failure"; it is *slow progress*. Rapid progress is not "success"; it is *rapid progress. We are, generally, ready to concede that a combination of factors, genetic and environmental, is responsible for the height and weight of the child. We are not yet, generally, ready to concede that a combination of factors, genetic and environmental, is responsible for the rate of learning.* Yet it is. The brain and its nerves are organs (inherited genetically), no more and no less than the heart and the circulatory system (inherited genetically), whose function we judge by blood pressure and the like. True, the environment is a factor in the development of all organs. It would be prudent then—and only prudent—not to label the child a success or a failure if the child is working to capacity in the judgment of teachers, psychologists, social workers, and parents. In short, report cards need to be redesigned to note a child's continuous progress, not a crossing from grade placement to grade placement, or from one label to another (A, B, C, D, or Passing, Failing, Satisfactory, or Unsatisfactory). Rather, the child's progress needs to be related to a possible destination, perhaps in a project, perhaps in a program of instruction, perhaps in progress in overcoming a disability.

At a certain point, possibly at the intersection of primary school (ages 6 to 9) and intermediate school (ages 10 to 12), a determination of stages of progress needs to be made. But in no case is this a final determination. It is a determination of progress under modes of instruction, styles of instruction, programs, and the like. Certainly remediative programs—where children seem to be learning at a slow rate of progress—will have been set up for children seven or eight years of age. It is at this point, if not earlier, that the need for extensive remediation should be determined and established, possibly using other modes of instruction or computer-assisted instruction. Wherever a child is not benefiting from instruction, reassessment is necessary. There are a sufficient number of specially designed individual achievement tests which are useful. By the age of nine, sufficient information, built up through observation by a minimum of five to seven teachers, one or more psychologists and social workers, a guidance officer assigned to the child, and the parent, will be available to enable a judgment to be made on a future program for the child. No doubt this will include an estimate of strengths and deficiencies, excellence and weakness, gifts, opportunities, and destinations. Perhaps at this time—the crossing of the primary and intermediate years—a provisional and tentative assessment of *aptitude* (not ability) should be made. Perhaps it is at this time that a curriculum and program of instruction for each child can be effectively designed. For it is in the intermediate school—no later—that a program of small group learning (no more than seven children in a group, no more than four groups to a class) should be designed. In my view, it is still too early for the LAP, or individualized instruction, except for the rare cases of the gifted child.

Inevitably and irresistibly we have been drawn to the model of a school as "life sample." The model of the current life sample is clear: what happens in school is a model of what happens in life; success in school presages success in life; and, inevitably, failure in school results in failure in life. The equating of the school with "all of education" for the young has done its mischief. But it is not true that success in school presages success in life. Success in school generally presages further success in school—or in similar activities.

Once the equation *success in school = success in life* was established, however vaguely, the school's assessment of a boy's or girl's achievement in gain of knowledge or skills became a matter of exceeding importance. And assessments of IQ which "predicted" the probability of success or failure became matters of predicting economic success. Efforts to set the matter straight have been of questionable success; efforts to demonstrate that success in schooling predicts further success in schooling and is not necessarily a prediction of success in life were of little avail—and are still so. But to consider schooling as part of education and not the whole of education, and thus to deal successfully with antecedents of the transformation of the schools as part of an educational system—the purpose of this book—requires precisely this: *the redefinition of the school.* Put another way, in terms increasingly familiar: For what is the school to be held accountable? More fairly, in the context of our society: What can the schools do—and become?

One can yield to a black pessimism as one reads reports in the newspapers and listens to accounts on TV of the failures of schooling. Thus Walter Cronkite and Charles Collingwood, in a TV report titled "Is there anyone out there learning?" concluded that 13% of the young were functionally illiterate. True, this should not be and we *must* attend to the 13%. But what of the other 87%? What of the position of the United States as a leading world power in living standard, in possibilities of choices, in possibilities for change, in technology overall, not only in potential for industrial leadership and military defense. (Evidence suggests it is *the* leading world power, given periods of decline during years when its purposes and decisiveness lie fallow.)

Rational inquiry would lead to the conclusion that a powerful nation is not built on the failure of a considerable number of its diverse school systems. Rational inquiry would suggest that certain schools *and* communities in the United States have "failed" (and I would say

229

"temporarily") in their early efforts with the new populations of students, the new minorities who have not yet accepted, and are therefore not complaisant with, the social function of the schools. "Limited" because the school does not in itself prepare for all of life; life does that. "Powerful" because in the main the school is a template of the culture and prepares the young for the cultural exchange necessary to life in our society, a cultural exchange consisting of not only language and numbers, but also the language and skills of habituation in past, present, and future. The school does intend to prepare the young for civilized encounter. And it assesses the young both in their capacity to garner fair success in the knowledges, values, and skills that are the school's task and in their overt behavior in acknowledging the function and dominion of the school in these aspects. In a word, schools are not equipped to accommodate rebellion, to acquiesce to a rejection of the school's purpose.

What, then, happens when a sizable population of the young does not accommodate to the school environment? Seemingly, this was true in the 1890s to 1920s, when sizable minorities, fresh from foreign countries flooded the United States. The young did not quickly accommodate to the schools, and the schools did not accommodate the young; some 40 to 60% (the data vary) did not complete secondary school. As time went on, the accommodation expanded. Still, in 1930, the data suggest that four out of ten did not complete high school. Yet the comparison of the kinds of minority then and now fails at a crucial point of analysis: then, the minorities were fleeing persecution, or unpromising environments, or oppressions of various sorts, and coming to a land of promise for the young, if not for the immigrants themselves. Now, it seems when the minorities consider themselves oppressed in their own land, there is no land of promise to which to flee. Society and schools both symbolize the oppressor, imagined or not. And so adults, who consider themselves oppressed, and their young are at war with school and society.

According to a National Education Association survey, one-third of the nation's teachers would not enter teaching if they were to begin their careers again. This is assessment by teachers of the environment in which they teach. Conversely, reported attacks on teachers by students indicate an assessment by the young of the schools in which they learn. We should not come to unwarranted conclusions, however. The attacks on teachers did not occur in sanative school environments where an appropriate ecology of achievement was at work. Further, even in the schools where such attacks did occur, the vast majority of students (more than 98%) did not participate in them.

The NEA report leaves no doubt that the present school environment is not the environment essential to the school: teachers and students in wholesome exchange engaged in the pursuit of knowledge, of skills, of excellence. The "psychological safety" (Carl Rogers's phrase) required of a sanative school environment is surely in danger. So is its merchandise of hope. The validity of assessment of students, through their work and through measures developed in school environments in which the validity of tests could be effectively determined, is surely open to question when environments are *not* conducive to effective work, or when students are at war with society and with the schools which are the agents of society. It seems that the schools cannot remain islands stable amidst the turbulence. Or is this a matter of the moment? I believe not. I believe a reassessment and a renewing of the function of the schools is mandated, not only because our society is at a turning point, but because the schools, as templates, as mirrors of society, are at a turning point as well.

A Place to Turn:
At the Turning Point

Granting that we wish to allow all children, all youth, to fulfill their powers in the pursuit of their individual excellence, what kind of redirection in schooling is required? Granting, with Philip Phenix, that the "human intelligence is too rare and precious a thing to squander on haphazard programs of instruction," what redirection is required? And, as a consequence, what is required of the environment of the school?

W. H. Auden and Lewis Mumford tell us, each in his own way, "we must love each other or die." Paul Ehrlich and Barry Commoner and René Dubos—and before them, John Muir and Leopold, and all conservationists and ekisticians—tell us, in effect, "we must love our environment or we die." Laurence Kohlberg, in investigating moral behavior, comes to the not so astonishing conclusion that children "who understand justice act more justly" than those who do not. At once he unites the cognitive and affective, concepts and values.

What is being called for is a school that mends differences, one that understands that as children are valued so they value themselves, one that heals injury to the valuing self. In an ethical society, ethicists are clearly necessary.

Memorandum: On Renewing Schooling and Education

If everyone, every child, all the young are to be in school, then one cannot deny the needs of variety. If each and every one of us was of equal ability, perhaps we would not be as strong a nation. That forest, that sea, is the most provident and that environment most viable, most sanative, which makes provision for the variety of its inhabitants. Variability itself is the guarantee of our freedom, if only because an open society requires the different skills and the wide variety of contributions of its people. Our schools need to be prototypes of what is prized in our culture, not what is despised. Inequities are surely to be examined, but not exploited; deprivation, oppression, disadvantage are surely to be analyzed, but as means to amelioration, not as destiny. Real obstacles, real threats, real problems, real conflicts are to be examined, but against a past where the obstacles, threats, problems, conflicts were not only more perilous but were overcome. A problem is not augury. Teachers are, or should be, *in loco parentis,* and under this care—because teachers should be trained in caring—a child can survive failure and learn from it. A school and a teacher are able to give a child a second chance, and a third. And still another. For a teacher, to repeat, is in the ministry of mercy.

It is easy to criticize the schools. The easy critics are easily satisfied by blaming the schools and not the community, or vice versa, or identifying children or youth as the culprits. Generally, most critics of the schools are almost always sanctified by one advantage: they have not taught, or, having taught and found that their ideas were not generally adopted, they have fled the schools in an idealistic pique. Criticism is easier than craftsmanship, Zeuxis told us long ago. And the craftsmanship required to improve the schools is not mainly or solely that of criticism—no more so than rancorous criticism of democracy is mainly curative.

For example, it is easy to criticize the Pilgrims or Puritans or Cavaliers or the Spanish or the French for their obvious failures in not bringing a heaven to the New World, for not building a new Atlantis, a Utopia, immediately. It is easy, too, to criticize the Continental Congress and its Constitution—for surely that did not ameliorate all ills; it was not enough—and the freeing of enterprise, for that was not enough; and the freeing of the slaves, for that was not enough; and schooling for everyone, for that was not enough. And the civil-rights movement, for that was not enough.

It would be more acceptable for the French to criticize their schools for their "failures" in World War II, for the French boast that their restricted secondary schools (enrolling about 20% of the population) and special universities prepare their leaders. And what of the British?

Surely failures in their economy, in leadership, could be laid to the schools, for their special schools are considered to be the source of their leaders. Of course, French or British schools are no more responsible than are American schools for the faults of their societies. If there is a relationship between schooling and the failure of societies, the argument for cause and effect needs to be reversed.

Not to burden the reader further, any invention is an evolution in thought, purpose, and deed. A society grows in a complex social evolution; so does any of its root agents—such as government, such as socialization, such as justice, such as education. And education has been a talisman to Americans: education was to retrieve any society from its morass; "basic skills" were somehow always to advance the education that was to redeem America as symbol and reality. The school has not failed; rather, the schools have been given too meager a purpose, and too meager support, and at the same time an overwhelming task: to be ameliorative of the ills of society.

We are required, then, to build schools that nurture individuals who are as competent as they are compassionate. For a strong case can be made that it was the surge of weakness in society when it yielded certain responsibilities for the development of curriculum and instruction to the so-called rebels in the Rebellion of the 60s that began the undermining of the schools. In yielding to incompetence, the arts of compassion—which are almost always interpreted as signs of weakness by those who use threat or force to gain their objectives—are perforce also lost.

Across our nation, in spite of what appears to be an apparent mistrust of schooling, curricular plans and methods of instruction are turning from a system of conveying to the child traditional knowledge in a rigid way to a system where the child uses his own individual powers in the ardent pursuit of his various excellences. "Ardent" is the word. The teacher prompts and motivates individual children to express what they know, value, and feel, and to which they respond most ardently. Teachers know there are varieties of excellence, found in a variety of children, which have a place in an open society.

In such a school system a child can and should learn in all possible ways: by voice, by book, by machine, by investigation, and above all, by example. A teacher cannot be replaced by a machine; a lecturer can. A machine can do as well as most lecturers, although, of course, the brilliant lecturer conveys not only the subject but also life itself.

In reflecting on the modes of curriculum, instruction, and evaluation, I have been answering in part the all-important question posed earlier: What kind of a world do we want for our children? But in counterpoint, the question also raised is: What is our image of the child? I have said that our conception of the child is of one who will in time grow to the measure of the civil and civilized, one who will accept the constraints of truth, beauty, justice, love, and faith, and live by them. In effect, we have survived because we have valued and returned to valuing these measures. These measures are indeed assessments, not only of humanity, but also of the competent human. If schooling is to produce competent young, prepared to flourish in and advance the civil life of an open society, we are required to assess the question whether the school, in a society at a turning point, can achieve such a purpose in an environment hostile to the purpose. The answer is "no." But the answer also is that our schools can, and should, and indeed must become environments in which what is best and noble in our culture is prized and practiced. Whenever schools have been prized by the young grown mature and adult, it is because they have been places for the development of the habitual vision of greatness. In other words, our thesis remains intact: the renewing of schooling and education lies in a new and precious amalgam of school *in* society where both serve an educational system—a renewed system of education, to be sure. It is this new educational system that can and should furnish the model of a life sample. This new system has its pieces lying about, waiting to be discovered, and ready to be assembled. A renewing of schooling and education can serve the requirements of an open society, a noble society, which is about to address itself to a fresh surge toward its ideals, its ends, to the beacons that have been guide as well as a benison for all who have read its history.

In spite of the absurdities and contradictions of life, we are obliged not to lose sight of these ends. We know the lesson: after boundless confusion, we have faced our enemies with clear eyes and these enemies continue to be the same: ignorance, meaninglessness, mindlessness, inhumanity.

Our task remains to grasp the courage to know and the courage to be, to continue our road to high competence and a compassion equal to competence. And in so doing to become ever truer, kinder, gentler, warmer, quieter, and withal wiser, firmer, and ever stronger—and thus to assure a boundless strength.

7. Regarding Development of an Ecology of Achievement in *Education*

A Necessary Prologue

My efforts to define the intent and content of "schooling" and "education" in the different contexts of past and present reforms, innovations, and movements, in the context of curriculum, instruction, and evaluation have been efforts not only to clarify the terms but also to disabuse the future of the need for continued polemic on the matter. In this I am sure that I am naïve. The polemic is not always intended to serve clarity.

How useful it would have been if the writings of John Holt (*Why Children Fail*), Jonathan Kozol (*Death at an Early Age*), Charles Silberman (*Crisis in the Classroom*), and Ivan Illich (*Deschooling Society*) had been put in the context of *education* and not of *schooling*. Neil Postman would not have needed to remark, in his *Teaching as a Conserving Activity:* "The essential facts of American *education* are as obvious as they are immovable." He was referring to *schooling,* because he continues, "To change what the students and teachers do to each other, or how and where they do it, would require sustained and rigorous criticism, accompanied by the invention of multiple alternatives of a practical nature." (Precisely: it would require the innovation of an educational system.) Nor would he need to comment on his facing in a different direction from that in his earlier book, *Teaching as a Subversive Activity* (1967). For he is talking about education, and alternately about schooling, and both his books are essential for a comprehensive discussion. How useful it would have been if countless writers, all well-meaning, had not proposed the engrafting on the schools of the functions of enormously diverse environments outside the ecology of schools, but had seen what Bailyn, Cremin, de Lone, and others had seen as a disjunction between schooling and education. In other words, our schools have been "successful" when they have met the objectives of the communities that support them, but our educational system has "failed" because it does not exist—not yet.

It continues to be disquieting to listen to discussions of what is "wrong" with our "educational system" when it is clear that what is being discussed are the objectives and achievements of schools with limited powers, powers granted by discrete communities or legal entities. What is being discussed in this book is the *renewing of school systems that are part of a vaster educational system,* and in this chapter in particular the initial steps in the design of an educational system. When Jencks demonstrates a discordance between schooling and economic success, he is underscoring for us the fact that economic success is rightly the outcome of a complex consisting of schooling, training, education, and work per se, which is the property of an *educational system,* but not discretely of school systems.

On the other hand, when one speaks of "improving" *the* "school system," those who have studied our schools search in vain for a national school system. What we have are a wide variety of schools in a variety of communities; few of these schools are joined in that integrative device that characterizes a system. Indeed, some have noted that the strength of the American school is its diversity. But, diversity and local control need not—and should not—mean disregard by a given community of fruitful policy and theory practiced by existing outstanding schools over the country.

In any event, before further massive ad-hoc experimentation with the lives of children takes place, before further demonstrations of the uses of children as implements of psychosocial warfare (the kinds of uses we have seen in the "wars of education" since schooling was identified as a vast public concern and codified as an institution), we should take pause and consider whether we want an educational system. If we do—and we think we do—then we shall find the fragments of one of the best, if not the best, educational system lying about. A beginning must be made. One such suggestion for the design of an educational system— inadequate because all the information necessary is not available—is offered here. Fine minds exist which can develop a more fruitful design.

We do not need more money. We do not need to abolish local control. We do not need the "inspectorate" of French, Japanese, or Italian schools, or even Russian schools. We should have learned by now that schools reflect a culture, and we do not effectively copy the habits of other cultures reflected in their schooling and education. This is not to say we cannot learn from their successes and failures—and from their practices.

We need a change in structure. We need, therefore, a design that embraces the host of magnificent educational opportunities (with schooling as a major factor) extant in the United States. Then, and only then, will we be able to make available to each and all, at whatever age, equal educational opportunity for equal educational achievement throughout life. Until an educational system is devised, we will be obliged to serve the expedient, therefore inadequate, the temporary and ad-hoc, therefore wasteful, the victory of the powerful polemic, therefore pendulation from one extreme to another. In the end, harm will be done.

Once we become concerned with the development of a system qua system, we are at once constrained to consider not only means but also ends. Further, these means and ends must be clearly perceived as dependent on each other; means and ends are inextricably one. For example, in curriculum, what is taught (means) determines what is to be known (end). What is known (end) determines what is to be taught (means). The teaching art itself (a means) is not consummated until there is a response (an end) by the one taught, the learner. If the end is growth in knowledge, values, and skills, growth in competence and compassion, then the means must be devised to serve that end. If the end is an individual whose behavior is changed by education, and thus constrained to maintain and sustain a vision of excellence and greatness, then the means are to be developed to maintain and sustain that end. For, generally speaking, behaviors are maintained and sustained by their consequences. Individuals who sustain a vision of excellence and greatness will in turn sustain an educational system that is the means to achieving the vision, and the kind of education that maintains it.

The *Antigone* tells us that nothing vast enters the life of man without a curse (for "a curse" read "unimagined problems"). If we want to ideate something as vast as civilization, and if we assume that schooling of the young is prelude to it, must we accept the attendant, strait-jacketed curse? Schools are to control the way children express themselves as well as their conduct during the time they submit themselves to schooling.

The argument Aristotle put forth so long ago in *Politics* still rages. Indeed, it summarizes succinctly the burden of most criticisms of schooling. (I hesitate to comment on a text by Aristotle, but although he used the term "education," his context seems to be that of "schooling.")

It is clear that there should be legislation about education and that it should be conducted on a public system. But consideration must be given to the question, what constitutes education and what is the proper way to be educated. At present there are differences of opinion as to the proper way to be educated. At present there are differences of opinion as to the proper tasks to be set; for all peoples do not agree as to the things that the young ought to learn, either with a view to virtue or with a view to the best life, nor is it clear whether their studies should be regulated more with regard to intellect or with regard to character. And confusing questions arise out of the education that actually prevails, and it is not at all clear whether the pupils should practice pursuits that are practically useful, or morally edifying, or higher accomplishments—for all these views have won the support of some judges and nothing is agreed as regards the exercise conducive to virtue, for, to start with, all men do not honor the same virtue, so that they naturally hold different opinions in regard to training in virtue.

Even so, Aristotle was then dealing with a relatively simple problem: the "schooling" or the "education" of the elite. We have exacerbated our curse: we force schooling on every child. If for this reason only, we should embark on the design of an *educational system*—which, in effect, will include a schooling system. Because an open society must make education available to all, because an open society depends on informed and thoughtful opinion, the educational system will be bound to affect *all,* not only those who succeed in schooling.

Essentials: The Development of a System

Other ages have engaged in a special nonsense, and it may be that ours will be engaged in endless discussions on the distinction between human and the machine that is designed to collaborate in mental function: the computer. Even now the discussion proceeds as if the machine were independent of its inventor, as if the machine built itself, as if human beings did not decide to build a machine, to achieve the means toward that end. We build our environment (machines included) with intent or by default, and in turn the environment affects our behavior. It is thus difficult to entertain a discussion of mechanical systems to illustrate the essential meaning of system, for at once those of us who teach are offended by the comparison of an educational system given over to humane and human needs and ends with a system given over to sustaining machines. Nevertheless, the comparison is illuminating; it directs but does not confine thought. In addition, a system is self-evaluating, for if it does not work, it directs attention to the malfunctioning part, enabling correction. We were alarmed when the gauges and meters in the servomechanism in a nuclear energy plant (at Three Mile Island) were not properly read, or did not work, for the safety of thousands of people living in the area was jeopardized. Nuclear energy plants are as safe as their monitoring devices (servomechanisms) are effective in enabling the plant to work as a system.

In our telephone system—a remarkable network of some billions of interconnections—a connection (a call) requested by means of a statement of seven numbers for a local call, a few more numbers for long distance, and a few more still for an international call brings together two or more people, two or more minds. Incredible! At once we know when it does not work (no ring) and we can then ask for intervention to correct the failure.

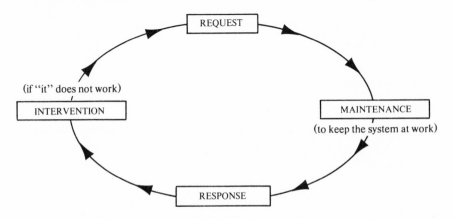

The system is closed, and we are informed when the system fails to work by the failure of the response—the ring of the phone in a distant place. To maintain a functioning telephone system requires constant intervention when malfunction is signaled and constant maintenance (every moment of the day) to prevent malfunction.

So, too, the body is a system. In fact, by the term "system" we imply that it is organized to do its work; we speak of the body's organization; we speak among others of its skeletal, or nervous, or circulatory, or digestive system; we speak of the body, a living system, as organism—organized for life. A stomachache signals a malfunction of the digestive system, and we may intervene with a known remedy or call in an expert to prescribe the remedy. Examination by stethoscope, then electrocardiogram or angiogram, informs an expert of a malfunction of the circulatory system, and remedies are prescribed. Of course, we should like the malfunction to be detected early. These days we may even intervene to remedy malfunction with mechanical devices—kidney machines for renal malfunction, pacemakers for certain malfunctions of the heart, and the like. The body is a system, served by component systems. Either malfunction signals the need for intervention, or regular examination (the medical or dental checkup) may offer information that will recommend intervention.

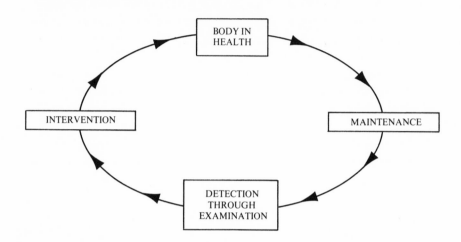

Curiously enough, the body has its own system of maintenance and intervention: homeostasis. For example, in a healthy body glucose (a sugar) is maintained at a concentration of .01% in the blood. Glucose is central to the body chemistry of sustaining energy for body function. A number of substances secreted by the body, known as hormones and enzymes, maintain this concentration of glucose at .01%. If it is not so maintained (due perhaps to diabetes, where the hormone insulin is lacking), the glucose concentration rises (in diabetes because insulin acts to assist the body in using glucose for the kind of energy needed to maintain life activities). If the body requires additional glucose, say, in an emergency—a burst of speed needed by a runner, excessive energy required during an accident or called for when fear dictates the body's action—another hormone, adrenaline (produced by the adrenal glands), is called into action. Adrenaline acts on muscle cells and the liver so that a substance, glycogen (so-called animal starch), is broken down by enzymes to produce more sugar. These activities are orchestrated by an organ known as the hypothalamus in conjunction with the pituitary gland, both above the roof of the mouth. This is but one example of the many devices built into the body system—a homeostatic system—to keep the body in a steady or "balanced" state. When our body remains in an unbalanced, or unhealthy, state, we call upon physicians to intervene. If we do not, injury or death may intervene. Often the body heals itself through its homeostatic system. But note: a homeostatic system returns the body to satisfactory function; it does not save the body in moments of dire emergency (say, insulin shock, with no one around to give assistance). The organism, as system, may not then endure. On the other hand, a social system or educational system may endure the death of one of its human members, but it acts to maintain the social system, or educational system, or economic system.

The educational system to become a system should perhaps become, in essence, an ecological system: that is, it should be made up of systems that serve it. A thermostatic control, or computer control (in the telephone system), or homeostatic control is not a good enough model. The educational system needs to change in accordance with the impending and demanding changes of societies, and thus its control should be at once homeostatic (characterizing the social state of a given school) and ecological (characterizing the psychosocial-political state of the community and society).

The educational system, being subject to change, needs to have somewhat the same system as the prehistoric oceans: able to heal themselves in catastrophe, able to make room for evolving organisms, yet able to sustain themselves over geologic time. An educational system should have the ecological interaction needed to achieve stability and balance, should be able to accommodate change without upheaval, should be able to withstand catastrophe—even as the United States has over the past 200 years or so. And the birth of an educational system may undergo similar pangs, including certain Articles of Confederation, and/or the doctrines that preceded them. Indeed, the model of our government designed by our Constitution is a decent model to begin with. It is a guide, not a book of recipes.

To repeat, we do *not* yet have an educational system. In a number of communities we have schooling systems that are efficient—that is, they serve the communities' special aims (means and ends are adjusted to serve those aims). But "failures" of some young people are permitted, and "failures" in attainment of necessary knowledge, values, and skills are not consistent with the function of an open society, dependent on the healthy social function of its citizens. Failures of the young are permitted even in essentials; there are those with "functional illiteracy"—verbal and mathematical illiteracy—and this is unsupportable in a society soon to enter a postindustrial age. Failures of health in the young are permitted; for example, "drug cultures," in which the young do damage to themselves even to the point of killing their own bodies. And this, too, is insupportable. It is a grave indictment of a society that it permits self-immolation of its young, and even of its adults, by a new and unnecessary chemistry—drugs which damage the homeostatic function of the body, even unto prolonged brain damage and death.

There are schools that do not utilize the most effective methods in curriculum and instruction; there are "good" schools and "bad" schools in neighboring communities, and this is insupportable. It is insupportable precisely because a system developed for superior function does not support relative malfunction. At the least, all school systems should be *aware* of the excellent schools around them, or in the nation; they should be aware of useful and efficient modes of conserving, transmitting, rectifying, and expanding knowledge, values, and skills.

In a telephone system it is the mode of transmission of information that is the system. *What* is transmitted—knowledge, values, and skills—is the significant element in an educational system. And in an educational system the benefits accruing to the informed—children, the young, the adults—are even more important. Not only are they informed, but also they are taught how to seek new information. That is, they may maintain a homeostatic educational system within them within an ecological system that surrounds them—an ecology of achievement maintained by the society. An educational system is not a manufacturing system, where one speaks of raw material in and finished product out, where one speaks of input and output. The young at any one point in development are ends in themselves, and at any one point—infant, child, adolescent—are in themselves the means to further development. In a telephone system, *how* something is transmitted is of supreme worth; in an educational system *what, how,* and *to whom* information is transmitted is of supreme worth.

In short, in the telephone system the machine is of supreme value; in an educational system each individual is of supreme value. It is this environment that constitutes the educational system, and as environment it is subject to the servomechanisms of the system. The single central device is the teaching and learning act; these are not separate acts but one. There is no teaching unless there is learning; that is the essence of instructed learning. In the response of the young to the teaching act we have the essential observable phenomenon that is our servomechanism, our feedback device. It is the mechanism that enables the learner to maintain an ecology of achievement in learning—that is, in the simplest sense, a lack of an adaptive behavior or some significant or vital knowledge is the stimulus for the learner's "learning system" to respond. The response is the search for new and reliable information and ways of changing one's behavior.

We may then proceed to the construction of the elements that may well make up the essential environments constituting our educational system. Its components are all the systems that enter into the education —not just the schooling—of the young. Foremost are the following tasks that society might take upon itself. They are given in order, perhaps, but all are, in a sense, first and foremost.

1.   Those who plan and are active in building the educational system —home school, preschool, primary, intermediate, transitional, preparatory, and apprentice and intern schools—need to be concerned with what Robert Havighurst, in *Human Development and Education* called "developmental tasks of youth." These developmental tasks are, in more familiar terms, aims of personal growth and development; they are the aims of education. The reason, it seems, for the failure to adopt Havighurst's developmental tasks as applying to schooling is that the tasks were then and are now applicable to an educational system. The phrase "developmental tasks" is at once one of those from which pragmatists recoil, but is, if taken seriously, a useful and important guide to planning an educational system within the ecology of achievement described here. Perhaps that term could be modified: developmental tasks are the "essential behaviors" required of a citizen in an open society, and essential behaviors are the "basics" of an educational system. (If the term is not useful, another will surely come into use.) Developmental tasks or essential behaviors are simply the tasks of growth every child, every girl and boy, every young man and woman living in an open, postindustrial, techno-electronic society must go through to lead a competent—even if not happy—life. For example, everyone must or at least should find some way of achieving good health, decent relationships with neighbors, satisfying work. Without worthwhile ends (aims) and means for attaining them, our educational system is not of service, it is not the servomechanism a system demands; it is instead, sloppy, it is wasteful of people and treasure, and it is held suspect. To put a central statement in terms applicable to an educational (not schooling) system: the behavior of the young is shaped and maintained by the essential behaviors an open, competent, and compassionate society sees as critical to its well-being and the well-being of its young. These essential behaviors are thus the true "basics" of an educational system.

2.   Curriculum and instruction need to be conjoined with the best practice. We know better how to do what we are doing. For example, if we reduced the lecture by 50% across the board, and em-

phasized "response" (synonym: individual work by the learner), we should improve effectiveness in instruction dramatically—assuming, of course, that what is designed to be learned (in curriculum) is worthwhile, that the curriculum balances the verbal (linear-sequential) with the spatiovisual (holistic and intuitive), and, further, that the curriculum comprises *balanced* offerings of the realms of meaning, which Phenix offers as a compendium of knowledge, attitudes, skills—in a word, experience serving life.

3.   The requirements of an ecology of achievement in schooling (as part of education) need to be considered. The requisite resources of nation, community, the private sector, parents, and students must be brought to bear confidently and competently on the business of learning and development—the prime business of the young in the school years.

4.   The aspects that are characteristic of a system should be examined. What is required, in effect, is adherence to a theory of instruction and curriculum that corresponds to an assertion of systems theory. That is, means should be evaluated in the realization of ends. The system needs to undergo constant testing with a variety of assessments, appraisals, and measures—paper-and-pencil tests, standardized tests, criterion-referenced tests, work by students (with independent evaluation), practical tests, observations by teams of experts, and so on. The tests should be used for purposes of guidance, as are the maturing-independence units suggested here as one approach to instruction that embraces not only the small group but also the individual learner. Tests are *never* (and the word is chosen carefully) to be used as a basis for judgment of a final destination of the learner. Accountability is to be had if it is based on decent expectation, competence, and compassion. But accountability begins with the statement of decent (that is, realizable) expectations, and these are to be asserted in a description of what it is to be a young man or woman aged sixteen to nineteen in a decent society. A decent society is given over to humane ends, where each individual is nurtured because in the end it is the individual who nurtures society; a society where opinion and behavior are not coerced but are the result of balance of opposing opinion; a society where opportunity is available for the fullest measure of achievement of which an individual is capable; a society in which a habitual vision of excellence and greatness— an essential behavior of an educated person—is to be sustained and maintained by young and old. Furthermore, teachers cannot

be held accountable for the outcomes of schooling if they are not given the support and the means by which to attain the outcomes.

Surely in the United States there are minds that can be gathered to develop these ends of education (and others certain to be developed). These ends are in a real sense the building blocks for the lifelong search for personhood, for that point in life which justifies living a life. It is to insist that an educational system cannot be built without a scheme, a model, a plot, of the kinds of lives the system will enhance. Certainly school buildings, day schools, TV stations, even homes cannot be built without making the environment fit for experience utilizable in a sanative life. Such planners, such people, such minds exist.

Essential Aims of Education: Essential Behaviors for the Young in an Open Society

---

Let us consider essential behaviors in harmony with the constants of the environment that are the hallmarks of an educational system, an environment in which the young fulfill their powers in the pursuit of excellence.

Because essential behaviors are the requirements of growth the young undertake to fulfill whether in school or not, we need to employ the entire environment to catalyze their development. The school cannot take on in 6/24ths (six hours) of the day the 24/24ths of life's tasks, problems, achievements, dreams. Certain developmental tasks of the young, for example, are to secure a healthy body, to attend to those tasks of self-expression and conduct that are basic to securing satisfying work, to have respect for individuals within the community without regard to race, sex, or creed. But the attainment of these behaviors is not limited to 6/24ths of the day, the time given over to schooling.

So, too, it is obvious that unless home and family attend to cleanliness, diet, and elementary care, the barest prerequisites for health cannot be secured; if alcohol and drugs are readily available to the young at home or in the community, and decent behaviors codified in statute and law are not enforced, it is footless to embark in school on programs of education dealing with the effects of drugs and, particularly, the excessive use of tobacco and alcohol on bodily health. It is equally clear that unless the family and the community make available opportunities for the individual to practice the elements of self-expression and decent conduct, schooling cannot achieve its ends and the schools cannot be held accountable. Obviously, a community in which life and property are hostage to violence cannot expect its schools to correct the injustices the community condones. To guarantee the school's function, then, is to ensure an educational environment in which the individual, the group, the school, the community, the nation can function, and thus to ensure an educational system in which schooling is a major function, but not the only one. When all the elements in a community—parents, teachers, federal and local agencies—collaborate, "discipline problems" are capable of solution. To "run free," any mechanism—say, a locomotive, a car, a hospital—must have its parts adjusted to smooth function. So must the school and the community. This is only reasonable.

Perhaps the most salient of developmental tasks of schooling might be viewed as indispensable to arming the young for fruitful development of the essential behavior required in a postindustrial society. We arm ourselves for defense with the view of maintaining our integrity as a nation, and we should arm the young for participation in society to maintain the integrity of the individual and the integrity of society. We would see, then, any individual (the emphasis is on *individual*) emerging from his or her early education (including schooling) armed with the equipment necessary to fulfill his or her powers in the pursuit of excellence. An educational system, as compared and contrasted with a schooling system, is defined by its aims and the structure devised to attain these aims: an *ecology of achievement in education* over and above an ecology of achievement in schooling. Perhaps the essential behaviors, behaviors essential to a matrix of behaviors fitted to an ecology of achievement in education and aimed at sustaining visions of excellence and greatness, can be considered under the following eleven heads:

1. *Facility in expression.* Surely schooling ought to equip the young with literacy and numeracy (verbal-numerical skills such as listening, speaking, reading, numbering, writing) sufficient to get and keep a job or proceed with further education. But these "basics" are not sufficient for the *education* of an individual destined to act responsibly in a postindustrial world.

2. *Facility in self-expression.* Literacy and numeracy are but one mode of self-expression. There are boys and girls who achieve competence in literacy and numeracy but have special abilities and achieve excellence in poetry, literature, music, art, dance, drama, athletics, and the variety of modes of self-expression characteristic of a rich culture.

   Early schooling is precisely the time when all the modes of

expression imbedded in the written and oral symbolic modes, as well as those grounded in the audio-spatiovisual, are the grist for the developing mind and body. It is certainly conceivable that by the end of the intermediate grades the various and idiosyncratic potentialities of the young for expression in the bread-and-butter symbolic modes of language and mathematics, and self-expression in the variety of spatiovisual (holistic, iconic, and enactive modes), should be on record. By the end of the transition period, it is not impossible for boys and girls to have partial mastery of a skill in at least one mode of expression other than language and mathematics —whether in poetry, painting, music, dance, or gymnastics is not so much the point. It is to say that to be able to achieve a potential in modes other than language and mathematics one should have opportunity for immersion in them. It is to suggest that the curriculum of the preschool, primary, intermediate, and transition schools should be balanced in the "basics" of language, mathematics, and the humanities (including the arts) even as the "basics," the knowledges, values, and skills in the social sciences and sciences requisite to an open society based in technology, are acquired.

It is necessary, too, for the young to gain an ability to express themselves in a second, or even a third, language. This may become a matter not only of cultural necessity, but of economic necessity as well. TV brings cultures of other lands to the young, and the airplane brings the young face to face with the people of other lands, other commitments, and other persuasions.

3. *Modes of conduct.* By the end of the primary years, children should have acquired modes of conduct that enable them to work well with others in the activities of the school whether involved directly in learning, or in play, or in social interchange. Surely the elements of courtesy are obligatory. But more than that, it is obvious that an open society depends fully on the active social interchange of its members, not merely on the behaviors inspired by tolerance, but on those based in respect. It is eminently desirable that by the end of the transitional school the modes of curriculum and instruction will have begun to foster continued growth in character. To re-emphasize, an individual should have an education that offers him or her a rich opportunity to become truer, kinder, gentler, warmer, humbler, quieter, and withal stronger, firmer, and wiser. Competence is not the sole aim of education. An educated person is surely as compassionate as competent. Otherwise, he or she is merely learned.

It should be clear that I am not pressing for inculcation of a special point of view, a special or single religious or "moral" purpose. Nor am I pressing for the inculcation through the schools of any special faith. Children should have acquaintance with the major religious faiths, for these faiths are ever present. More important, faith in oneself, in family, in nation, in one's belief is a bulwark against despair and is a basis for defense of one's belief, whether social, political, or religious. However, I do press for what David Riesman calls "moral scrupulosity." (As a case aside, but to the point, how "useful" it would have been if we had understood the nature of the Shiite and Suni aspects of Islam in our relationship with Iran.)

4. *Facility in modes of inquiry.* The objects and events—that is to say, the many environments—of what we call "society" are in constant change. Education is, therefore, never static; its dynamism requires facility in modes of inquiry that enable the young and the adult to determine what is valid, what is based on evidence, and whether that evidence is based on valid modes of inquiry. It is clear, generally speaking, that the aims and methods of scientific inquiry are not understood. Facts, hypotheses, and theories that are *not* testable are not part of science. Thus scientific inquiry does not include within its domain the body of religious practice and religious belief. The beliefs of a religion are not readily discarded as are the hypotheses of a science. For the citizen in an open society, modes of seeking and evaluating evidence are necessary tools. The "methods of intelligence" (often called "scientific methods") are devices of research integral to the subject matters called "the sciences," "the social sciences," and to certain areas of the humanities; they should be part of the armament in the essential behaviors of the young whether they become experts and use the modes of inquiry as part of their work or use them in an understanding sufficient to evaluate data placed before them. The maturing-independence approach advocated affords constant practice in the use of a variety of modes of inquiry.

5. *Modes of participation in an open society.* The social sciences (including the field called "conservation") are replete with accounts of successful and unsuccessful behavior in the solution of social and political problems. The sciences are similarly replete with accounts of behaviors in the solution of problems in the physical and natural world. The same holds true for the arts and humanities in the solution of problems concerning the human condition

and human conduct. But it is the utilization of the past and the melding of tradition and innovation in application to the present that are stimulated by modes of instruction proposed here. Symbolic, synoptic, synoetic, empiric, esthetic, and ethical probes are to be part of the subject matters that form the curriculum of the schools. The study of history particularly is more than a recounting of facts in a chronology. It is a conceptualization of the promise of a nation.

6. *The acquiring of fitness in vocational skills.* Throughout, the participation of the learner essential to completing work in the acquisition of knowledge, values, and skills in all the stages of schooling, work-study opportunities and the initiation of the young into renumerative work at least in the apprentice and intern schools, and the activities in the work place explicated in the next section, are to be developed to give the young the experience necessary to get and keep a job. The *educational system* (not to be equated with the school system) is precisely the device to make available opportunity for constant retraining (constant education, if you will) to enable those who wish it to fit themselves for new vocations. Such fitness applies to the great variety of vocations available in our society—to the physician or electrician seeking to manage a new technology; to the housewife seeking to enter the professions or the marketplace; to the "retired" who wish to fit themselves for new enterprise. A postindustrial society demands new skills and the recognition of the major impact on the work place of computerized technology.

7. *Modes of achieving and maintaining physical and mental health.* Certainly the case for the maintenance of physical health need not be pressed. We have advanced to the point of requiring "intrusive medical techniques" (immunization) as a requirement for attending school. And we shall advance in our curricular and instructional modes in teaching care of the body through diet, exercise, rest. Considerations involving mental health will be pressed. Essentially, character education, based on the "character-rooted passions," presses for examination of the kinds of "prudence values" —values that seem self-evident—for the maintenance of health (including diet, alcohol, smoking, drugs). In turn, prudence values press upon the uses of rest and exercise as well as knowledge and skills necessary for the prevention and amelioration of "new" diseases—hypertension, cardiovascular disease, cancer. Certainly the newer knowledges pertaining to aging are essential. Mainly, a

new ecology of habits is required; home, community, and school *must* intervene to secure the physical health as well as the mental health of the young. For example, the drug habit is not a convenience but a danger to the life of the individual and the life of society, but it may well be a first sign of emotional imbalance.

8. *Modes of coming to terms with age-mates of different sex.* The essential behaviors needed to deal with the newer "moralities," newer "values," new relationships between the sexes make it obligatory for the young to acquire knowledges not hitherto considered part of schooling. One of these areas of knowledge is often called "sex education," which, of course, includes more than the functions of sex per se. Whether sex education is conducted in the schools, at home, or in a place of worship is not the main point, but it is essential that it become part of the *education* of the young. Each community should decide where education in such knowledge and behavior should be conducted. The home has not always been effective in this area. "Sex education" as rubric involves early understanding of the relationships between the sexes beginning in early childhood, and commands the knowledges, values, and skills in social and individual behavior demanded by the most explicit and often poignant cognitive and affective behavior. To be avoided, if possible, are the trauma, both physical and mental, of teen-age pregnancy, teen-age marriage, and broken marriages affecting children and adults.

9. *Modes of maintaining and sustaining the environment.* The past years have fostered the recognition of our dependence on a sanative environment, but the conviction that care of the environment is an individual responsibility is not yet common. Searching for scapegoats is all too common; for example, the focus too often is on industrial disregard of the needs of the environment whereas in fact industrial management is responsive to its clients: buyers and sellers who demand its products. A new ethic is required, and its building is part of the education proposed.

10. *The achievement of a world view.* The impact of the living-room TV classroom has not yet been fully acknowledged. The world is becoming a global state, if not a "global village," as Marshall Mc-Luhan has suggested. "Global state" is perhaps more apt, if only because the state of the globe is ready fare on TV as well as in print media. Although instructional materials available to all schools stressed the interdependence of the inhabitants of the globe, it was not until events involving not only the globe, but also the universe,

were brought to the living room that the need for a world view became imperative. When the activities of OPEC, revolution in Iran, the incredible vision of American hostages held in "retribution" for past history, the evolution of Zimbabwe (Rhodesia), and other new states, landings on the moon, terrorist activities in Munich, discussions at the United Nations on resolutions having wide impact, visits of satellites to Mars and Jupiter made "real" by pictures, a shuttle to and from space, Three Mile Island, a coronation, a crime, a war—when such events are brought in intimate association by TV and radio to a small or large group, it is sheer cavil to argue whether or not events displayed on TV affect behavior. The young are, in effect, citizens of a nation and participants in global events. Aside from knowledge of a second language, knowledge of the world's history is of increasing importance.

11. *The achievement of self-esteem, or a self-concept.* All in all, the essential behaviors sketched here in broad strokes are the warp and woof of "self-concept." A self-concept, which is an antecedent of self-esteem, depends, of course, on the totality of the development that results from the interplay of heredity and environment.

Education, in the sense employed here, is comprised of all the elements of the environment that act to initiate and modify effective responses to the environment, that maintain the integrity of the individual, the group, and society—planned and unplanned actions which change behavior. Education is thus both cause and effect of a lifelong search for personhood, of a sustained vision of high purpose, of excellence and greatness.

Are these *all* the essential behaviors with which the young are to be armed? The answer waits upon a plan for the development of an educational system. It would be arrogant to assume otherwise.

Essentials of an Educational System: Lifelong Education

There are no comforting answers to the problem of making available to all youth kinds of satisfying work while they prepare themselves for a vocation that will give them sufficient remuneration and sustain integrity, if not a sense of worthwhileness, or pride. But that is precisely what an educational system must do—for *all,* not *part* of its population of young. It must *prepare* for work; not *guarantee* work. The guarantee of work is the province of society, not of an educational system.

Consider, if you will, that the schooling system we have probed in past chapters, which is part of an educational system, is intended to meet the common and special needs of the great and rich variety of the youth of the nation. There will be those who, gifted in a variety of abilities, sure of their opportunity and destination, will leave in good time. Their year of special service will be especially enriching to them and those they serve. There will be a good population ready for a postschool education. The vast majority, 90% at least, will have the competencies (more than minimum) to enable them to accommodate to the next stage of their education: work to fit them for a place in society, remunerative work that enables them to contribute their skills to the advance of the community and society.

Our society makes available rich opportunities for employment to the young who have decent cognitive and affective capacity and ability, and thus are capable of acquiring the level of success in academic areas (those based in linear-sequential processing) that would sustain them in college or university. Let us assume a system of financial incentives, including loans to be repaid in a reasonable time, so that all who are able and so motivated can and do go to college. Similarly, assume incentives available so that those who are able do go to community college (two years). At this moment, let us not break the argument on the rocks of the question Is college worthwhile for all who aspire to attend it? Let us consider the bare question of finding suitable and honorable work for those who have left the preparatory school (our "new" secondary school). A good number—more than 60%—will apply for college entrance. What of the rest? What aspects of further education are available to them?

Recall that all the young who are of "leaving age" (having fulfilled the requirements) are now to be given opportunity for one year of service to the community and society generally. A number who take advantage of this year of moratorium—a year to find a suitable guide to the future—may find a door to explore the kind of work that may satisfy them: work in these areas, given only by way of example:

• Health services (nursing, paramedical services, medical or dental technicians, including X-ray, therapy, and other specialized treatment)

• Institutes and academies to prepare those interested in pursuing the arts (design, painting, music, dance)

• Vocational colleges and institutes to prepare, for example, com-

puter programers and refrigeration, air-conditioning, and home-appli-
ance repair persons
- Academies to prepare police, fire-fighting, postal personnel, and
the like
- Industrial institutes in the automotive industries, machine crafts,
transportation (trucking and general)
- Armed services, not only in military aspects of service, but also as
a way to enter the skilled crafts of maintenance of aircraft, ships, machines, and to continue a career in the armed services
- Home services (maintenance, electricity, plumbing, TV, mechanics)
- Community services, generally those involved in health care (home
visits), park and sanitation services, care of the very young, the disabled,
the indigent, the handicapped aged
- New areas of work, part of a postindustrial area not yet known or
contemplated

The complex of academies, institutes, vocational colleges, community colleges, universities, and institutions devoted to conservation,
community, and armed services (except for those that lead directly from
the secondary school and for which the latter is considered a prerequisite
function) is not considered a part of the educational system of this
country. But these components are, and should be. The fact is that in
the United States the young are not *fixed* in their initial vocational
selections. The young who leave high school may sooner or later select
various successive fields of work, including the university. Those who
enter the university may leave to participate in other areas of a lifework.
The destiny of American youth is opened by choice, though not necessarily free choice, because choice is bound by ability and education.

Preparation for work of whatever kind should, in a postindustrial
society, be considered a part of the educational system. For the purpose
of an educational system (note: not a school system) is to be no less
than *full* preparation for life fit for an open society, one in which every
citizen seeks fitness of purpose and fulfillment in satisfying work. In our
society, preparation for work is a practical and essential goal.

We come at once to the problem of extending the education through
work of those who for one reason or another do not excel or, given the
circumstances, do only passably well in the preparatory school. It is
true that modes of curriculum and instruction (such as the maturing-
independence model of learning) have attempted to assure competency
in literacy and numeracy. For all general purposes, functional illiteracy
will no longer be a problem—or at least not a problem of major con-
tention (and soon enough, because it is a "priority"). There will still

be young who for one reason or another cannot yet profit from the kind of education full participation in work can give. Still, in a society where accomplishment and achievement are marks of fitness, suitable work must be found for them. Vocational training, in the ordinary sense of the word, may not be the answer. But training for useful service in the community may well be. One need not look far—and we should not consider this make-work, but work of fundamental importance to the individual and society. Again, by way of example:

There is need for a *construction corps* to assist in the considerable task of rehabilitating decaying cities and communities. There are varieties of work with tangible rewards in rehabilitating a block of houses, a playground, a park, or the like—work that needs doing and that would afford a measure of integrity and a breathing space, allowing certain of the young to take stock. These are safe havens which society should furnish; these havens are better than jail or the idleness that breeds crime and the drug culture. Federal, state, and local funds—funds from the public and private sectors—can and should be made available for this purpose and the services that follow.

There is need for a *conservation corps* to care for the environment, to reconstitute the land and water, to replant forests, to restock lakes, ponds, and rivers, to maintain scenic roadsides and parks.

There is need for a *home service corps* to care for the aged and the indigent. In a nation whose health services are dedicated to eliminating infectious and functional disease, the average life span is expanding and will expand. But not all of the aged will be capable of caring for themselves.

These are prosaic tasks, but as we consider the problem in all its extensions, these are some ways of sustaining all the young in the initial stages of finding satisfying work. The purpose: to learn the skills and attitudes required to sustain oneself in the work place.

This is not—in any way—to set aside the incredible programs of education, training, and retraining that are part and parcel of the policy of corporate industry. These many programs have often been called "on-the-job training," but this, too, is a simplistic term. Harold Clark and Harold Sloan's valuable analysis of industrial programs in *Classrooms in the Factories* has indicated the extent of this vast but loose enterprise, which in truth consists of parts of an "educational system." Generally, industrial programs are open to employees who qualify, but they are based on a diagnosis of qualifications or lack of them, and therefore of areas in which training should be established (including programs in language and mathematics); progressive units of work where the employee's progress is constantly appraised; and advance to a job utilizing the new knowledge or skill.

It is not uncommon for a specific industry to subsidize the education of individuals in schools, colleges, and universities in undergraduate, graduate, and postgraduate levels. Clark once estimated that the funds expended in education (teaching and learning) by industry exceeded the amounts spent in schooling.

To press the point from another view, our life span is increasing (no, catapulting), and it is not unreasonable to permit certain of the young—those who have not yet found themselves an initial foothold in society—a period up to twenty-five years of age for their personal and singularly unique experiment in development.

We have not begun to consider the education of those who, having left the work force at any stage, not exclusive of retirement, wish to continue their education, for purpose of retraining or for the purpose of sustaining their life work.

How is this to be done? Who is to do it? Who is to support so massive an effort?

Solutions are necessary; and if necessary, possible; and if possible, open to invention. An examination of alternatives is in order. The kind of educational system we now require must accommodate lifelong education. We must have nothing less than an end to haphazardness. That is just what "system" means—that ends be related to means; that ends satisfy means; that ends and means be evaluated in terms of each other; that unsatisfactory ends suggest without qualification unsatisfactory means, and vice versa.

Essentials: A Gathering of Minds and Resources

Early in the development of schooling in the colonies, and early in the development of the Union, and finally in the codification of rule, custom, and law by the Founding Fathers into the Constitution, the dominant principle was clearly this: to protect the rights of the individual against the "tyranny" of central government. Schooling—simply a right to know, to be informed—was *not* to be a function of central government. The danger of the uses of control over minds by a central authority (European schooling was the example) was ever present, as indeed it should be. Thus local control over schooling and local financing were established as policy; thus some 16,000 school districts are now in site, each a local subgovernment, as it were, with funds drawn from local taxes. Political control by the central government was avoided, but the crushing demands for funding of schooling to maintain the "rising tide of expectation" of a population soon to be 250 million were not. The requirements imposed on local school governments (school districts) by federal and state laws to educate each and all were not foreseen by the usually farsighted Founding Fathers. Nevertheless, the Constitution was flexible enough; the intent of its preamble was clear: it permits modification of existing codification. Nor were the requirements foreseen of an education in a techno-electronic age, in a meritocratic society, in a culture where space colonies are projected, where interdependent global relationships are needed for defense or for survival of economies, where first, second, and third worlds exist, and where events are no longer isolated by barriers—solid (land), liquid (oceans), or gaseous (air). Nor were life spans of seventy-five to one hundred years foreseen, or the intimacy forced by travel at the speed of mach 2 (by air) and the transmission of word and image at the speed of light (by TV).

Local initiative and control of the schooling of the young must be protected, but the function of state and federal initiatives in education should also be sustained. It is clear that local funding must be supplemented by federal funds, even though these are not always wisely allocated. For example, it is estimated that there are 12 to 14 billions of federal Title I funds (funds essentially for young children, in elementary school) that are returned to communities on a revenue-sharing basis. But the funds are not (perhaps one should say "not yet") concentrated in areas or communities of greatest need. The model of distribution is perhaps analogous to one that requires distribution of winter heating oil to all states, "sun belt" or "snow belt," on the basis of population rather than need. Yet the requirements in funds, other resources, and talent in the development of new curriculums and instructional modes geared to programs necessary, for example, to the education and special training and retraining of teachers, to the development of effective curriculums, to the isolation of innovations that work, to the care of individual excellence and handicap, are so extensive and so demanding that few, if any, communities can sustain the burden. Nor can any single group now serving *education* sustain the entire burden—not the federal government; not state departments of education; not schools of education, which prepare teachers; not publishers who prepare instructional materials (and the curriculums that undergird them); not TV corporations;

not communications industries, which will soon supply additional instructional materials in varieties of knowledge and skills through satellites, computers, cassettes and/or discs, Bildschirm texts, or through Telex models or TV sets, which will become part of the educational system. Certainly the federal government cannot of itself be the source of funds and minds. Nevertheless, a vast offensive to develop an educational system is required; *it must be mounted.*

In a sense, the word "offensive" is precisely descriptive; the equivalent of a "war" needs be mounted. But, as we shall see, what is proposed is that once the objective of the offensive is reached, the *organization* that achieved the objectives should be disbanded. The *structure* (as compared and contrasted with organization) that is invented to make the educational system function should, however, be maintained and sustained, and modified to fit what is inevitable: *change.* As has been suggested, the problem is structural, not intellectual. To repeat, there are individuals with the needed proclivity for inventiveness, and what seems clear is that no new funds are required; they are already available. It will be necessary to attend to the type of organization or structure that needs inventing, the type of organization that might catalyze the invention and the source of funding, and a major invention of how a co-ordinated structure might function in the solution of a major educational problem: the lifelong education of Americans—all Americans, at all ages and conditions of development.

A Structure: Meant to Be Struck Down and Constantly Reinvented

---

First, certain objectives; second, the genre of organizations already in place; third, a possible organization to mobilize effort; fourth, its funding; fifth, some comments, perhaps gratuitous, on a ground in policy— these will be sketched in all brevity to clarify *purpose* rather than final organization. It would be imprudent, not to say arrogant of this writer, at this point, to make recommendations that should come out of the sustained deliberation of the finest minds, deliberation that evaluates validity. And these deliberations should not come out of a "conference"—one of the great social diseases of modern cultures. The finest minds can design more effective means of deliberation. There is valid research and there are a host of valid questions and situations to challenge the validity of the research that exists. Sad experience with conferences and educational treatises shows that too many of the individuals who attend conferences, or look to summaries of "educational research," are wont to use statements as data. If they listen long enough, attend enough conventions, read enough reports, listen to enough "experts," they will surely find that in any conference on education (as in other scholarly pursuits) it is sporting to disagree, and that in the end the reporters of educational research will agree on two or more statements, each in profound disagreement with the other. For example, Jon Schaffarzick and Gary Sykes, reporting in a most effective manner, in *Value Conflicts and Curriculum Issues,* the contributions of a recent conference and reflecting the deliberations of respected leaders in schooling, nonetheless were obliged to report a certain position (an honest one, to be sure) thus: "The vigorous exchange of views concerning the possibility of a nonpolitical dimension in curriculum development illustrates again the depth of ideological difference underlying seemingly innocent positions. That the structure of knowledge itself might be the result of a political process is, to some, unthinkable. To others, that it might *not* seems unthinkable."

And then there are those incredible statements that are the refuge of schoolman and scholar, researcher and scientist, when driven by fatigue and frustration. I once took part in a collaboration of research scientists, respected scholars in science and psychology, and selected teachers in the surge of innovation in curriculum of the 1955–1965 period. After a day of fatiguing discussion and frustrating work (for there was a dearth of valid data on the effectiveness of curriculum and instruction), it was reassuring to hear how little was known by these highly respected scientists (some Nobelists) and psychologists. One heard what have been called "BLKS," that is, statements incapable of proof or disproof, such as:

"The teacher is the key."

"Parents don't care."

"Education isn't respected in the United States."

"Those who want to work will learn."

"If you work students hard, they will work harder."

The participants, splendid scientists all, were in fact acknowledging how little was known about the teaching process, though they would recoil in horror were such simplistic statements made in their own fields of research. Perhaps certain BLKS are intuitively "true"; however this may be, the truth or falsity of a statement must be tested. If true it will conform to fact; if false it will not. That is precisely the point: we know little of a "science of education"; we know a great deal about what works. But we really do not know why it works. We are at the stage perhaps that early practitioners of agriculture and animal husbandry once encountered: they grew plants well, but knew nothing of photosynthesis; they knew that if they mated like animals, the offspring might have the characteristics of these animals, but they had no idea of sperms and eggs, of the transmission of chromosomes, of DNA. So there is a vast literature in education and schooling on what works (and sometimes a valid explanation), but there is no science of education or schooling. But *we need to know what is valid,* and we can, and should, establish criteria for valid research and practice in sight of carefully conceived aims and objectives.

To emphasize once again, schooling and education are art-sciences of practice, not yet of the laboratory. And teaching, in its finest examples, seems to be a personal invention and a performing art. Like other performing arts, it can be exercised by its trained practitioners. But what valid data are to be applied to the improvement of teaching? Another word, highly relevant on this aspect, by Lee Cronbach, an eminent scholar in the field of learning, schooling, and education, is important:

> We have, on one hand, the view of education as cultural transmission, which hints strongly that it is the teacher's job to know the answers and to put them before the pupil. On the other, we have the view of education as growth, arguing that the only real and valuable knowledge is that formulated by the pupil out of his own experience. The second position, which appeals to liberal, humanitarian, and instrumentalist biases, has a long history. In the last thirty-odd years the bias favoring do-it-yourself learning has been very strong, as educators and psychologists have united in attacks on teacher dominance and pupil conformity. Consequently, we have had almost none of the cut-and-thrust debate needed to define issues and to expose implications or fallacies of the evidence.

It is for the reasons stated above, particularly the masterful summation by Cronbach, that I have taken care not to be overly critical, if I have been critical at all, of experiments that purport to show that one method of instruction or one type of curriculum, one type of administration or schooling, has been superior to another. It is for the reasons stated above and for the reasons to follow that I suggest that programs designed, for example, for the amelioration of disadvantage, for the advancement of the gifted, for the training of teachers and administrators in the teaching of specific fields, say, mathematics or the humanities and arts, need to be examined in the context of an ecology of achievement *within* a school system *within* an educational system by valid methods of inquiry. An opportunity to develop such an ecology of achievement within an educational system seems to me desirable before we develop alternative school systems, including voucher systems or ad-hoc systems of any sort. We speculate, until the evidence is in, that the reason for the success of the "elites" is that they are able, with the means at their disposal, to construct for themselves out of the fragments of the educational system lying about a fairly complete and relatively effective educational system. This is not to say that the young—with the advantages of such a specially devised educational system—will achieve certain "success." We do not yet know the limits of success in the complex society in which we live; certainly we cannot predict the elements of such success in the coming postindustrial society. This in itself requires careful study before, during, and after the event. Let us anticipate the design of the first educational system on planet Earth (in modern times, of course). By way of suggestion the design would embrace at least these two elements:

1.   Consideration of the aims and objectives of an *educational system*
•   *The founding of an educational system serving more than 250 million Americans,* including some 60 million to 80 million children, adolescents, and postsecondary adults, some 140 million to 150 million adults in the work force, and some 50 million mature, retired, and elderly. The educational system should not in any manner or form supplant local school systems, but should develop a *structure* in which the liberty of communities to educate their young is catalyzed and supported by a clear exposition of what is known to be best in teaching and learning and what works.

There are excellent schools in existence; there is competent leadership (that is, cadres of acknowledged leaders in administration, curriculum, and instruction, in scholarship and community and corporate affairs) that can make available demonstrable (in the sense that what is demonstrable may be visually examined in practice in one or more schools) and competent (in the sense that suitable evaluation is available) forms of curriculum and instruction suitable to the great variety of individuals (in whose diversity lies our strength). It is notably American, and characteristic of an open society, to combine forms that seem, at first, opposed—for example, leadership without coercion and freedom of choice in participation. In any event, the net result of such innovation would be the existence of demonstration models of effective school systems within an educational system within an ecology of achievement in communities strategically placed throughout the United States. These could not be ignored; their success would be demonstrated and communicated by TV, at least, but necessarily supported by other competent means. A competition for excellence—which Americans prize—would be set in motion. But it would be competition for demonstration of excellence in educational methods, and educational methods applicable to schooling in an open society.

• *The formulation of valid theory and design in instruction, curriculum, and evaluation; the catalysis of innovation in curriculum, instruction, and evaluation in education as well as in schooling; the design of the administrative structures required for individualized and group instruction.* The innovations would and should include the development, where need has been demonstrated, of curriculums, instructional materials such as general books, textbooks, and realia of all kinds, including laboratory manuals, films and filmstrips, TV programs, satellite programs, cable TV, cassettes and discs, computer-assisted instruction, and new technologies in general which accommodate the idiosyncratic teaching and learning styles of individuals and groups in school and out of school. For example, the computer is about to enter the home. Cassettes, discs, and cable TV are already there. But there is also an acknowledged dearth of useful programs. Methods and designs of instruction to fit the needs of a variety of modalities for lifelong education will need to be developed.

In sum: curriculums, instruction, evaluation, and administration are to be developed for school systems, within educational systems and for elements of an educational system, existing outside of public schooling systems. That is to say, the educational system will, of course, encompass curriculums, instructional modes, evaluation, and administration over and above a schooling system. For example, certain curriculums for TV instruction, certain programs in denominational schools, may well have content unacceptable to the public schools.

• In respect of new programs developed, *the development of methods of education, training, and retraining for teachers and/or supervisors and administrators.* Like physicians, teachers need constant professional retraining. Just as the physician uses existing knowledge and research on which to base performance, so, too, does the teacher. In the end, doctors, writers, artists, and teachers are performers, and are to be judged by their science and their art. It is in singularly poor taste to criticize teachers for failing to have knowledges and skills for which they were not hired (standards had not been set or were not available), or for the lack of certain knowledges and skills when they were hired (available standards were ignored). There are useful methods of selecting teachers who have the knowledges and skills required for *beginning work* in instruction. There are in existence excellent works on the education and training of teachers. But there is a need for the training of teachers for instruction on TV and cassette. The presentations, to be effective, require the response of the viewer (the learner). The technique is in its infancy.

• *The reviewing of researches that exist and selection of those that have demonstrated validity* not only in the classroom and other types of instruction but also through the kind of replication of research that is the hallmark of scientific methods.

• *The planning and catalyzing of those new researchers that are required* on the basis of probes to identify the critical problems requiring investigation. Because research often highlights the true nature of the problem, and redirects research, a time limit cannot be set for selection of a problem when the problem is not yet defined.

• *The selecting of problems that are major and basic.* These will be opportunities to identify a host of subsidiary problems, long and short term.

• *The catalysis of continued development of valid methods of evaluation* that serve the ends of demonstrating the effectiveness of curricular, instructional, and administrative modes in schooling and education. This is but an attempt to unite formal testing with evaluation coming out of formal instruction—for example, instructed learning, including individualized instruction and group instruction.

2.   The genre of organizations that may become parts of a functioning educational system (a definition of a *system* that may be applicable is perhaps this: "an aggregation or assemblage of objects united in interaction or interdependence so as to form an integral whole")

• Clearly these "aggregations" are already in place (the list is not in any order and certainly is not complete, but it is offered by way of example):

    Public and private schools and their supporting communities and institutions: the great variety of pupils, teachers, school boards, superintendents, principals, supervisors, Parent-Teacher Associations (PTAs)

    Colleges and universities

    University schools of education

    Academic departments that prepare teachers in special fields

    Teachers colleges and teacher-training institutions and institutes

    State and city departments of education

    The Department of Education—recently organized

    The U.S. Office of Education (USOE) and the National Institute of Education (NIE)

> Such organizations as the National Science Foundation, particularly its Education Division, and the National Endowment for the Humanities
> Organizations of teachers
> Organizations of administrators
> Organizations of supervisors
> Scholarly organizations
> Publishers of instructional materials and tests; developers of curriculums and tests
> Authors of instructional materials
> Commercial and educational TV
> Authors of critiques of schooling and education
> Industry concerned with the education of employees
> Labor organizations concerned with the education of workers
> Private foundations, especially those concerned with education
> Industrial groups concerned with the development of machines used in education—computers, cassettes, films, and the like
> Journals and newspapers concerned with educational practice
> Task forces (such as the Carnegie Foundation Study Groups)
> Nonprofit educational institutes
> Vocational institutes (proprietary and the like)
> Armed Forces Educational Institutes
> Study groups, of enormous variety

A certain truth is this: *At present,* schools are indeed affected by the variety of pronouncements, products, decisions, practices, promotion devices, and pressures generated by most, if not all, the groups mentioned above. In fact, administrators and teachers are often crushed by the conflicting demands coming out of these groups.

It is a fact that the schools draw on all these resources to effect classroom practice. Further, by wide dissemination of projects directed at changing functions and practices in schooling, co-ordination of effort could be effected. How might this be effected?

• *A loose, benign, but effective organization* to bind the interdependent parts of an educational system noted above in the development of an educational system, to improve curriculum and instruction in schooling and education by bringing the most effective methods to bear on them, and to introduce newer and newer and more effective methods coming out of valid research. How might this be accomplished?

First, a digression, perhaps—though perhaps not so. The creation of special organizations, later to be disbanded, is nothing new; it is characteristic of all great campaigns. In World War II, the Allied Command was created; in the Curricular Revolution of 1957, stimulated by a variety of events, a variety of organizations was created: PSSC (The Physical Science Study Committee), SMSG (School Mathematics Study Group), CHEMS (Chemistry), PE (Project English), A-LM (Audio-Lingual Method—for study of languages), the Science and Mathematics Groups under the Educational Division of the National Science Foundation, and others under various scholarly societies (with funds from federal government and foundations). Perhaps the preparation, retraining of teachers, and effective utilization of the multitude of programs developed would have been facilitated and sustained, and a measure of confusion as well as certain failures would have been avoided, had a benign co-ordination been possible. What kind of special organization, established to begin the design of an educational system, might be developed? *Perhaps* a *germ* of a suggestion is to be found in the following:

It may be desirable to empower the present National Research Council or the National Institute of Education or officials of the Department of Education, or other groups acting as a consortium to find five to nine individuals of demonstrated scholarship, organizing ability, and leadership in public affairs to be a Commission on Educational Systems (CES) for a period of no more than three years. These members of CES should have experience in schooling, education, industry, society, and politics, and should have the trust of the various component educationally oriented groups (public and private) listed previously. CES would function as an initial organizing board and would be disbanded once the planning effort has been made. National and local effort in developing an educational system should not in any manner or form be headed by CES. Above all, one should avoid an effort that begins with a convention. Nevertheless, to maintain the parts of a structure that can be reassembled in need, a Standing Committee with but *one* power needs to be instituted. The one power would be: to develop a roster (as did the Office of Scientific Research and Development, OSRD) of individuals contributing to advances in education; these, of course, are not to be confined to the teaching community per se. This roster might be available to all communities—the individuals to be available for consultation without expense to any specific communities—to assist in the development of a community's educational system.

Thus, CES might be disbanded once it has done the following three things:

1. Developed a new and efficient roster of contributors to education
2. Accomplished the organization of a National Educational Clearing-

house (including at least a National Computerized Library of print and visual media in schooling and education). Such a clearing-house might, among other elements, contain a definitive collection of materials developed for use in curriculum, instruction, evalua-tion, administration, and supervision however and wherever pro-duced; a roster of individuals with demonstrated capacities in these areas; and a reference library of demonstrably valid research affect-ing schooling and education. ERIC (Educational Resources In-formation Center) already exists and may form a base for such a clearinghouse.

3. Effected perhaps the nomination and selection of individuals to staff five (no more) groups provisionally titled Regional Authori-ties for Educational Advancement (RAEA). These individuals would come out of the five areas where the five RAEAs would sit: the Northeast, the Southeast, the Midwest, the Southwest, the West. Each RAEA might perhaps consist of no more than five commis-sioners, representing in broad measure the educationally oriented constituencies listed before. The term of appointment might well be five years over a staggered period, but in any event an RAEA should not have a co-ordinating function for a period of longer than twelve years. Continuing duties of an RAEA for another eight years (beyond the twelve) would be strictly those of assisting states in its region in the evaluation of "pilot" schools instituted as "demonstration schools," and assisting states in the development of reports to be circulated widely of effectiveness of educational policy and practice in those schools.

What might the RAEA do? (Certainly these suggestions are not all-inclusive, for the functions should grow in accordance with the need.) In order of relative but not absolute importance, the functions of the RAEAs might, perhaps, include these five:

1. Assisting the states in the development of demonstration schools and programs which use the most effective methods in administra-tion, supervision, curriculum, and instruction. The number of schools selected, as well as their sites, should be sufficient so that each might serve as an *accessible* school demonstrating effective methods for surrounding schools or school systems. Why not a traveling cadre of observers who would act as consultants and de-scribe what they observe? This has not worked in the past. Other-wise why have the descriptions and critiques (say, Silberman's, or

the excellent attempts of Goodlad's IDEA) not been effective? My best guess is that linear-sequential (verbal) descriptions are not as effective as they might be. The written report is distillable, and good teaching practice must be seen whole to be believed, first; to be appreciated, second; to be adopted, third. The teaching art, the practice within the classroom, is holistic, spatiovisual, and loses a great deal—perhaps the essential—in purely verbal description. Similarly, TV reporting of excellent teaching practice is also dismally ineffective. So much of it is highly selective and focuses only on the successful and the dramatic. The classroom is a whole; its "intelligent failures" in instruction are as important as those "demonstration lessons" that are staged. Teachers who come to learn in a clinical situation rightly suspect the demonstration lesson to be contrived. In this they have the professional's sixth and seventh senses to note what is unfamiliar and surprising to the performer, to sense what is not possible of duplication in their own situations (unless there is a radical change in practice).

2. Assisting states in the institution of curricular and instructional projects as well as administrative and supervisory initiatives to develop "schools without failure," perhaps to develop projects designed to meet the requirements of equal opportunity in schooling with regard to varied abilities, aptitudes, gifts.

3. Instituting critical curricular and instructional research—valid research—to evaluate promising existing reports of valid research within the region. This should permit variability and a certain degree of competition. To be avoided is the centralization of educational policy in one inspectorate or commission (in the French style, for example).

    The aim is clear: each child, each of the young, should be able to advance to full capacity in accordance with general and special ability and aptitude.

4. Developing a design of a system (part of the educational system) with devices to supplement the schooling system; for example, work-study programs, TV programs for parents, the home school, the apprentice and intern schools, and the like. Each state within the region would select those components of the design which would complement its own educational system.

5. Designing an *educational system for lifelong education*. This, of course, goes beyond a schooling system. It does not exist—not yet. It would include educational devices and programs for the young in those "essentials of behavior" the schools are not equipped to

embrace. It would embrace the full life span of all. It would never be compulsory for adults but would, as the educational system develops, offer attractive opportunities to advance life and living. It would continue to furnish opportunities for the fulfillment of one's powers in the pursuit of excellence at all stages of life. Although certain suggestions for the education of prospective parents have already been made in Chapters 3, 4, and 5, it would not be useful, in a small book, to go further. But certain comments may be permissible. If nothing else were done in the development of an educational system beyond the restructuring of schooling and development of programs for the education of parents in the rearing of infants and children and in the nurturing of the adolescent years, great steps will have been taken in the development of an educational system. If, further, the educational system embraced efforts at ensuring the continued growth of adults in social, political, and economic affairs—including retraining for the new work of a post-industrial society—a tremendous step would be taken in advancing lifelong education. If, in addition, programs were devised—whether for viewing at home or in "classes" in the evening—that probed the understandings necessary for life in a richly endowed multi-racial society clearly pluralistic in its social, political, and economic understandings, an additional giant step would be taken. Education, in the coming postindustrial society, cannot end with school or college. It is lifelong and should not be haphazard.

Funding

At this point, the nature of funding is sheer conjecture, and it is offered with considerable diffidence. A National Educational Development Bank, with power to issue bonds backed by federal and national banking institutions, might be one useful mode. An Educational Trust Fund to be allocated to the RAEAs might be one source of funds. Corporations wishing to contribute might be offered substantial tax credits. In any event, funding might be a pooling of federal, state, and local funds, as well as funds from foundations and from industry.

Whatever the mode of establishing funding, it seems clear that no additional funds than are now allocated to education need be brought into play. Even the roughest calculation of the resources allocated to education by the components of the sprawling educational establishment, which could make up the flexible, noncoerced parts of an educational system, amounts to $130 to $170 billion (some say more, by $20 billion or so) per year. This is not an inordinate amount in an economy embracing a GNP of about $3 trillion—and growing. What is being suggested is that in the interests of free enterprise the component institutions support a kind of NATO of education for a brief period in order to secure a future harmony.

In sum: however the renewing of schooling and education is to come about, it must be effected. We can no longer afford the cost in lives and treasure subject to the cycles of ascent, decline, and fall of schooling and education characteristic of the past. A recognized educational system of which the schooling system is a part will supply at least part of the ameliorative. A society that understands *nature* and *nurture* will supply the other. Each will nourish the other in the ecology of achievement stressed here.

The "eternal vigilance" demanded of a just society embodied in the experiment in personal fulfillment and pursuit of excellence that is the bedrock of our democracy is nowhere more essential than in its founding of an educational system dedicated to securing the civilization that is its promise. Surely the people of a democracy are its major resource. Surely they are *the* resource capable of generating that habitual vision of greatness which is the mark of the educated person. Surely such a person, in constant growth, in the fulfillment of personal powers, characteristically seeking excellence in self-expression and conduct, is equally able to encompass experience in search of meaning, in search of those guides to full expression and conduct that have characterized the educated over centuries past. Should we not find a way to neutralize with evidence, reason, judgment, and compassion the all-too-easy assumptions of those who condemn our school systems without exception and wish to eliminate them, and those who wish to use the schools to reform society in a certain image? It may be time to challenge all assumptions and established practice, but it is *never* the time to experiment with children, never the time for ad-hoc methods, the effect of which on growth and personality of the developing child and its future cannot be demonstrated.

Surely it remains for us to chart a new course for the development of a powerful system called an "educational system," strongly supported and ever renewed by the society that is its watershed. The course should be continuous, constant, and consistent in its direction: the development of inordinate personhood and of a sustained vision of greatness.

A life is at once a fact and the fact perhaps most prized by its owner. A life occurs once; it is precious; it is not to be used as an implement of another's political, social, and psychological warfare.

The creation of a school, a school system, an educational system is a noble act pre-eminently concerned with a humane use of human beings. To sustain a school, its young, and its teachers requires an act of renunciation. One is obliged to renounce whim and fancy or hasty augury coming out of one's own foreboding. Out of such renunciation is born the civility and the comity that nourish the young and their teachers and the competence and compassion that nourish civilized society.

A single life cannot outwit time, but perhaps the contributions of an educated people, gracious and civil and informed and acting in concert, may triumph. Thus we may prevail.

Bibliography

Principal References: these are in accord with specific references or quotations to be found in the chapters indicated.

Additional References: these are books, papers, and documents I had occasion to consult as I considered the thesis of the book. They may be useful to the reader.

Chapter 1

Principal References

Bailyn, Bernard. *Education in the Forming of American Society*. Chapel Hill: University of North Carolina Press, 1960.

Cremin, Lawrence A. *The Genius of American Education*. New York: Vintage Books, Random House, 1966.

————. *American Education: The National Experience 1783–1876*. New York: Harper & Row, 1980.

Chapter 2

Principal References

Broudy, Harry S. *The Real World of the Public Schools*. New York: Harcourt Brace Jovanovich, 1972.

Cremin, Lawrence A. *The Transformation of the School: Progressivism in American Education, 1876–1957*. New York: Vintage Books, Random House, 1964. For quotations on progressive education, see pp. 168 and 348.

Goodlad, John, et al. *Looking Behind the Classroom Door*. Worthington, Ohio: Charles H. Jones, 1974. P. 33.

Illich, Ivan D. *Deschooling Society*. New York: Harper & Row, 1971.

Silberman, Charles E. *Crisis in the Classroom: The Remaking of American Education*. New York: Random House, 1970. P. 159.

Bibliography

Additional References

Anthony, Albert S. "Twenty Unprinciples for Successful Innovation." *The Clearing House* 46 (1971): 32–34.

Association for Supervision and Curriculum Development. *A New Look at Progressive Education.* Washington, D.C.: National Education Association, 1972.

Bestor, Arthur. *The Restoration of Learning.* New York: Alfred A. Knopf, 1955.

Dix, Lester. *A Charter for Progressive Education.* New York: Teachers College Press, 1939.

Duke, Daniel L. *The Retransformation of the School.* Chicago: Nelson-Hall, 1978.

Havelock, Ronald G. *A Guide to Innovation in Education.* Ann Arbor: Center for Research on Utilization of Scientific Knowledge, Institute for Social Research, 1970.

Hillson, Maurie, and Hyman, Ronald T. *Change and Innovation in Elementary and Secondary Organization.* New York: Holt, Rinehart & Winston, 1971.

Hunter, Madeline. "Innovations—What Is Expected? Probing the Concept Theoretically and Practically." *National Association of Secondary School Principles Bulletin,* February 1973, pp. 1–91.

Jelinek, James J. *Principles and Values in School and Society.* Tempe, Ariz.: Far Western Philosophy of Education Society, 1976.

Miles, Matthew B., ed. *Innovation in Education.* New York: Teachers College Press, 1964.

Sarason, Seymour B. *The Culture of the School and the Problem of Change.* Boston: Allyn & Bacon, 1971.

Unruh, Adolph, and Turner, Harold E. *Supervision for Change and Innovation.* Boston: Houghton Mifflin, 1970.

Vaughan, Maury S. "Change in Education: The New and the Not So New." *School and Society,* October 1971, pp. 341–344.

von Haden, Herbert I., and King, Jean Marie. *Innovations in Education: Their Pros and Cons.* Worthington, Ohio: Charles A. Jones, 1971.

Chapter 3

Principal References

Bell, Daniel. *The Coming Post-industrial Society: A Venture in Social Forecasting.* New York: Basic Books, 1973.

Coleman, James S. "Equal Schools or Equal Students." *The Public Interest,* Summer 1966, p. 74.

———. "Coleman on the Coleman Report." *Educational Researcher* 1 (March 1972): 13.

Bibliography

Coleman, James S., *et al. Equality of Educational Opportunity.* Washington, D.C.: U.S. Department of Health, Education, and Welfare, 1966.

de Lone, Richard H. *Small Futures: Children, Inequality and the Limits of Liberal Reform.* Written for the Carnegie Council on Children. New York: Harcourt Brace Jovanovich, 1979. P. xiv.

Harrington, Michael. *Decade of Decision: The Crisis of the American System.* New York: Simon & Schuster, 1980. P. 264.

Jencks, Christoper, *et al. Inequality: A Reassessment of the Effect of Family and Schooling in America.* New York: Basic Books, 1972. P. 264.

Swanson, Gordon. "As I See It. . . ." In *Christoper Jencks: In Perspective.* Arlington, Va.: Association of School Administrators, 1973. Pp. 56–61.

Additional References

Austin, Gilbert R. *Early Childhood Education: An International Perspective.* New York: Academic Press, 1976.

Brameld, Theodore. *The Climactic Decades: Mandate to Education.* New York: Praeger, 1970.

Clark, Kenneth. *Dark Ghetto.* New York: Harper & Row, 1965.

Clignet, Remi. *Liberty and Equality in the Educational Process.* New York: John Wiley & Sons, 1974.

Conant, James B. *Education in a Divided World.* Cambridge, Mass.: Harvard University Press, 1948.

Cronbach, Lee J., and Suppes, Patrick, eds. *Research for Tomorrow's Schools.* New York: Macmillan, 1969.

Della-Dora, Delmo, and House, James E., eds. *Education for an Open Society.* Washington, D.C.: Association for Supervision and Curriculum Development, 1974.

Deutsch, Martin, *et al. The Disadvantaged Child.* New York: Basic Books, 1967.

Dewey, John. *The School and Society.* Rev. ed. Chicago: University of Chicago Press, 1915. (Originally published in 1899.)

Ellul, Jacques. *The Technological Society.* New York: Alfred A. Knopf, 1964.

Erikson, Erik H. *Childhood and Society.* 2d ed., rev. New York: W. W. Norton, 1963.

Fantini, Mario D., and Weinstein, Gerald. *The Disadvantaged: Challenge to Education.* New York: Harper & Row, 1968.

Freire, Paulo. *Pedagogy of the Oppressed.* New York: Herdes & Herdes, 1972.

Galbraith, John Kenneth. *The New Industrial State.* Second edition. Boston: Houghton Mifflin, 1971.

Graham, Patricia A. *Progressive Education from Arcady to Academe: A History of the Progressive Education Association.* New York: Teachers College Press, 1967.

Bibliography

Hunt, J. McVicker. *The Challenge of Incompetence and Poverty.* Urbana, Ill.: University of Illinois Press, 1969.

Kahn, Herman, *et al. The Next Two Hundred Years: A Scenario for Americans and the World.* New York: William Morrow, 1976.

Karier, Clarence J.; Violas, Paul; and Spring, Joel, eds. *Roots of Crisis: American Education in the Twentieth Century.* Chicago: Rand McNally, 1973.

Mosteller, Frederick, and Moynihan, Daniel P., eds. *On Equality of Educational Opportunity: Papers Deriving from the Harvard University Faculty Seminar on the Coleman Report.* New York: Vintage Books, Random House, 1972.

Moynihan, Daniel P., ed. *On Understanding Poverty.* New York: Basic Books, 1969.

Myrdal, Gunnar. *An American Dilemma.* New York: Harper & Row, 1962. (Originally published in 1944.)

Rawls, John. *Theory of Justice.* Cambridge, Mass.: Harvard University Press, 1971.

Riessman, Frank. *The Culturally Deprived Child.* New York: Harper & Row, 1962. Chapter VII, "The Slow Gifted Child."

Rist, Ray C., ed. *Desegregated Schools: Appraisals of an American Experiment.* New York: Academic Press, 1979.

Sarason, Seymour B. *The Culture of the School and the Problem of Change.* Boston: Allyn & Bacon, 1971.

Seymour, Whitney N., Jr. *Why Justice Fails.* New York: William Morrow, 1973.

Spring, Joel. *Education and the Rise of the Corporate State.* Boston: Beacon Press, 1972.

Toffler, Alvin. *Future Shock.* New York: Random House, 1970.

Wirth, Arthur G. *Education in the Technological Society.* Scranton, Pa.: Intext Educational Publishers, 1972.

Woodring, Paul, and Scanlon, John. *American Education Today.* New York: McGraw-Hill, 1963.

Chapter 4

Principal References

Austin, Gilbert R. *Early Childhood Education: An International Perspective.* New York: Academic Press, Inc., 1976.

Ausubel, David P.; Novak, Joseph D.; and Hanesian, Helen. *Educational Psychology: A Cognitive View.* Second edition. New York: Holt, Rinehart & Winston, 1978.

Brandwein, Paul F. "A General Theory of Instruction." *Science Education* 63 (1979): 285–297.

Bibliography

———. *The Gifted Student as Future Scientist*. New York: Harcourt Brace, 1955. Pp. 65–68.

Bruner, Jerome S. *On Knowing: Essays for the Left Hand*. Cambridge, Mass.: The Belknap Press of Harvard University Press, 1962.

———. *The Process of Education*. Cambridge, Mass.: Harvard University Press, 1960 and 1977.

———. *The Relevance of Education*. New York: W. W. Norton, 1971. P. 68.

———. *Toward a Theory of Instruction*. Cambridge, Mass.: The Belknap Press of Harvard University Press, 1966.

Coopersmith, Stanley. *The Antecedents of Self-Esteem*. San Francisco: W. H. Freeman, 1967. Pp. 236–237.

Cronbach, Lee J. "The Logic of Experiments in Discovery." In *Learning by Discovery: A Critical Appraisal*, Lee S. Schulman and Evan R. Keisler, eds. Chicago: Rand McNally, 1966.

Cuban, Larry. "Determinants of Curricular Change and Stability 1870–1970." In *Value Conflicts and Curriculum Issues*, Jon Schaffarzick and Gary Sykes, eds. Berkeley, Calif.: McCutchan Publishing, 1979. Pp. 141–196.

Donaldson, Margaret. *Children's Minds*. New York: W. W. Norton, 1979.

Gagne, Robert M. *The Conditions of Learning*. New York: Holt, Rinehart & Winston, 1965.

Hosford, Philip L. *An Instructional Theory: A Beginning*. Englewood Cliffs, N.J.: Prentice-Hall, 1973.

National Science Foundation, Office of Program Integration. *What Are the Needs in Precollege Science, Mathematics, and Social Science Education? Views from the Field*. Washington, D.C.: National Science Foundation, Office of Program Integration, Directorate for Science Education, 1979, SE80-9.

Novak, Joseph D. *A Theory of Education*. Ithaca, N.Y.: Cornell University Press, 1977.

Rogers, Carl R. *On Becoming a Person*. Boston: Houghton Mifflin, 1961.

Additional References

Ashton-Warner, Sylvia. *Teacher*. New York: Simon & Schuster, 1963.

Ausubel, David P. *Educational Psychology: A Cognitive View*. New York: Holt, Rinehart & Winston, 1978.

Bloom, Benjamin S., ed. *Taxonomy of Educational Objectives: The Cognitive Domain*. New York: David McKay, 1956.

Bode, Boyd H. *Modern Educational Theories*. New York: Macmillan, 1927.

Bremer, Anne, and Bremer, John. *Open Education: A Beginning*. New York: Holt, Rinehart & Winston, 1972.

Cronbach, Lee J. *Educational Psychology*. New York: Harcourt Brace Jovanovich, 1963.

Bibliography

Dewey, Evelyn. *The Dalton Laboratory Plan.* New York: E. P. Dutton, 1922.

Flanders, Ned A. *Analyzing Teaching Behavior.* Reading, Mass.: Addison-Wesley, 1970.

Foshay, Arthur W. *The Professional in Education.* New York: Teachers College Press, 1979.

Gartner, Alan; Kohler, Mary; and Riessman, Frank. *Children Teach Children: Learning by Teaching.* New York: Harper & Row, 1971.

Georgiades, William, and Clark, Donald C., eds. *Models for Individualized Instruction.* New York: MSS Information, 1974.

Georgiades, William, *et al. Take Five: A Methodology for the Humane School.* Chalmette, La.: St. Bernard School Board, 1979.

Goodlad, John I., and Anderson, Robert H. *The Nongraded Elementary School.* New York: Harcourt Brace Jovanovich, 1963.

Goodlad, John I.; Klein, M. Frances; *et al. Behind the Classroom Door.* Worthington, Ohio: Charles A. Jones, 1970.

Gross, Ronald, and Osterman, Paul, eds. *High School.* New York: Simon & Schuster, 1971.

Hilgard, Ernest R., and Bower, Gordon H. *Theories of Learning.* New York: Appleton-Century-Crofts, 1966.

Hillson, Maurie, and Bongo, Joseph. *Continuous-Progress Education: A Practical Approach.* Palo Alto, Calif.: Science Research Associates, 1971.

Holt, John. *How Children Fail.* New York: Pitman, 1964.

————. *How Children Learn.* New York: Pitman, 1967.

Howard, Eugene R. "Developing Sequential Learning Materials," *National Association of Secondary School Principals Bulletin,* May 1970, pp. 159–168.

Howes, Virgil M. *Individualization of Instruction.* New York: Macmillan, 1970.

Hudgins, Bryce B. *Problem Solving in the Classroom.* New York: Macmillan, 1966.

Inhelder, Barbel, and Piaget, Jean. *The Growth of Logical Thinking from Childhood to Adolescence.* New York: Basic Books, 1958.

Jackson, Philip. *Life in Classrooms.* New York: Holt, Rinehart & Winston, 1968.

Jelinek, James J., ed. *Improving the Human Condition: A Curricular Response to Critical Realities.* Washington, D.C.: Association for Supervision and Curriculum Development, 1978.

Joyce, Bruce, and Weil, Marsha, eds. *Perspectives for Reform in Teacher Education.* Englewood Cliffs, N.J.: Prentice-Hall, 1972.

Kohl, Herbert. "Teaching the Unteachable," *The New York Review,* 1966.

Krathwohl, David R., ed. *Taxonomy of Educational Objectives: Affective Domain.* New York: David McKay, 1956.

Bibliography

Lewis, Arthur J., and Miel, Alice. *Supervision for Improved Instruction.* Belmont, Calif.: Wadsworth, 1972.

Mager, Robert F. *Preparing Instructional Objectives.* Belmont, Calif.: Fearon, 1962.

Mason, Robert E. *Contemporary Educational Theory.* New York: David McKay, 1972. Chapter 3.

Massialas, Byron G., and Zevin, Jack. *Creative Encounters in the Classroom.* New York: John Wiley & Sons, 1967.

National Society for the Study of Education. *Adapting the Schools to Individual Differences.* Twenty-fourth Yearbook, Part II. Bloomington, Ill.: Public School Publishing, 1925.

————. *The Activity Movement.* Thirty-third Yearbook, Part II. Chicago: University of Chicago Press, 1934.

Oettinger, Anthony G., and Marks, Sema. *Run, Computer, Run.* Cambridge, Mass.: Harvard University Press, 1969.

Parkhurst, Helen. *Education on the Dalton Plan.* New York: E. P. Dutton, 1922.

Plowman, Paul D. *Behavioral Objectives: Teacher Success Through Student Performance.* Chicago: Science Research Associates, 1971.

Popham, W. James, and Baker, Eva L. *Systematic Instruction.* Englewood Cliffs, N.J.: Prentice-Hall, 1970.

Postman, Neil, and Weingartner, Charles. *Teaching as a Subversive Activity.* New York: Delacorte Press, 1969.

Pratte, Richard. *Contemporary Theories of Education.* Scranton, Pa.: International Textbook, 1971.

Raths, Louis E.; Harmin, Merrill; and Simon, Sidney B. *Values and Teaching: Working with Values in the Classroom.* Columbus, Ohio: Charles E. Merrill, 1966.

Rugg, Harold, and Shumaker, Ann. *The Child-centered School.* New York: Arno Press and *The New York Times,* 1969. (Reprint of a book first published by World Book Company in 1928.)

Saettler, Paul. *A History of Instructional Technology.* New York: McGraw-Hill, 1968.

Schaefer, Robert J. *The School as a Center of Inquiry.* New York: Harper & Row, 1967.

Shiman, David A.; Culber, Carmen M.; and Lieberman, Ann. *Teachers on Individualization: The Way We Do It.* New York: McGraw-Hill, 1974.

Shulman, Lee S., and Keislar, Evan R., eds. *Learning by Discovery: A Critical Approach.* Chicago: Rand McNally, 1966.

Silberman, Charles E., ed. *The Open Classroom Reader.* New York: Random House, 1973.

Skinner, Burrhus F. *Contingencies of Reinforcement: A Theoretical Analysis.* New York: Appleton-Century-Crofts, 1969.

————. *The Technology of Teaching.* New York: Appleton-Century-Crofts, 1968.

State of New York, Office of Education Performance Review. *School Factors Influencing Reading Achievement: A Case Study of Two Inner City Schools.* March 1974.

Stevens, Leonard. *Alternative Education within the Public Schools.* Croft Leadership Action Folio, Number 59. Waterford, Conn.: Croft Educational Services, 1973.

Strain, Phillip S.; Cooke, Thomas P.; and Appolloni, Tony. *Teaching Exceptional Children.* New York: Academic Press, 1976.

Tanner, Daniel. *Using Behavioral Objectives in the Classroom.* New York: Macmillan, 1972.

Taylor, Calvin W. *Creativity: Progress and Potential.* New York: McGraw-Hill, 1964.

Torrance, Ellis P. *Guiding Creative Talent.* Englewood Cliffs, N.J.: Prentice-Hall, 1962.

Trump, J. Lloyd, and Baynham, Dorsey. *Focus on Change: Guide to Better Schools.* Chicago: Rand McNally, 1961.

Tyler, Ralph W. *Basic Principles of Curriculum and Instruction.* Chicago: University of Chicago Press, 1949.

Ulich, Robert, ed. *Three Thousand Years of Educational Wisdom.* Cambridge, Mass.: Harvard University Press, 1954.

Waller, Willard. *The Sociology of Teaching.* New York: John Wiley & Sons, 1965.

Washburne, Carleton W., and Marland, Sidney P., Jr. *Winnetka: The History and Significance of an Educational Experiment.* Englewood Cliffs, N.J.: Prentice-Hall, 1963.

Westbury, Ian, and Bellack, Arno A., eds. *Research into Classroom Processes.* New York: Teachers College Press, 1971.

Chapter 5

Principal References

Bogen, Joseph E. "Some Educational Aspects of Hemispheric Specificity," *UCLA Educator* 17.2, Spring 1975.

Cuban, Larry. "Determinants of Curricular Change and Stability 1870–1970." In *Value Conflicts and Curriculum Issues,* Jon Schaffarzick and Gary Sykes, eds. Berkeley, Calif.: McCutchan Publishing, 1979. Chapter 4.

Gazzaniga, Michael J. "Review of the Split Brain," *UCLA Educator* 17.2, Spring 1975.

Holton, Gerald. *Introduction to Concepts and Theories in Physical Science.* Reading, Mass.: Addison-Wesley, 1952. Pp. 271–272.

Johnson, Mauritz. *Intentionality in Education: A Conceptual Model of Cur-*

Bibliography

ricular and Instructional Planning and Education. Albany, N.Y.: Center for Curricular Research and Services. 1977.

McDonald, James B. In *Confronting Curriculum Reform,* Elliot W. Eisner, ed. New York: Little, Brown, 1971. P. 126.

Molnar, Alex, and Zahoric, John A., eds. *Curriculum Theory.* Washington, D.C.: Association for Supervision and Curriculum Development, 1977.

Phenix, Philip H. *The Realms of Meaning: A Philosophy of the Curriculum for General Education.* New York: McGraw-Hill, 1964.

——. "The Use of the Discipline as Curriculum Content," *Educational Forum* 26 (1962): 275–276.

Stern, Fritz, ed. *The Varieties of History.* New York: World Publishing, 1956. P. 13.

Tanner, Daniel, and Tanner, Laurel. *Curriculum Development: Theory into Practice.* New York: Macmillan, 1975.

Tyler, Ralph W. *Basic Principles of Curriculum and Instruction.* Chicago: University of Chicago Press, 1950.

Wittrock, Merle C. "The Generative Process of Memory," *UCLA Educator* 17.2, Spring 1975.

Additional References

Alder, Richard R. *Humanities Programs Today.* New York: Citation Press, 1970.

Alexander, William M. *The Changing High School Curriculum.* Second edition. New York: Holt, Rinehart & Winston, 1972.

Bode, Boyd H. *Modern Educational Theories.* New York: Macmillan, 1927.

Brandwein, Paul F-. *The Reduction of Complexity.* New York: Harcourt Brace Jovanovich, 1977.

Broudy, Harry S. *The Real World of the Public Schools.* New York: Harcourt Brace Jovanovich, 1972.

Broudy, Harry S.; Smith, B. Othaniel; and Burnett, Joe R. *Democracy and Excellence in American Secondary Education.* Chicago: Rand McNally, 1964.

Bruner, Jerome S. *The Process of Education.* Cambridge, Mass.: Harvard University Press, 1960.

Combs, Arthur W., ed. *Perceiving, Behaving, Becoming.* Washington, D.C.: Association for Supervision and Curriculum Development, 1962.

Commission on the Reorganization of Secondary Education. *Cardinal Principles of Secondary Education.* Washington, D.C.: U.S. Bureau of Education, 1918.

Davis, Oscar L., ed. *Perspectives on Curriculum Development: 1776–1976.* Washington, D.C.: Association for Supervision and Curriculum Development, 1976.

Dewey, John. *The Child and the Curriculum.* Chicago: University of Chicago Press, 1956. (Originally published in 1902.)

Bibliography

Doll, Ronald C. *Curriculum Improvement*. Boston: Allyn & Bacon, 1970.

Educational Policies Commission. *Education for All American Children*. Washington, D.C.: National Education Association, 1948.

Fisher, Bernice. *Industrial Education: American Ideals and Institutions*. Madison, Wis.: University of Wisconsin Press, 1967.

Ford, G. W., and Pugno, Lawrence. *The Structure of Knowledge and the Curriculum*. Chicago: Rand McNally, 1964.

Foshay, Arthur W. *Curriculum for the 70's: An Agenda for Invention*. Washington, D.C.: National Education Association, 1970.

Gardner, John W. *Excellence*. New York: Harper & Row, 1961.

Glass, Hiram Bentley. *The Timely and the Timeless*. New York: Basic Books, 1970.

Goodlad, John. *Planning and Organizing for Teaching*. Washington, D.C.: National Education Association, 1963.

Grobman, Hulda. *Developmental Curriculum Projects: Decision Points and Processes*. Itasca, Ill.: F. E. Peacock, 1972.

Hofstadter, Richard. *Anti-Intellectualism in American Life*. New York: Alfred A. Knopf, 1963.

Inglow, Gail M. *The Emergent in Curriculum*. Second edition. New York: John Wiley & Sons, 1973.

Jarrett, James L. *The Humanities and Humanistic Education*. Reading, Mass.: Addison-Wesley, 1973.

Jelinek, James J., ed. *Improving the Human Condition: A Curricular Response to Critical Realities*. Washington, D.C.: Association for Supervision and Curriculum Development, 1978.

Kohlberg, Laurence. "Education for Justice." In *Moral Education*. Cambridge, Mass.: Harvard University Press, 1970.

Krathwohl, David R., ed. *Taxonomy of Educational Objectives. Affective Domain*. New York: David McKay, 1956.

Krug, Mark M. *What Will Be Taught: The Next Decade*. Itasca, Ill.: F. E. Peacock, 1972.

Lawler, Marcella R., ed. *Strategies for Planned Curricular Innovation*. New York: Teachers College Press, 1970.

Leese, Joseph; Frasure, Kenneth; and Johnson, Mauritz, Jr. *The Teacher in Curriculum Making*. New York: Harper & Row, 1961.

Maclure, J. Stuart. *Curriculum Innovation in Practice*. Report of the Third International Curriculum Conference. London: Her Majesty's Stationery Office, 1968.

Mason, Robert E. *Contemporary Educational Theory*. New York: David McKay, 1972. Chapter 3.

May, Philip R. *Moral Education in School*. London: Methuen Educational, 1971.

McNally, Harold J., and Passow, A. Harry. *Improving the Quality of Public School Programs*. New York: Teachers College Press, 1960.

Bibliography

National Society for the Study of Education. *American Education in the Postwar Period: Curriculum Reconstruction.* Forty-fourth Yearbook, Part I. Chicago: University of Chicago Press, 1945.

National Society for the Study of Education. *The Curriculum: Retrospect and Prospect.* Seventieth Yearbook, Part I. Chicago: University of Chicago Press, 1971.

Passow, Harry A., ed. *Curriculum Crossroads.* New York: Teachers College Press, 1962.

Peddiwell, J. Abner. Foreword by Harold Benjamin. *The Saber-Tooth Curriculum.* New York: McGraw-Hill, 1939.

Phenix, Philip H. *Education and the Common Good: A Moral Philosophy of the Curriculum.* New York: Harper & Row, 1961.

———. *Realms of Meaning.* New York: McGraw-Hill, 1964.

Piaget, Jean. *The Moral Judgment of the Child.* New York: Free Press, 1965.

———. *The Psychology of Intelligence.* New York: Harcourt Brace Jovanovich, 1950.

Raths, Louis E.; Harmin, Merrill; and Simon, Sidney B. *Values and Teaching: Working with Values in the Classroom.* Columbus, Ohio; Charles E. Merrill, 1966.

Report of the Harvard Committee. *General Education in a Free Society.* Cambridge, Mass.: Harvard University Press, 1945.

Saylor, J. Galen, and Alexander, William M. *Planning Curriculum for Schools.* New York: Holt, Rinehart & Winston, 1974.

Schwab, Joseph J. *The Practical: A Language for Curriculum.* Washington, D.C.: National Education Association, 1970.

Smith, Mortimer, ed. *A Decade of Comment on Education, 1956–1966.* Washington, D.C.: Council for Basic Education, 1966.

Snow, C. P. *Two Cultures and the Scientific Revolution.* New York: Cambridge University Press, 1959.

Taba, Hilda. *Curriculum Development: Theory and Practice.* New York: Harcourt Brace Jovanovich, 1962.

Tanner, Daniel. *Secondary Curriculum: Theory and Development.* New York: Macmillan, 1971.

Tanner, Daniel, and Tanner, Laurel. *Curriculum Development: Theory into Practice.* New York: Macmillan, 1975.

Taylor, Harold E., ed. *The Humanities in the Schools.* New York: Citation Press, 1968.

Thomas, Russel. *The Search for a Common Learning: General Education, 1800–1960.* New York: McGraw-Hill, 1962.

Trump, J. Lloyd, and Miller, Delmas F. *Secondary School Curriculum Improvement.* Second edition. Boston: Allyn & Bacon, 1973.

Ulich, Robert, ed. *Education and the Idea of Mankind.* New York: Harcourt Brace Jovanovich, 1964.

Whitfield, Richard. *Disciplines of the Curriculum*. London: McGraw-Hill, 1971.

The yearbooks and other volumes published by the Association for Supervision and Curriculum Development, Suite 1100, 1701 K Street, NW, Washington, D.C. 20006.

Chapter 6

Principal References

Brandwein, Paul F-. *The Gifted Student as Future Scientist*. New York: Harcourt Brace Jovanovich, 1955.

Brody, Erness Bright, and Brody, Nathan. *Intelligence: Nature, Determinants, and Consequences*. New York: Academic Press, 1976. P. 7.

Georgiades, William; Hilde, Reuben; and McCauley, C. Grant. *New Schools for a New Age*. Santa Monica, Calif.: Goodyear Publishing Company, 1977.

Getzels, J. W., and Jackson, P. W. "The Highly Intelligent and the Highly Creative Adolescent: A Summary of Some Research Findings." In *The Third University of Utah Research Conference on the Identification of Creative Scientific Talent*, C. W. Taylor, ed. Salt Lake City, Utah: University of Utah Press, 1959. Pp. 46–57.

Glickman, Charles. "Mastery Learning Stifles Individuality," *Educational Leadership*. November, 1979.

Jensen, Arthur. "How Much Can We Boost IQ and Scholastic Achievement?," *Harvard Educational Review*. Cambridge: Mass.: Harvard University Press,

Klausmeier, Herbert J.; Rassmiller, Richard A.; and Saily, Mary. *Individually Guided Elementary Education*. New York: Academic Press, 1977.

Lewontin, Richard. "The Fallacy of Biological Determinism." *The Sciences*. March/April 1976.

Skinner, Burrhus F. *Walden II*. New York: Macmillan, 1948.

Terman, L. M., and Oden, M. H. *The Gifted Group at Mid-Life*. Stanford, Calif.: Stanford University Press, 1959.

Torrance, E. Paul. *Guiding Creative Talent*. Englewood Cliffs, N.J.: Prentice-Hall, 1962. P. 59.

Torshen, Kay Pomerance. *The Mastery Approach to Competency-Based Education*. New York: Academic Press, 1977. Pp. 17–18.

White, Sheldon. "Social Implications of I.Q." *The National Elementary Principal* 54 (1975): 13–14.

Additional References

Advisory Council on Vocational Education. *Vocational Education: The Bridge Between Man and His Work*. Washington, D.C.: U.S. Government Printing Office, 1968.

Bibliography

Austin, Gilbert R. *Early Childhood Education: An International Perspective.* New York: Academic Press, 1976.

Bloom, Benjamin S.; Hastings, J. Thomas; and Madaus, George F. *Handbook on Formative and Summative Evaluation of Student Learning.* New York: McGraw-Hill, 1971.

Callahan, Raymond E. *Education and the Cult of Efficiency.* Chicago: University of Chicago Press, 1962.

Drost, Walter H. *David Snedden and Education for Social Efficiency.* Madison, Wis.: University of Wisconsin Press, 1967.

Englemann, Siegfried. *Preventing Failure in the Primary Grades.* New York: Simon & Schuster, 1969.

Erikson, Erik H. *Childhood and Society.* New York: W. W. Norton, 1963.

Featherstone, Joseph. *Schools Where Children Learn.* New York: Liveright, 1971.

———. *Informal Schools in Britain Today.* New York: Scholastic Book Services, Citation Press, 1971.

Gallagher, James J., ed. *Teaching Gifted Students: A Book of Readings.* Boston: Allyn & Bacon, 1965.

Getzels, Jacob W., and Jackson, Philip W. *Creativity and Intelligence.* New York: John Wiley & Sons, 1962.

Holt, John. *How Children Fail.* New York: Pitman, 1964.

Houts, Paul L., ed. *The Myth of Measurability.* New York: Hart, 1977.

Hunt, J. McVicker. *Intelligence and Experience.* New York: Ronald, 1961.

Husén, Torsten, ed. *International Study of Achievement in Mathematics.* New York: John Wiley & Sons, 1967. Vols. 1, 2.

Jensen, Arthur R. "How Much Can We Boost IQ and Scholastic Achievement?" *Harvard Educational Review,* Winter 1969.

Lazarus, Mitchell. (in press) *Goodbye to Excellence: A Critical Look at Minimum Competency Testing.* National Association of Elementary School Principals, 1980.

Lessinger, Leon M., and Tyler, Ralph W., eds. *Accountability: Systems Planning in Education.* Homewood, Ill., Charles A. Jones, 1973.

Moynihan, Daniel P., ed. *On Understanding Poverty.* New York: Basic Books, 1968.

Piaget, Jean. "Theory of Intelligence," Chapter 14. In H. B. and N. M. Robinson, *The Mentally Retarded Child.* New York: McGraw-Hill, 1965.

Raup, R. Bruce, *et al. The Improvement of Practical Intelligence.* New York: Harper & Row, 1950.

Riessman, Frank. *The Culturally Deprived Child.* New York: Harper & Row, 1962. Chapter VII, "The Slow Gifted Child."

Robinson, Halbert B., and Robinson, Nancy M. *The Mentally Retarded Child.* New York: McGraw-Hill, 1965. "Theories of Learning as Related to Mental Retardation," Chapter 13.

Sexton, Patricia C., ed. *School Policy and Issues in a Changing Society.* Boston: Allyn & Bacon, 1971.

Smith, Eugene, and Tyler, Ralph W. *Appraising and Recording Student Progress.* New York: Harper & Row, 1942.

Stephens, J. M. *The Process of Schooling.* New York: Holt, Rinehart & Winston, 1967.

Stocker, Joseph, and Wilson, Donald F. "Accountability and the Classroom Teacher," *Today's Education* 60 (1971): 41–56.

Trump, J. Lloyd, and Georgiades, William. "How to Evaluate the Quality of Educational Programs," *National Association of Secondary School Principals Bulletin,* May 1975, pp. 99–103.

Turnbull, William W. "The Uses of Measurement in Individualized Education," *National Association of Secondary School Principals Bulletin,* May 1970, pp. 80–87.

Tyler, Ralph W., and Wolf, Richard M., eds. *Crucial Issues in Testing.* Berkeley, Calif.: McCutchan Publishing, 1974.

Chapter 7

Principal References

Clark, Harold F., and Sloan, Harold S. *Classrooms in the Factories.* Rutherford, N.J.: Fairleigh Dickinson University, 1958.

Havighurst, Robert. *Human Development and Education.* New York: David McKay, 1953. Pp. 111–159; see also p. 162.

Postman, Neil. *Teaching as a Conserving Activity.* New York: Delacorte Press, 1979. P. 5.

Schaffarzick, Jon, and Sykes, Gary, eds. *Value Conflicts and Curriculum Issues: Lessons from Research and Experience.* Berkeley, Calif.: McCutchan Publishing, 1979.

Additional References

Aiken, Wilford M. *The Story of the Eight-Year Study.* New York: Harper & Row, 1942.

———. *Thirty Schools Tell Their Story.* New York: Harper & Row, 1942.

Beale, Howard K. *A History of Freedom of Teaching in American Schools.* New York: Charles Scribner's Sons, 1941.

Bell, Daniel. *The Reforming of General Education.* New York: Columbia University Press, 1966.

Bloom, Benjamin S. *Stability and Change in Human Characteristics.* New York: John Wiley & Sons, 1964.

Bowles, Samuel, and Gintis, Herbert. *Nightmares and Dreams: Capitalism and Education in the United States.* New York: Harper & Row, 1975.

Brameld, Theodore. *The Climactic Decades: Mandate to Education.* New York: Praeger, 1970.

————. *Patterns of Educational Philosophy.* New York: Holt, Rinehart & Winston, 1971.

Braun, Robert J. *Teachers and Power.* New York: Simon & Schuster, 1972.

Bronfenbrenner, Urie, and Condry, J. C., Jr., *Two Worlds of Childhood: U.S. and U.S.S.R.* New York: Russell Sage Foundation, 1970.

Bunker, Frank Forest. "Reorganization of the Public School System," *U.S. Bureau of Education Bulletin* #8. Washington, D.C.: Government Printing Office, 1916.

Bushnell, David S., and Rappaport, Donald. *Planned Change in Education: A Systems Approach.* New York: Harcourt Brace Jovanovich, 1971.

Carnoy, Martin, ed. *Schooling in a Corporate Society: The Political Economy of Education in America.* New York: David McKay, 1972.

Chamberlin, Charles Dean, *et al. Did They Succeed in College?* New York: Harper & Row, 1942.

Conant, James B. *The American High School Today.* New York: McGraw-Hill, 1959.

————. *The Education of American Teachers.* New York: McGraw-Hill, 1963.

Coons, John E.; Clune, William H., II; and Sugarman, Stephen D. *Private Wealth and Public Education.* Cambridge, Mass.: The Belknap Press of Harvard University Press, 1970.

Crary, Ryland W. *Humanizing the School.* New York: Alfred A. Knopf, 1969.

Cronbach, Lee J., and Suppes, Patrick, eds. *Research for Tomorrow's Schools.* New York: Macmillan, 1969.

Cronin, Joseph M. *The Control of Urban Schools: Perspective on the Power of Educational Reformers.* New York: Free Press, 1973.

Danforth Foundation and the Ford Foundation. *The School and the Democratic Environment.* New York: Columbia University Press, 1970.

Della, Delmo; Della, Dora; and Hurse, James, eds. *Education for an Open Society.* Washington, D.C.: Association for Supervision and Curriculum Development, 1974.

Dewey, John. *Democracy and Education.* New York: Macmillan, 1916.

————. *The Sources of a Science of Education.* New York: Horace Liveright, 1929.

Dewey, John, and Dewey, Evelyn. *Schools of Tomorrow.* New York: E. P. Dutton, 1915.

Drucker, Peter F. *Technology, Management and Society.* New York: Harper & Row, 1970.

Erikson, Erik H. *Childhood and Society.* New York: W. W. Norton, 1963.

Eurich, Alvin C., ed. *High School 1980.* New York: Pitman, 1970.

Fantini, Mario. *Public Schools of Choice: A Plan for the Reform of American Education.* New York: Simon & Schuster, 1973.

Bibliography

Flexner, Abraham. *A Modern College and a Modern School.* New York: Doubleday, 1923.

Friedenberg, Edgar Z. *Coming of Age in America.* New York: Random House, 1965.

Fromm, Erich. *The Sane Society.* New York: Holt, Rinehart & Winston, 1955.

Gartner, Alan; Kohler, Mary; and Riessman, Frank. *Children Teach Children: Learning by Teaching.* New York: Harper & Row, 1971.

Georgiades, William. *How Good Is Your School? Program Evaluation for Secondary Schools.* Reston, Va.: The National Association of Secondary School Principals, 1978.

Georgiades, William; Hilde, Reuben; and McCaulay, C. Grant. *New Schools for a New Age.* Santa Monica, Calif.: Goodyear, 1977.

Glasser, William. *Schools Without Failure.* New York: Harper & Row, 1969.

Glatthorn, Allan A. *Alternatives in Education: Schools and Programs.* New York: Dodd, Mead, 1975.

Goodman, Paul. *Compulsory Mis-Education.* New York: Vintage Books, 1964.

Graubard, Allen. *Free the Children: Radical Reform and the Free School Movement.* New York: Pantheon, 1972.

Greer, Colin. *The Great School Legend: A Revisionist Interpretation of American Public Education.* New York: Basic Books, 1972.

Gross, Ronald, and Gross, Beatrice, eds. *Radical School Reform.* New York: Simon & Schuster, 1969.

Harnum, Willis W. "The Nature of Our Change in Society: Implications for Schools." In *Curriculum & the Cultural Revolution,* Purpel, David E., and Belanger, Maurice, eds. Berkeley, Calif.: McCutchan, 1972.

Havighurst, Robert J.; Smith, Frank L.; and Wilder, David E. *A Profile of the Large-City High School.* Washington, D.C.: National Association of Secondary School Principals, 1970.

Hechinger, Fred M. *The Big Red Schoolhouse.* Garden City, N.Y.: Dolphin Books, 1962.

Herriott, Robert E., and Hodgkins, Benjamin J. *The Environment of Schooling: Formal Education as an Open System.* Englewood Cliffs, N.J.: Prentice-Hall, 1973.

Hofstadter, Richard. *Anti-Intellectualism in American Life.* New York: Alfred A. Knopf, 1963.

Holt, John. *Freedom and Beyond.* New York: E. P. Dutton, 1972.

Illich, Ivan D. *Celebration of Awareness: A Call for Institutional Revolution.* Garden City, N.Y.: Doubleday, 1970.

———. *Deschooling Society.* New York: Harper & Row, 1971.

Jackson, Philip W. *Life in Classrooms.* New York: Holt, Rinehart & Winston, 1968.

Bibliography

Joyce, Bruce, and Weil, Marsha, eds. *Perspective for Reform in Teacher Education*. Englewood Cliffs, N.J.: Prentice-Hall, 1972.

Kaestle, Carl F. *The Evolution of an Urban School System: New York City, 1750–1850*. Cambridge, Mass.: Harvard University Press, 1973.

Kohl, Herbert R. *The Open Classroom*. New York: Random House, 1969.

————. *36 Children*. New York: New American Library, 1968.

Krug, Edward A. *The Shaping of the American High School*. New York: Harper & Row, 1964.

Lieberman, Myron. *Education as a Profession*. Englewood Cliffs, N.J.: Prentice-Hall, 1956.

Lurie, Ellen. *How to Change the Schools: A Parent's Action Handbook on How to Fight the System*. New York: Random House, 1970.

Macdonald, James B.; Wolfson, Bernice J.; and Zaret, Esther. *Reschooling Society: A Conceptual Model*. Washington, D.C.: Association for Supervision and Curriculum Development, 1973.

Marien, Michael, and Ziegler, Warren L. *The Potential of Educational Futures*. Worthington, Ohio: Charles A. Jones, 1972.

Martin, Everett Dean. *The Meaning of a Liberal Education*. Garden City, N.Y.: Garden City Publishing, 1926.

National Commission on the Reform of Secondary Education. *The Reform of Secondary Education*. New York: McGraw-Hill, 1973.

National Society for the Study of Education. *The Elementary School in the United States*. Seventy-second Yearbook, Part II. Chicago: University of Chicago Press, 1973.

————. *Uses of the Sociology of Education*. Seventy-third Yearbook, Part II. Chicago: University of Chicago Press, 1974.

Nearing, Scott. *The New Education*. New York: Arno Press and *The New York Times*, 1969. (Reprint of the volume published by Row, Peterson in 1915.)

Neill, A. S. *Summerhill*. New York: Hart, 1960.

Open Court Editorial Advisory Board. *Papers on Educational Reform*. Vols. I and II. LaSalle, Ill.: Open Court, 1970, 1971.

Phillips, A. Craig, ed. *Education for Tomorrow*. Raleigh, N.C.: North Carolina Department of Public Instruction, 1976.

Postman, Neil, and Weingartner, Charles. *Teaching as a Subversive Activity*. New York: Delacorte, 1969.

Rand Corporation. *How Effective Is Schooling?* Santa Monica, Calif.: The Rand Corporation, 1972.

Rathbone, Charles H., ed. *Open Education: The Informal Classroom*. New York: Citation Press, 1971.

Raup, R. Bruce, *et al. The Improvement of Practical Intelligence*. New York: Harper & Row, 1950.

Raywid, Mary Anne. *The Ax-Grinders*. New York: Macmillan, 1962.

Bibliography

Report of the Harvard Committee. *General Education in a Free Society.* Cambridge, Mass.: Harvard University Press, 1945.

Rice, Joseph M. *The Public School System of the United States.* New York: Century, 1893.

Rickover, Hyman G. *American Education: A National Failure.* New York: E. P. Dutton, 1963.

Riessman, Frank. *The Culturally Deprived Child.* New York: Harper & Row, 1962. Chapter VII, "The Slow Gifted Child."

Rogers, Carl R. *Freedom to Learn.* Columbus, Ohio: Charles E. Merrill, 1969.

Rokeach, Milton. *The Nature of Human Values.* New York: Free Press, 1973.

Roszak, Theodore. *The Making of a Counter Culture.* Garden City, N.Y.: Doubleday, 1969.

Saettler, Paul. *A History of Instructional Technology.* New York: McGraw-Hill, 1968.

Schaefer, Carl J., and Kaufman, Jacob J. *New Directions for Vocational Education.* Lexington, Mass.: D. C. Heath, 1971.

Schaefer, Robert J. *Schools for the 70's and Beyond: A Call to Action.* Washington: Center for the Study of Instruction, National Education Association, Main Report, 1971.

Schramm, Wilbur, and Roberts, Donald. *The Process and Effects of Mass Communication.* Rev. ed. Urbana, Ill.: University of Illinois Press, 1971.

Scribner, Harvey B., and Stevens, Leonard B. *Make Your Schools Work.* New York: Simon & Schuster, 1975.

Sexton, Patricia Cayo. *The American School: A Sociological Analysis.* Englewood Cliffs, N.J.: Prentice-Hall, 1967.

Skidelsky, Robert. *English Progressive Schools.* Middlesex, England: Penguin Books, 1969.

Skinner, Burrhus F. *Beyond Freedom and Dignity.* New York: Alfred A. Knopf, 1971.

Smith, B. Othaniel, ed. *Research in Teacher Education: A Symposium.* Englewood Cliffs, N.J.: Prentice-Hall, 1971.

Spring, Joel H. *Education and the Rise of the Corporate State.* Boston: Mass.: Beacon Press, 1972.

Study Commission on Undergraduate Education and the Education of Teachers. *The University Can't Train Teachers.* 1972.

Toffler, Alvin, ed. *Learning for Tomorrow.* New York: Random House, 1974.

Tractenberg, Paul. *Testing the Teacher: How Urban School Districts Select Their Teachers and Supervisors.* Foreword by Eleanor Holmes Norton. New York: Agathon Press, 1974.

Trump, J. Lloyd, and Georgiades, William. *How to Change Your School.*

Reston, Va.: The National Association for Secondary School Principals, 1978.

Ulich, Robert, ed. *Three Thousand Years of Educational Wisdom.* Cambridge, Mass.: Harvard University Press, 1954.

U.S. Department of Labor. *U.S. Manpower in the 1970's: Opportunity and Challenge.* Washington, D.C.: U.S. Government Printing Office, 1971.

Wesley, Edgar B. *NEA: The First Hundred Years.* New York: Harper & Row, 1957.

Whitehead, Alfred North. *The Aims of Education.* New York: Macmillan, 1929.

Williams, Richard C.; Wall, Charles C.; Martin, W. Michael; Berchin, Arthur. *Effecting Organizational Renewal in Schools: A Social Systems Perspective.* New York: McGraw-Hill, 1974.

Wittes, Simon. *People and Power: A Study of Crisis in Secondary Schools.* Ann Arbor, Mich.: The University of Michigan, 1970.

Index

psychosocial development of child, 36,
40, 106, 144, 206
vs. intellection, 40, 41–42
psychological services, 211
public health industry, 79
public-service year, 90–91, 213–14
tasks for students in, 212, 213, 224,
225, 226
see also apprentice or intern school
publishers of instructional materials,
256, 263

quality of life, *see* "good life"
"Quincy System," 32, 36

racial groups:
equality of achievement in schooling
for, 74
integration of, 65
see also disadvantaged; minorities
Rassmiller, Richard, *Individually
Guided Elementary Education,*
206, 282
reading assignments, 98, 100, 112, 124
reading difficulties, programs for
children with, 13, 41
see also remediation
reading skills, 27, 32, 36, 40, 50, 52,
59, 89, 132, 164, 192, 217
instructional methods to teach, 99
elementary school lesson, 119–20
maturing-independence approach,
123
"realms of meaning," 165–70, 177–78,
180, 244
Realms of Meaning, The (Phenix),
165–66, 279
Real World of the Public Schools, The
(Broudy), 48, 271
records, 136
reform:
education and, 8
of schools, 27, 51–52, 56, 141, 175–
76, 182–86
administrative and instructional
changes required for, 37, 48, 49
by evolution, 26, 28, 42, 55
by revolution, 26, 27, 28
elements common to, 42, 44, 55,
182
movements distinguished from
innovations, 40–41

past attempts at, in U.S., 30–53,
59–61, 84, 143, 144–45, 176,
264
pendulation in, 39–40, 143, 144–
45, 176, 177–78, 182, 185, 205
progressive education, *see* progressive education movement
reform through schools before,
24–25, 31–49 *passim*
by revolution, 26, 27, 28
through schools, 28
before reforms of schools, 24–25,
31–49 *passim*
Regional Authorities for Educational
Advancement (RAEA), 265
reinforcement, 107, 108, 150, 205
explanation of principle of, 46
in home environment, 218–20
of teachers, 37, 112, 137, 138, 142
Relevance of Education, The (Bruner),
100, 275
religion, 168, 169, 170, 248
religious institutions, 9, 67, 261
remediation, 211, 212, 213, 220, 221
discovering needs for, 123, 124,
226, 228
see also disadvantaged; learning, as
individualized; "special opportunity" in schooling
report cards, 228
research, 69
educational, *see* educational research
statistical models applied to social,
22–23, 67, 88
retardation, absolute vs. relative,
130
retirement and retired, 82, 249
role in future educational system,
211, 212, 224, 226
revenue-sharing, 256
Riesman, David, 248
Rogers, Carl, 108, 231
On Becoming a Person, 105, 275
Rousseau, Jean Jacques, 150

Saily, Mary, *Individually Guided Elementary Education,* 206, 282
Salzburg Seminar in American Studies,
62
SATs, *see* Standard Aptitude Tests
Schaffarzick, Jon, 258, 284
scholarly organizations, 263, 264
scholastic aptitude tests, *see* tests
and testing, "intelligence,"